Renaissance Literature
and Its Formal Engagements

Renaissance Literature and Its Formal Engagements

Edited by
Mark David Rasmussen

palgrave

Permissions

"Veni Coronaberis," from *New and Collected Poems 1952–1992.* Copyright © 1994 by Geoffrey Hill. Reprinted by permission of Houghton Mifflin Co. All rights reserved.

The Kitchenmaid [De keukenmeid] by Johannes Vermeer. Courtesy of the Rijksmuseum, Amsterdam.

"Veni Coronaberis," from *Geoffrey Hill: Collected Poems.* Copyright © 1978, 1985 by Geoffrey Hill. Reprinted by permission of Penguin Books, Ltd.

RENAISSANCE LITERATURE AND ITS FORMAL ENGAGEMENTS
© Copyright Mark David Rasmussen, 2002. All rights reserved. No part of this book may be used or reproduced in any manner whatsoever without written permission except in the case of brief quotations embodied in critical articles or reviews.

First published 2002 by
PALGRAVE™
175 Fifth Avenue, New York, N.Y. 10010 and
Houndmills, Basingstoke, Hampshire RG21 6XS.
Companies and representatives throughout the world.

PALGRAVE is the new global publishing imprint of St. Martin's Press LLC Scholarly and Reference Division and Palgrave Publishers Ltd (formerly Macmillan Press Ltd).

ISBN 0–312–29360–7 paperback
ISBN 0–312–29359–3 hardback

Library of Congress Cataloging-in-Publication Data
Renaissance literature and its formal engagements / edited by Mark David Rasmussen.
    p. cm. Includes bibliographical references and index.
    ISBN 0–312–29360–7 (alk. paper)—ISBN 0–312–29359–3 (pbk.: alk. paper)
    1. English literature—Early modern, 1500–1700—History and criticism. 2. Renaissance—England. 3. Literary form. I. Rasmussen, Mark David, 19530
PR418.L57 R48   2002
820.9'003—dc21   2001035954

A catalogue record for this book is available from the British Library.

Design by Letra Libre, Inc.

First edition: January 2002
10 9 8 7 6 5 4 3 2 1

Printed in the United States of America.

Contents

Introduction: New Formalisms?   1
   Mark David Rasmussen

I.
Toward a Historical Formalism

Between Form and Culture: New Historicism
and the Promise of a Historical Formalism   17
   Stephen Cohen

Shakespeare and the Composite Text   43
   Douglas Bruster

The Politics of Aesthetics:
Recuperating Formalism and the Country House Poem   67
   Heather Dubrow

Marston's Gorge and the Question of Formalism   89
   Joseph Loewenstein

II.
Renewing the Literary

Learning from the New Criticism:
The Example of Shakespeare's Sonnets   115
   Paul Alpers

Undelivered Meanings: The Aesthetics of Shakespearean Wordplay   139
   Mark Womack

The Poetics of Speech Tags   159
   William Flesch

Flirting with Eternity: Teaching Form and Meter
in a Renaissance Poetry Course   185
   Elizabeth Harris Sagaser

❖ ❖ ❖ ❖ ❖

Afterword: How Formalism Became
a Dirty Word, and Why We Can't Do Without It   207
   Richard Strier

Contributors   217
Index   219

Introduction

New Formalisms?

Mark David Rasmussen

The aim of this collection is to encourage a shift in the study of English Renaissance literature, a shift toward a fuller and more self-conscious engagement with questions of form.
  Why is such a change needed now? Briefly, because the field has moved too far away from these questions lately, in favor of modes of analysis that for all of their methodological sophistication tend to interpret Renaissance works as bundles of historical or cultural content, without much attention to the ways that their meanings are shaped and enabled by the possibilities of form. To be sure, something along these lines has been happening in virtually every area of literary study today, as part of the movement toward cultural studies.[1] But it is a particularly ironic development in the field of Renaissance literature, since over the years that field has been so fertile in providing objects of formalist scrutiny. Indeed, the history of British and American formalisms during the century just past might almost be written as a series of responses to English Renaissance texts. One need only recall T. S. Eliot's championing of the metaphysical poets, or the centrality of the poetry of Donne and Shakespeare to the criticism of Cleanth Brooks and William Empson, to recognize the programmatic importance of this body of literature for the brand of Anglo-American formalism that came to be known as the New Criticism.[2] The great battles between that version of formalism and what is now often called the "old" historicism were fought over English Renaissance poems, in the debate between Brooks and Douglas Bush over Marvell's "Horatian Ode," or in the controversy so engagingly recounted by Richard Strier between Empson and Rosemond Tuve over George Herbert's poem "The Sacrifice."[3] One might cite A. Kent Hieatt's discoveries about numerological patterning in Spenser's *Epithalamion*, or Stephen Booth's minute attention to the linguistic intricacies of Shakespeare's Sonnets, as two other examples, very

different in kind, of the extraordinary responsiveness of previous generations of critics to the formal properties of the English Renaissance literary text.[4]

Renaissance studies changed overnight with the publication in 1980 of Stephen Greenblatt's *Renaissance Self-Fashioning*.[5] Certainly most work published in the field since the early eighties has been shaped by its engagement with Greenblatt's new historicism, whose prominence within Renaissance studies today is unmatched by any critical method in any other area of British, American, or comparative literary study. As several analysts of the new historicism have noted, its successes as a critical method may largely be attributed to its ability to negotiate the twin pitfalls of a formalist criticism perceived to be essentially ahistorical, on the one hand, and a politicized mode of ideology critique perceived to be reductive of textual meanings, on the other.[6] More specific to the thoroughly overdetermined triumph of the method within Renaissance studies is the often-noted tendency of contemporary academics to find their own post-modern alienation mirrored in the anxieties of works produced at the inception of modernity, as those anxieties find voice in new historicist accounts.[7] For our purposes, though, the really crucial point is that made by Stephen Cohen in his essay for this volume, in which he demonstrates that new historicist critical analyses were originally far more oriented than they are today toward questions relating to literary form and its function within culture. Whether, in Heather Dubrow's witty formulation, we see in the title of an early new historicist anthology, "The Forms of Power and the Power of Forms in the Renaissance," an embrace of power by forms, or a relegation of forms to the margins, form remains an unmistakably prominent part of the mix.[8] Indeed, much of the early influence of Greenblatt's book was surely due to its providing a series of breathtaking readings of such canonical works as More's *Utopia,* Wyatt's lyric poetry, Spenser's *Faerie Queene,* and Shakespeare's *Othello*—readings not formalist in their scope, but directed toward the total explication of the literary text that had also been the goal of the New Critical interpretations with which they were in dialogue.[9] Simply put, Greenblatt's readings often seemed to do a better job of explaining what was going on within these works than previous, mainly New Critical, accounts had managed to do, and so supplanted the authority of those accounts; but both Greenblatt's subsequent work and that of his followers has set aside such explication as its goal, in favor of the mining of literature for evidence of cultural practices. This later version of the new historicism takes Renaissance culture rather than literature as its central concern, dipping only intermittently into the literary text as one manifestation of that culture among many.[10] While the allure of Greenblatt's early readings was largely responsible for the prestige of new historicist method within the academy, and particularly within Renaissance studies, it is this second version of the new historicism that now dominates published work within the field. Much of this work has been valuable, but in recent years many have come to feel that the new historicist paradigm, at least in its present orientation toward cultural studies, appears to be exhausted, its initial excitement now long since cooled.

That is the situation that this volume addresses. The authors of the essays collected here disagree about many things, but all of them, I think, share a sense that what is needed within the field today is a renewed commitment to engaging questions of form. Such a sense is increasingly making itself felt throughout the literary academy, in all areas of study.[11] Indeed, as Ellen Rooney has argued in a recent essay, the current "flight from form" serves to impoverish not just literary studies, but cultural studies as well, slighting the disciplinary specificity of each.[12] As Rooney also maintains, any genuine attempt to reinvigorate formalist analysis must work through the theoretical developments of recent years, rather than bypassing them out of a nostalgia for formalisms past; if it is to have a legitimate claim on our attention, a renewal of formalist inquiry must address both the history and the needs of our present moment.[13] Such a freshly theorized formalism might be expected to take two main directions, either inflected toward the historical/cultural or toward the literary/aesthetic, as the grouping of the essays in this volume is intended to suggest.

So, all four essays in the volume's opening section, "Toward a Historical Formalism," share a commitment to a critical practice that at least one contributor, Douglas Bruster, believes is already finding its place within the field, though not yet as a theoretically self-conscious movement. If that is so, the need for some initial reflection upon the aims and methods of such a historicized formalism is more than met by the four essays in this section, and especially by Stephen Cohen's opening contribution. As Cohen puts it, his essay aims to replace the new historicism's "oppositional narrative" of its own relation to formalist criticism with a "more complex network of influences acknowledged and unacknowledged, roads taken, passed by, or abandoned." So, while most standard accounts of the new historicism stress its indebtedness to the cultural anthropology of Clifford Geertz and to Michel Foucault's anatomies of discourse and power, Cohen chooses instead to emphasize the affinities of much early new historicist work with that of such Marxist diagnosticians of form and culture as Louis Althusser, Terry Eagleton, Fredric Jameson, and (especially) Raymond Williams.[14] Yet the influence of these thinkers has proved far more enduring within the field of cultural studies than within the new historicism, producing the especially piquant irony of our present intellectual moment, when, as Cohen observes, cultural critics perform formalist readings of nonliterary texts and practices, while literary scholars will themselves not to think about form. Cohen's essay provides, among other things, the most careful tracing yet to appear in print of the complex splinterings and affiliations between cultural studies and the new historicism. It also in passing effectively refutes an argument frequently made against formal readings of Renaissance literature: that since the very notion of the literary is a modern invention, to apply it to early modern texts is anachronistic. But English Renaissance authors, Cohen reminds us, did have a word for what we call (or used to call) literature. They called it "poesy."

In the opening section of his essay, Douglas Bruster succinctly defines the "new formalism" espoused, explicitly or implicitly, by all four essays in this section as "a critical genre dedicated to examining the social, cultural, and historical aspects of literary form, and the function of form for those who produce and consume literary texts." Both in his essay for this collection and in his most recent book, *Quoting Shakespeare,* Bruster finds himself intrigued by the role that source study, and particularly the analysis of verbal borrowing, might play within such a revitalized formalism.[15] Source study as a critical practice tends to be viewed dismissively today, though as Bruster points out the new historicism might itself be regarded as version of such study, with the literary work excavated as a source for the text of culture. More to the point, the analysis of verbal borrowing takes on new interest in the light of recent post-structuralist arguments about the multiply-determined authorship of Renaissance plays.[16] To interpret verbal borrowing as one element of these "composite texts," as Bruster terms them, is to gain access to rich cultural information embedded in literary data, a point amply demonstrated by the concluding section of Bruster's essay, which examines an apparent verbal borrowing from Nashe's *The Unfortunate Traveller* found in Shakespeare's *Henry V.* As Bruster notes, such a borrowing would not be likely to tempt the interest of a new historicist critic, nor would it engage a more traditional scholar drawn to recovering dialogues among high canonical works. Yet as Bruster's reading shows, a contemporary scholar operating in a seemingly old-fashioned critical mode, but armed with something like a postmodernist sense of textuality, may distill a wealth of social and cultural detail from the words.

As Bruster notes, the scholar most closely associated with the call for a "new formalism" in Renaissance studies is Heather Dubrow, who first used the phrase in print in the conclusion to her book *A Happier Eden,* published in 1990.[17] Dubrow's essay for this collection is a revised and expanded version of an article she published in *Modern Language Quarterly,* as part of a special issue, "Reading for Form."[18] The piece begins by examining some of the causes, both intellectual and institutional, for the recent hostility toward questions of form. Like Cohen and Bruster, Dubrow views this animosity as partly fueled by a reductive account of the various histories of formalist theory and practice, from Kant to the present. Her essay goes on to demonstrate the power of a historicized formalism through a series of dazzling readings of tropes in English Renaissance country house poems, showing how these tropes function both aesthetically and socially, to manage contemporary anxieties about hospitality and invasion. Dubrow follows this feast of close reading with a brief but refreshing (not to say palate-cleansing) consideration of similar issues in a modern novel, Kazuo Ishiguro's *Remains of the Day,* and she concludes by acknowledging both the value and the potential limitations of such a recuperation of formalism as a guest at the table of poststructuralist analysis. (About these limitations other contributors, in other essays, will have more to say.)

To students of literature today, metrical analysis may seem the most bloodless of critical pursuits, but as practiced by Joseph Loewenstein in the fourth of this opening cluster of essays, that mode of analysis comes lurching back to life. In a virtuoso piece of writing, Loewenstein construes Marston's unspeakable prosody—his "speech-stopping speech"—as a kind of bodily self-fashioning, an assertion of authorial identity that (like the retching and belches that fill out his lines) is less than fully under the playwright's control. Some of Marston's lines truly must be heard to be believed, and it is no small virtue of Loewenstein's essay that it allows us to hear them; but its larger purpose is to lobby for further and more detailed studies of prosody as somatic practice, a "cultural poetics of the throat" that would serve to embellish a "properly historical formalism." Such a project would take us very far indeed from counting stresses and finding the caesura.

In one way or another, all four essays in this opening section analyze the complex ways that form is implicated in culture. Whether such an analysis is felt to extend the reach of new historicist method or to recall that method to its original concerns, none of these four essays challenges the primacy accorded to culture over literature in recent critical discourse. Yet, as Heather Dubrow cautions in the conclusion to her essay, to weigh the cultural significance of forms is hardly to exhaust their uses or value. What (to put it crudely) of beauty? What of the literary? How are we to understand *these* aspects of form today? Questions like these are now being asked throughout the academy, but they are particularly charged within the field of Renaissance studies because that field's recent commitment to historicism and to cultural studies has been so absolute.[19] This, then, is the chief question that the four essays in the second part of this collection, "Renewing the Literary," are concerned to reckon with: how do we account for the distinctive power of literary language in a post-theoretical age? None of these four authors denies that form can do cultural work. But their efforts here focus on recovering a sense of the more specifically literary aspects of form that a predominantly cultural mode of analysis tends to neglect.

Paul Alpers' essay reopens the case of the Renaissance lyric in just these terms. It is certainly possible to construe lyric poetry as coded cultural discourse, and a number of new historicist studies have done just that.[20] But this is to slight the very aspects of lyric that make it distinctive: its heightened uses of formal literary language. For Alpers, what is needed today is a formalist account of lyric that acknowledges its literariness without falling into the chief methodological pitfall of earlier formalisms, their tendency to posit (and hence to confer) formal unity. Alpers' essay on modernist responses to Shakespeare's Sonnets offers the beginning of such an account. As Alpers notes, modernist critics like John Crowe Ransom and Yvor Winters were troubled by what Ransom wryly termed the "wonderful imprecision" of the Sonnets—that is, the way that individual poems tend to offer a series of disparate linguistic moments not readily assimilable to the total design prized by New Critical dogma. With the notable exception of Stephen Booth, modernist critics have either judged these poems to be failures or reined in their verbal extravagance by inferring a coherent dramatic speaker for each individual sonnet, a speaker responsible for that poem's peculiar effects. (Helen Vendler's massive commentary on the Sonnets is a recent instance of the latter approach.)[21] For Alpers, neither of these responses to the Sonnets fully succeeds at engaging the qualities that make the poems unique. Alpers believes that Kenneth Burke is the modernist critic best able to lead us to a convincing formalist account both of the Sonnets and of the Renaissance lyric more broadly conceived, for Burke's rhetorical conception of literature as a repertoire of "strategies for the encompassing of situations" allows us to discern the shifting identifications of the lyric speaker without having to reconcile those identifications into a larger coherence, whether of persona or of theme. While Burke does not isolate literature from other modes of discourse or require that literary works sustain a formal unity, he remains sensitive to the "individuality of literary works and the specifically literary usages that determine their individuality." A Burkean account of Renaissance lyric might thus be applicable to both canonical and noncanonical works, and might renew our sense of the literary by showing it operating in unexpected ways, in unexpected places.

One attraction of Alpers' approach is that it licenses readers to weigh a broad range of motives—cultural, psychological, aesthetic—as they come to terms with the rhetorical identifications of the text. By contrast, Mark Womack is uncompromising in his refusal to account for the distinctive power of literary language in any other than aesthetic terms. Womack takes as his topic wordplay in Shakespeare, and particularly the odd case of the undelivered pun, which occurs when the materials for a play on words almost, but not quite, come together. Whether we are reading or in the theater, such unrealized puns seldom reach our conscious understanding and mean, literally, nothing; and yet they help to establish an extra-logical coherence that brings delight. In paying attention to such trivial verbal events, and in declining the bait of interpretation, Womack knowingly follows the example of Stephen

Booth, but as Alpers points out, Booth's own commentary on Shakespeare's Sonnets does not always resist the urge to find thematic or dramatic coherence in verbal play.[22] More of a Boothian than Booth, Womack never slides into such thematizing. His refusal to regulate the "multiple and conflicting connotations of literary language" finds its ultimate (and most delightful) expression in the concluding pages of his essay, where Womack examines two instances of wordplay that would certainly have been unintelligible to Shakespeare and his contemporaries, and insists nonetheless that each represents a valuable part of our aesthetic experience of the play. A more impolitic assault on the chief of our present pieties—that to read works within their cultures is to follow the path of virtue—is hard to imagine.

Like Womack, William Flesch devotes his essay to an apparently trivial phenomenon, the poetic speech tag. Verbal markers like "sayd she" or "quod I" seem the most pedestrian of formal features, the poetic equivalent of punctuation, and yet Flesch argues convincingly that they offer paradigmatic and highly suggestive instances of the assimilation of matter to form. In the ways that they bring utterances into relation with their local context, accommodating quotation to metrical scheme and speech to narration, speech tags exemplify the very subject of poetry, the "telescoping [of] different modes or realms of expression." As Flesch demonstrates through a series of lovingly detailed readings of poems by (among others) Herbert, Wyatt, Sidney, Shakespeare, and Spenser, the range of functions performed by speech tags in poetry produced during the Renaissance, before the modern typographic convention of quotation marks, is impressively supple and large. In all of the instances that Flesch cites, we see the marginal speech tag redefine the poetic center in variously complex ways; among many other things, his essay shows how attending seriously to the insights of deconstruction may help to expand the range of formalist theory and practice.

Diverse as they are, the essays by Alpers, Womack, and Flesch share a devotion to literary reading—reading that is closely attuned to the nuances of literary language and form—without embracing the New Critical ideal of formal unity or coherence. The rallying cry for *this* "new formalism" might be "literary reading without organic form"; its task would be to discover how our sense of the literary might be refreshed, rather than set aside, as a result of the critical and institutional histories of the past twenty years.

The final essay in this cluster, by Elizabeth Harris Sagaser, addresses this question from a somewhat different perspective, asking how a sense of the literary might be renewed by practices within the classroom. Sagaser's beautifully impassioned essay details her own strategies for bringing students into physical, emotional, and intellectual contact with Renaissance lyric poetry, and so with the impossible desire that drives meter and rhyme, the wish to "master time and thwart mortality." Students steeped in formal verse come to experience some of the period's most basic fears and beliefs, and in this sense Sagaser's formalist pedagogy is deeply committed to a process of cultural address. But the culture under consideration—Renaissance culture—is not conceived of as inaccessibly "other" or estranged from our present concerns; its hopes and anxieties resonate with our own, and its poetic accomplishments can still give us strength. Sagaser's essay pairs suggestively with that by Joseph Loewenstein in this regard. Both essays address metrical topics, and both build on classroom experiences (as Loewenstein notes in his opening pages), but while Loewenstein's attitude toward the "history of creative unfreedom" in the Renaissance is jaundiced in a recognizably Foucauldian way, Sagaser admires the period and its values. She is joined in this by the other three contributors to this section, all of whom frankly and quite unfashionably celebrate the richness, complexity, and beauty of the literature they study. As a group, the essays in this section show how a return to formalist literary analysis, invigorated by the critical challenges of recent years, may help to counteract what Richard Rorty has pointed to as the most troubling aspect of the cultural studies movement, its attitude of self-protective "knowingness" toward works of the past.[23] The de-centered formalisms of Alpers, Womack, Flesch, and Sagaser avoid the totalizing impulse of formalisms past, but their openness to a range of literary effects may yet revive our capacity to admire, if only we are willing.

As many of the essays in both halves of this volume demonstrate, the distinction between historical and literary formalisms, however convenient, is far from absolute; often in the best critical writing these two versions of formalism work together. In his afterword to this volume, Richard Strier takes the cooperation between formalist analysis and historical criticism as his topic, bringing the collection to a suitably ecumenical close. As Strier demonstrates with great clarity and conviction, "internalist" readings of literary texts, focusing on literary features of those texts, may nonetheless bear real implications for historical analysis; and close reading techniques applied to nonliterary texts can turn up surprising data. In his conclusion, Strier draws on a pair of terms from analytic philosophy, "mention" and "use," to clarify the distinction between new historicist and formalist approaches. For Strier, what defines formalist criticism is above all the "premise . . . that *the work provides the initial context* for understanding the significance of any particular item in a text." That is a premise that neither Strier, nor the other contributors to this volume, feel inclined to abandon, for the cost of such abandonment is the loss of what is most distinctive in the object of their study—Renaissance literature—whether that object is viewed primarily from a historical/cultural or a literary/aesthetic perspective.

You have before you, then, a rich and diverse collection of essays, offering a range of approaches to Renaissance literature and its engagements with form. To be sure, not every critical method is included here; most conspicuous in its absence is any sustained reflection on how formalist approaches might be broadened by reckoning with the achievements of feminist scholarship in the field, and particularly the recovery of Renaissance literary texts written by women.[24] But the meal is ample and various, nonetheless. As a group, the essays ask us to reflect upon our critical practices and their histories, weighing carefully the claims of the cultural and the literary. In particular, the recent disparagement of formal analysis must be called into question by the critical and institutional histories offered by Stephen Cohen, Heather Dubrow, and Paul Alpers. Critical practices now out of favor are brilliantly revived, as well; so, to pick a few prominent instances, source study cannot look quite the same after Douglas Bruster has renewed it by bringing it into contact with post-structuralist textuality; and metrical analysis must be freshly understood after the essays of Joseph Loewenstein, William Flesch, and Elizabeth Sagaser. An especially pleasant feature of the volume (at least for its editor) is the number of beautifully nuanced readings that it provides; examples might include Bruster's teasing out of the implications of Shakespeare's verbal debt to Nashe, Dubrow's decoding of tropes in English country house poems, Womack's unmasking of impossible puns, and Flesch's painstaking analyses of the work of lyric.

In conclusion, what about the "new formalism"—or "new formalisms"—toward which the title of this introduction so imprudently glances? Of the eight authors collected here, only one, Douglas Bruster, uses the term to characterize his own approach. Such diffidence seems entirely justified, at a critical moment when claims of the "new" can only be viewed with skepticism. (That "New Formalism" also names a decade-long movement among contemporary poets may help to rule it out of account.)[25] It is not the ambition of this collection, or of its editor, to add another term to the critical lexicon. Nor is it the shared ambition of these eight authors to replace other critical approaches to Renaissance literature with the various formalisms they advocate. But if this volume can reopen the discussion of questions of form and of the literary, if its precedent can provide reassurance that such questions continue to be worthy of attention, and if it can help to extend the range of methods within Renaissance studies to include a revived and critically self-conscious formalist practice, then it will have more than served its purpose.

❖ ❖ ❖ ❖

This collection had its origin in a special session that I organized and chaired at the 1997 Modern Language Association convention, titled "Toward a New Formalism in Renaissance Studies." Paul Alpers, Heather Dubrow, Joseph Loewenstein, and Richard Strier presented papers at this session, and I would like to thank all of them for letting me put them up to it. The session at MLA was well-attended and widely discussed, and afterwards several people suggested that I assemble a collection of essays on the topic. In soliciting further contributions beyond the initial group of four, I sought authors whose work I found particularly exciting, including both established names within the field and some of its most notable rising stars. All wrote their essays on spec, through several stages of revision, for an editor they'd never met. This I took, and continue to take, as a sign of their commitment to engaging the topic this volume addresses, and for that commitment and for their cheerful hard work, I thank them. Special gratitude goes to Heather Dubrow; to my editor at Palgrave, Kristi Long; and to my dean at Centre College, John Ward, all of whom offered encouragement and advice at key moments. My own work on this project was supported by a summer grant from the Centre College Faculty Development Committee, and most of all by the love and good humor of my dear family: Helen, Ivan, and Petra.

Notes

1. For a recent diagnosis of the cultural studies movement and its "loss of form," see John Brenkman, "Extreme Criticism," *Critical Inquiry* 26 (1999): 109–127, especially pages 109–16, as well as Ellen Rooney, "Form and Contentment," *Modern Language Quarterly* 61 (2000): 17–40. Brenkman's essay has been reprinted in *What's Left of Theory? New Works on the Politics of Literary Theory*, ed. Judith Butler, John Guillory, and Keith Thomas (New York: Routledge, 2000): 114–36.
2. Eliot's famous essays "The Metaphysical Poets" and "Andrew Marvell" appear in *Selected Essays* (New York: Harcourt, 1932): 241–63; "The Language of Paradox," Brooks' equally influential reading of Donne's "The Canonization," appears as the introductory essay to *The Well Wrought Urn: Studies in the Structure of Poetry* (New York: Harcourt, 1947), 3–21, which also contains perhaps the most celebrated New Critical reading of a Shakespeare play, Brooks' study of image patterns in *Macbeth*, "The Naked Babe and the Cloak of Manliness," 22–49. For some of Empson's best-known responses to English Renaissance poems, see *Seven Types of Ambiguity* (New York: New Directions, 1949) and *Some Versions of Pastoral* (New York: New Directions, 1950). Of course, Coleridge's concept of "organic form," so foundational for New Critical method, finds its great exemplar in Shakespeare, as does Keats' notion of "negative capability," equally foundational for the New Critics' valuing of aesthetic disinterestedness; see R. A. Foakes, ed., *Coleridge's Criticism of Shakespeare* (Detroit: Wayne State University Press, 1989), 51–3, and Hyder Edward Rollins, ed., *The Letters of John Keats* (Cambridge: Harvard University Press, 1958): 2:193–4.
3. For the Brooks-Bush controversy, see Cleanth Brooks, "Criticism and Literary History: Marvell's 'Horatian Ode'," *The Sewanee Review* 55 (1947):

199–222; and Douglas Bush's rejoinder, "Marvell's *Horatian Ode*," *The Sewanee Review* 60 (1952): 363–76. Empson's reading of "The Sacrifice" is presented in *Seven Types of Ambiguity*, 226–33; Tuve's response, "On Herbert's 'Sacrifice'," appeared in *Kenyon Review* 12 (1950): 51–75. Strier's account of the controversy may be found in his *Resistant Structures: Particularity, Radicalism, and Renaissance Texts* (Berkeley: University of California Press, 1995), 13–26.

4. See A. Kent Hieatt, *Short Time's Endless Monument: The Symbolism of the Numbers in Spenser's "Epithalamion"* (New York: Columbia University Press, 1960); and Stephen Booth, ed., *Shakespeare's Sonnets* (New Haven: Yale University Press, 1977).

5. Stephen Greenblatt, *Renaissance Self-Fashioning: From More to Shakespeare* (Chicago: University of Chicago Press, 1980). Though Greenblatt's book set the new historicist paradigm, his emphasis on cultural agency in English Renaissance works had been anticipated by, among others, G. K. Hunter, *John Lyly: The Humanist as Courtier* (Cambridge: Harvard University Press, 1962); Stephen Orgel, *The Illusion of Power: Political Theater in the English Renaissance* (Berkeley: University of California Press, 1975); Richard Helgerson, *The Elizabethan Prodigals* (Berkeley: University of California Press, 1976); and Daniel Javitch, *Poetry and Courtliness in Renaissance England* (Princeton: Princeton University Press, 1978).

6. See, for instance, Vincent Pecora, "The Limits of Local Knowledge," in *The New Historicism*, ed. H. Aram Veeser (New York: Routledge, 1989), 183. This point is developed more fully by Stephen Cohen in his essay for this collection.

7. On this point, Jean Howard is especially astute; see her essay "The New Historicism in Renaissance Studies," *English Literary Renaissance* 16 (1986): 13–43, especially pages 15–17. Where New Critics found a wished-for unity in the verbal icon, new historicists recognize their own experience of dissonance and rupture. A remark of Greenblatt's in *Renaissance Self-Fashioning* memorably evokes the new historicist response to the past: "To experience Renaissance culture is to feel what it was like to form our own identity, and we are at once more rooted and more estranged by the experience" (175).

8. See Dubrow's essay for this collection, "The Politics of Aesthetics."

9. In the introduction to his collection *Aesthetics and Ideology* (New Brunswick: Rutgers University Press, 1994), George Levine similarly remarks on the "self-conscious literariness of Greenblatt's project" in *Renaissance Self-Fashioning* (8). An analogous point might be made, I believe, about the work of Louis Montrose that appeared in the late seventies and early eighties, particularly his essays on Elizabethan pastoral and on *A Midsummer Night's Dream*. This body of writing, second in its influence on students of Renaissance literature only to the work of Greenblatt, is again remarkable as a series of brilliant readings; the most important of Montrose's essays in this mode are "'The perfect paterne of a Poete': The Poetics of Courtship in *The Shepheardes Calender*," *Texas Studies in Literature and Language* 21 (1979): 34–67; "'Eliza, Queene of

shepheardes,' and the Pastoral of Power," *English Literary Renaissance* 10 (1980): 153–82; and "'Shaping Fantasies': Figurations of Gender and Power in Elizabethan Culture," *Representations* 2 (1983): 61–94. In all of these essays, Montrose is more explicitly interested than Greenblatt in the cultural functions of literary form, extending his analyses to works not highly valued within the New Critical canon, particularly Elizabethan pastoral poems. To the original readers of these essays, Montrose's interpretations suddenly made this body of literature seem as intriguingly full of tensions as a lyric by Donne. In an important article, Alan Liu has attacked the work of early new historicists as a disguised formalism that takes culture, rather than literature, as the object of its analysis; see his essay "The Power of Formalism: The New Historicism," *ELH* 56 (1989): 721–771. From this perspective, the strength of Greenblatt and Montrose's readings *as* readings reveals their weakness as cultural criticism.

10. That such explorations can prove powerfully illuminating on their own terms goes without saying; exemplary in this regard is Gail Kern Paster, *The Body Embarrassed: Drama and the Disciplines of Shame in Early Modern England* (Ithaca: Cornell University Press, 1993). Paster freely admits that she seeks to illuminate culture, rather than literature, through her work, though she believes that her project does have literary implications: "Throughout, new readings of plays, though they are sometimes an indirect product of the argument, are not an express goal. Reading Elizabethan-Jacobean plays is rather the *means* to the end of discovering the signifying properties of the humoral body and the disciplinary protocols of its long-term transformation in culture. But the signifying properties of the humoral body, and humoral theory in general, do make a significant difference to the reading of early modern plays, for they introduce an insistent materialism into locutions once understood solely as figuration" (21–2). Paster's readings usually tease out the cultural significance of particular moments within individual plays, rather than offering comprehensive critical interpretations; typical is her extended decoding of Malvolio's reference in *Twelfth Night* to Olivia's "Great P's" (30–4). Greenblatt's own most recent work on *Hamlet* seems increasingly drawn back to the ideal of explication, as he presents cultural anxieties about corporeality and remembrance as supplying the central, organizing conflict of the play, the heart of its mystery; see the chapter "The Mousetrap" in Catherine Gallagher and Stephen Greenblatt, *Practicing New Historicism* (Chicago: University of Chicago Press, 2000), 136–62, and Stephen Greenblatt, *Hamlet in Purgatory* (Princeton: Princeton University Press, 2001). In his "Prologue" to the latter work, Greenblatt confides, "My only goal was to immerse myself in the tragedy's magical intensity" (5), but he also admits that his study of the play's cultural contexts exerted a powerful pull of its own, an acknowledgement borne out by the book's structure: three chapters on Purgatory as a cultural institution, one chapter on ghosts in Shakespeare, and one chapter on the play.

11. Over the past several years three volumes of essays have considered the place of formal analysis within literary studies, mainly in relation to aesthetics: Levine, *Aesthetics and Ideology;* James Soderholm, ed., *Beauty and the Critic:*

Aesthetics in an Age of Cultural Studies (Tuscaloosa: University of Alabama Press, 1997); and Michael P. Clark, ed., *Revenge of the Aesthetic: The Place of Literature in Theory Today* (Berkeley: University of California Press, 2000). Perhaps the most helpful, as well as the most theoretically wide-ranging, collection of essays on this topic is the special issue "Reading for Form" that appeared as Volume 61, number 1 of *Modern Language Quarterly* (2000), edited by Susan J. Wolfson and Marshall Brown. This issue contains both an earlier version of Heather Dubrow's essay for this collection and Rooney, "Form and Contentment."

12. Rooney, "Form and Contentment": "Formalism is an unavoidable moment in the projects of both literary and cultural studies, fields that remain sufficiently entwined to engage one another's serious attention and sufficiently distinct to yield autonomous scholarship and rival disciplinary formations" (18). For Rooney, the "flight from form" (31) in both fields in favor of thematic or content-based interpretation amounts to nothing less than a "retreat from reading" (32) that has become endemic.

13. Rooney, "Form and Contentment": "To recover the category and work of form in literary and cultural studies is thus not to transcend the New Historicism, poststructuralism, cultural materialism, feminism, semiotics, postcolonialism, or any of the other critical interventions marking literary studies in the late twentieth century. Rather, the renewal of form as an operation intrinsic to reading enables literary and cultural studies fully to take the pressure of those interventions" (17).

14. For (literally) textbook examples of the standard account, emphasizing the influence of Geertz and Foucault, see "New Historicism and Cultural Studies" in *The Critical Tradition: Classic Texts and Contemporary Trends*, 2nd ed., ed. David H. Richter (Boston: Bedford Books, 1998), 1204–21, and the section "What Is the New Historicism?" printed in slightly different versions in several volumes of the "Case Studies in Contemporary Criticism" series, such as *James Joyce: The Dead*, ed. Daniel R. Schwarz (Boston: Bedford Books, 1994), 150–8.

15. Douglas Bruster, *Quoting Shakespeare: Form and Culture in Early Modern Drama* (Lincoln: University of Nebraska Press, 2000).

16. For influential discussions of Renaissance plays as collaborative enterprises not readily assimilable to modern notions of individual authorship, see among others Stephen Orgel, "What Is a Text?" in *Staging the Renaissance: Reinterpretations of Elizabethan and Jacobean Drama* ed. David Scott Kastan and Peter Stallybrass (New York: Routledge, 1991), 83–87; Peter Stallybrass, "Shakespeare, the Individual, and the Text," in *Cultural Studies*, ed. Lawrence Grossberg, Cary Nelson, and Paula Treichler (New York: Routledge, 1992), 593–612; Margreta de Grazia and Peter Stallybrass, "The Materiality of the Shakespearean Text," *Shakespeare Quarterly* 44 (1993): 255–83; and Jeffrey Masten, "Playwrighting: Authorship and Collaboration," in *A New History of Early English Drama*, ed. John D. Cox and David Scott Kastan (New York: Columbia University Press, 1997), 357–82.

17. Heather Dubrow, *A Happier Eden: The Politics of Marriage in the Stuart Epithalamium* (Ithaca: Cornell University Press, 1990), 259–70.

18. Heather Dubrow, "Guess Who's Coming to Dinner?: Reinterpreting Formalism and the Country House Poem," *Modern Language Quarterly* 61 (2000): 59–77.
19. For recent interest in the aesthetic, see Levine, *Aesthetics and Ideology;* Soderholm, *Beauty and the Critic;* and Clark, *Revenge of the Aesthetic.* It is worth mentioning that neither Levine's nor Soderholm's collection contains a single essay devoted to a Renaissance author or text; Clark's volume, a *festschrift* for Murray Krieger, contains one, "Marvell and the Art of Disappearance" by Stanley Fish.
20. For prominent instances, see Arthur Marotti, "'Love is not love': Elizabethan Sonnet Sequences and the Social Order," *ELH* 49 (1982): 396–428; and Marotti, *John Donne: Coterie Poet* (University of Wisconsin Press, 1986).
21. Helen Vendler, *The Art of Shakespeare's Sonnets* (Cambridge: Harvard University Press, 1997).
22. See the discussion in Alpers' essay of Booth's commentary on Sonnet 33, where he catches Booth recuperating syntactic doubleness as "a metaphor for the unexpected inconstancy the poem talks about," and so indulging in a bit of New Critical thematizing.
23. See Richard Rorty, "The Inspirational Value of Great Works of Literature," *Raritan* 16 (1996): 8–17; see also Matthew Greenfield, "What We Talk About When We Talk About Culture," *Raritan* 19 (1999): 95–113, which voices similar concerns about how "the jargon of cultural analysis serves . . . to protect us against the texts we study and the claims they make on us" (112). Graham Bradshaw has observed the ways being "estranged" increasingly overwhelms being "rooted" in Greenblatt's accounts of his own engagement with Renaissance culture; see Greenblatt's formulation quoted in note 7 above, and Graham Bradshaw, *Misrepresentations: Shakespeare and the Materialists* (Ithaca: Cornell University Press, 1993), 245–57.
24. Ilona Bell, *Elizabethan Women and the Poetry of Courtship* (Cambridge: Cambridge University Press, 1998), offers one instance of such an approach. Other critical methodologies with potent implications for a revived formalist practice might include Lacanian psychoanalysis and textual criticism. See, for the former, Marshall Grossman, "The Rhetoric of Feminine Priority in *Paradise Lost*," forthcoming in *English Literary Renaissance;* and, for a particularly challenging version of the latter, the work of the self-proclaimed textual un-editor Randall McLeod [Random Cloud], especially Random Cloud, "Fiat Flux," in *Crisis in Editing: Texts of the English Renaissance,* ed. Randall McLeod (New York: AMS Press, 1994), 61–172. Both Grossman and McLeod contributed essays to an earlier version of this collection, and the range of critical approaches represented here is diminished by their absence.
25. For programmatic collections of New Formalist poems and essays, see *Rebel Angels: 25 Poets of the New Formalism,* ed. Mark Jarman and David Mason (Brownsville: Story Line Press, 1996); and *After New Formalism: Poets on Form, Narrative, and Tradition,* ed. Annie Finch (Brownsville: Story Line Press, 1999).

Part I

Toward a Historical Formalism

Between Form and Culture

New Historicism and the Promise of a Historical Formalism

Stephen Cohen

Since its inception—or at least its christening—new historicism has proclaimed its antiformalism. The movement's critical oppositionality is implicit in its very name: "new historicism" not only distinguishes itself from an "old historicism" but also invokes the longstanding historicist/formalist opposition by appropriating for the former the adjectival bravado of the latter's chief American exemplar, the New Criticism.[1] The name was first used in its current sense by Stephen Greenblatt in the introduction to a collection of essays said to exemplify the critical movement he is generally credited with founding, and the context in which he uses the term confirms new historicism's oppositional roots: "diverse as they are, many of the present essays give voice, I think, to what we may call the new historicism, set apart from both the dominant historical scholarship of the past and the formalist criticism that partially displaced this scholarship in the decades after World War Two."[2] For Greenblatt, this formalism is closely identified with the New Critical orthodoxy of his own professional training in the 1960s, characterized by its decontextualization of literary works, its treatment of literature as "a fixed set of texts that are set apart from all other forms of expression and that contain their own determinate meanings. . . ."[3] The task of new historicism, then, was to recontextualize literature, not—as in the "old" historicism—as a privileged or transcendent reflection of its historical situation, but as one cultural discourse among others, not only "socially produced" but also "socially productive."[4]

With the institutionalization of new historicism, both the movement's antiformalist origins and its characterization of formalism as antihistorical and (thus) politically conservative have become critical commonplaces. For example, the Cambridge Studies in Renaissance Literature and Culture series, which traces its theoretical roots to the cultural revolution in Renaissance studies initiated by new historicism, describes that revolution as "a move away from formalism to a sense of literature as an aspect of social, economic, political, and cultural history."[5] Similarly, in a volume intended to introduce new historicism and its British counterpart, cultural materialism, to students, John Brannigan states that "the most powerful impetus behind the emergence of new historicism was to oppose formalist approaches to the study of literature," and that new historicism has succeeded in so doing by "opening new avenues in thinking about literature in relation to history and politics" and by "demystifying the privileged autonomy of the literary text, and placing literature in circulation with texts of all kinds."[6] Nor have new historicism's many critics objected to its characterization of formalism or its concomitant neglect of formal issues.[7] On the contrary, they have incorporated new historicism's condemnation of formalism as historically naive and politically quiescent into the much-repeated claim that in its treatment of Renaissance culture as a synchronic totality, new historicism itself harbors a residual formalism. According to this argument, as its name suggests, "cultural poetics" (Greenblatt's preferred term for new historicism) reads a culture like the New Critics read a literary text, containing tension, dissension, and subversion within a complex but ultimately unified whole; the result is new historicism's notorious inability to account for either genuine political resistance or historical change.[8]

Given the professional stature of new historicism, it is not surprising that the result of this programmatic antiformalism has been a dramatic decline in both the prestige and the overall practice of formalist scholarship in a Renaissance literary criticism increasingly dominated by historical and cultural studies. My purpose in this essay is not to challenge new historicism's valuation of New Critical formalism or to question the role of the latter in the development of the former, but rather to recontextualize new historicism, to remove it from the narrative of origins it has created for itself and resituate it in the broader critical context of the period of its emergence—a context that includes not only American New Criticism, but also a variety of continental and Anglo-American "left formalisms" that were grappling with the very sorts of historical and political issues refused by the New Critics. The story that emerges ends no more happily for formalism than does the conventional account of New Criticism's vanquishing at the hands of the new historicists; but by replacing new historicism's simple oppositional narrative with a more complex network of influences acknowledged and unacknowledged, roads taken, passed by, or abandoned, we may develop a richer sense of both what is at stake in the disengagement of cultural and formal studies, and what a truly historico-political formalism could be.

During most of the post-war period in which the New Critics dominated American literary criticism, the left-political criticism of literary form was virtually invisible in the American academy, not only because of the primarily Marxist affiliations of its practitioners, but also because of its foundation in a reflectionist model that was the polar opposite of New Criticism's doctrine of literary autonomy. Rooted in the base/superstructure model of what has since become known as "vulgar" Marxism, but best exemplified by its more sophisticated incarnations in Georg Lukács' writings on genre and style and Lucien Goldmann's Marxist structuralism,[9] this type of criticism saw literary forms as reflections of socioeconomic formations, historical situations, or class-based world views. Though avoiding the ahistorical idealism of New Criticism, the reflectionist model raises some of the same issues that the new historicists have noted in their critique of "old" historicism, particularly the unidirectional relation between history and literature that subordinates form as the product, rather than producer, of historical forces even as it privileges literary forms as sites of reflection. The chief alternative to the reflectionist model was an avant-garde aesthetic whose best-known exponent was Bertolt Brecht; it held that certain literary forms did not reflect but on the contrary defamiliarized our everyday (or ideological) perceptions of reality by means of a stylistic alienation effect that, in challenging a reader or audience's preconceptions, could lead to demystification and perhaps political agency. This model, however, was prescriptive rather than descriptive, offering not a complete materialist theory of literary form but instead a model of progressive aesthetic praxis; lacking a more general understanding of the interaction of history and form, it risked idealizing a historically specific effect as an intrinsic formal property.[10] Taken together, the two models—one a reflectionist historicism, the other a potentially idealist formalism—were in a sense the left-political equivalents of "old" historicism and New Criticism and placed similar limits on the political criticism of form as at once culturally productive and historically variable.

The 1970s, however, saw an unprecedented influx of theoretical works rethinking the relation between history, culture, and literary form, including Terry Eagleton's *Criticism and Ideology* (1976), Raymond Williams' *Marxism and Literature* (1977), Tony Bennett's *Formalism and Marxism* (1979), and Fredric Jameson's *Marxism and Form* (1971) and *The Prison-House of Language* (1972), which provided the foundation for his 1981 *The Political Unconscious*. This was in part a consequence of the continuing Anglo-American reception of the continental neo-Hegelian Marxisms of Lukács and the Frankfurt School, many of whose works were being published for the first time in English in the 1960s and 1970s. The primary impetus can, however, be traced to two of the period's seminal theorists, Williams himself and the French structuralist Marxist, Louis Althusser.

In his immensely influential (and controversial) 1969 essay "Ideology and Ideological State Apparatuses," Althusser outlined a theory of ideology that provided the tools for extracting literary form from the twin traps of passive reflectionism and superstructural determinism. By emphasizing that the relation between a society's economic mode of production and its various ideologies was not unmediated and pervasive but rather one of "determination in the last instance," Althusser allowed a relative autonomy to ideological apparatuses, which opened the door for a historical theory of literary forms as something other than direct reflections of economic forces and relations.[11] Moreover, at the heart of his theorization of the ideological state apparatus is an insistence on ideology as socially productive, the driving force behind the shaping of subjects capable of perpetuating a society's means of production. Althusser's own account of the primary means of this ideological subjectification—a Lacanian model of interpellation that begins even before birth, so that one is "always-already a subject"—has been critiqued as excessively totalizing and pessimistically inescapable. Nonetheless, his insistence on the plurality and potentially conflictual relative autonomy of ideological apparatuses invites an examination of the specific effectivity of literature as a means of both subjection and resistance.[12]

While in "Ideology and Ideological State Apparatuses" Althusser identifies literature as a part of both the cultural and the educational ideological apparatuses (143 and 155, respectively), in his writings on art he assigns it a position not within ideology but between ideology (mystification) and science (knowledge), capable, through an "internal distantiation" from the ideology of which it partakes, of allowing us to "see" or "perceive" but not "know" (in the scientific sense) that ideology.[13] The implications of Althusser's gnomic comments are worked out not in his own work but in that of Pierre Macherey, "the first Althusserian critic."[14] Macherey's theory is essentially formalist: working from the premise of the relative autonomy of the literary, he holds that a text does not simply reflect the ideological constructions that provide its raw material but instead shapes or works them in accordance with its own unique formal requirements. By thus giving ideologies shapes not their own, literature reveals—to criticism—the gaps and contradictions of ideology that are invisible in its more elusive, fluid everyday manifestations, allowing us to "see" them in the Althusserian sense. As numerous critics have noted, however, despite its rigorous historical-materialist foundations, Althusser and Macherey's theory of literature partakes of the same sort of formalist idealism as that of the Russian formalists: by assigning to literature a single, defining function (both theorists use this revelatory property to distinguish between "authentic" and "debased" literature[15]) ultimately independent of the historical and ideological materials that it contains, they essentialize the literary as an ahistorical, transcendent category.[16]

The Althusserian influence on Anglo-American criticism of the 1970s is most evident in English theorist Terry Eagleton's *Criticism and Ideology*, the most systematic and successful extrapolation of the value of Althusser's work for a historical theory of literary form. Adapting Macherey's emphasis on the relative autonomy of literary form and ideological content to the later Althusser's insertion of the literary into the network of ideological apparatuses, Eagleton lays the groundwork for a truly historical-materialist formalism by insisting on the ideological function of literary form itself. In his schematic second chapter, "Categories for a Materialist Criticism," Eagleton distinguishes between General Ideology (the overall category for the set of discourses and apparatuses that construct the subjects necessary to perpetuate the dominant mode of production), Authorial Ideology (the author's specific insertion into the General Ideology), and Aesthetic Ideology (a subset of the General Ideology that includes the ideological content of literary traditions, genres and conventions). His third chapter, "Towards a Science of the Text," explores the implications of these distinctions. Like Macherey, Eagleton holds that the literary text does not simply reflect those elements of the General Ideology that comprise its materials but instead through its form shapes or "produces" them (by analogy with a theatrical performance's production of a dramatic text).[17] Literary form is thus functional, a part of a material practice; but while for Macherey that function is uniform and external to ideology, for Eagleton it is neither. Form—both conventional forms and the individual text's unique adaptation of them—is itself ideological, and as such its working of the text's (ideological) content is a historically variable ideological function. The intersection of Aesthetic and General Ideologies—ideologies of form and content[18]—in a given text is, then, ideology to the second power, or the ideologically determined aesthetic "production" of ideological materials. Moreover, while the text's ideologies of form and content are both aspects of the General Ideology, the relative autonomy of ideological apparatuses denies their intersection in individual texts a consistent social function: instead, the result may be cooperation or contradiction, both to varying degrees. Ultimately, however, Eagleton is interested not in the implications of his theory for a model of literature's social function, but—like Althusser and Macherey—in its value to the Marxist critic seeking to expose the obscured contours of ideology: his concluding paragraph is an Althusserian gesture toward literature's privileged status as "the most revealing mode of experiential access to ideology that we possess. . . . more immediate than that of science, and more coherent than that normally available in daily living itself" (101). While not going so far as to idealize literary form by removing it from the historical and ideological, Eagleton's emphasis on the text's utility to the critic rather than its effect on the reader leaves to others the fuller theorization of the literary text as socially productive as well as produced.

Before turning to the chief figure in that endeavor, it will be useful to explore the importance of Althusser to the work of America's foremost political theorist of literary form in the 1970s and 80s, Fredric Jameson.[19] Like Eagleton's, Jameson's work is explicitly Marxist, but while *Criticism and Ideology* is very much indebted to an Althusserian structuralist Marxism, Jameson's roots—as his *Marxism and Form* suggests—are in the continental Hegelian tradition. As a result, his relation to Althusser in his major work on the political theory of form, *The Political Unconscious,* is one of constructive opposition. In order to resist Althusser's replacement of Hegelian expressive causality with a model of structural causality that emphasizes the relative autonomy of different social fields determined only "in the last instance" by a totalizing social structure, Jameson offers a more flexible version of expressive causality for literary criticism, tempering its homological relation between literature and history/society with difference, mediation, and conflict, and supplementing its passive reflection with a more complex theory of literary—and specifically formal—function.[20] In his discussion of "the ideology of form" (98–100), Jameson describes transtextual literary forms as having their own ideological contents, appropriate to the general mode of production out of which they emerged. But even as specific historical situations are shaped not by a single dominant mode of production but by the uneven conflict between multiple coexistent modes, so too in Jameson's model literary texts are not simple reflections of a single form (and its informing ideology) but rather layered and potentially conflictual "field[s] of force in which the dynamics of sign systems of several distinct modes of production can be registered and apprehended" (98). Moreover, as Jameson elaborates in his ensuing discussion of genre criticism,[21] the content or meaning of these forms is not fixed: because genres embody not transhistorical essences but historically specific economic modes or ideological positions, the function of that embodiment will be historically variable. As time passes, a genre's signifying abilities may wane or alter, and users may change certain aspects to maintain the basic form's relevance; consequently, when reading a given text it is as important to trace its genres' histories and note the variations of their individual textual manifestations as it is to identify their original meanings. Like Eagleton's intersections of ideologies of form and content, Jameson's historically specific juxtapositionings of a text's multiple formal structures may have multiple and variable effects, resulting in "harmon[y]" or "contradiction," "coexistence" or "tension" (141). Jameson too does not pursue the implications of his treatment of genre for a fuller theory of the cultural function of literary texts; but the very complexity of the questions he raises indicates his value to a historico-political theory of form that refuses to reduce all literature to a single, predictable meaning or function.[22]

The conception of literary form as productive rather than merely reflective that informs both Eagleton's and Jameson's work receives its fullest articulation in the "cultural materialism" of Raymond Williams.[23] Approaching Marxism from a left-humanist perspective, Williams rejects the economic determinism of the Marxist base/superstructure model in favor of a concept of "productive forces" that includes the cultural as well as the economic; according to Williams, culture is not a superstructural reflection of more basic economic relations but is rather one set of practices among others within a hegemonic—but not strictly deterministic—social system. Thus, to use one of Williams' most influential constructions, culture is not a collection of artifacts or products to be broken down by analysis into their constituent or determinant components, but rather a range of practices to be situated in relation to the conditions that enable them, which they in turn perpetuate or modify.[24] For Williams, then, literature is neither apart from nor simply determined by society, but is itself an integral part of the ongoing social process of hegemonic consolidation, resistance, and change: in a much-quoted summation that is a repudiation as much of Althusserian aesthetic exceptionalism as of New Critical transcendence, Williams insists that "we cannot separate literature and art from other kinds of social practice, in such a way as to make them subject to quite special and distinct laws. They may have quite specific features as practices, but they cannot be separated from the general social process."[25] Williams' dictum is not, however, a rejection of formalism, but a call for its reconceptualization.[26] As the chapters "Conventions," "Genres," and "Forms" in *Marxism and Literature* make clear, literature's "specific features as [a] practice" include the literary conventions that inform individual texts; but to understand their role in and as social practice they must be subject to a formal analysis that is also a thoroughly historicized analysis of their social origins and functions.[27] As in Jameson's account, such an analysis entails an awareness of both the historical variability of a form's effect and the uncertain interactions of conventional forms with the specific contents of their individual realizations.

As important as Williams' insistence on literature as a part of "the general social process" would seem to be for the development of a truly historical formalism, its effects have been mixed. The greatest impact of Williams' theory of culture as social practice has been not in literary studies per se, but in the burgeoning field of cultural studies, which takes as its enabling premises Williams' description of culture's social efficacy as well as his expansion of the concept to include not only "high" culture but popular, mass, and alternative culture as well.[28] The relationship between literary and cultural studies has been an ambivalent one. On the one hand, cultural studies has borrowed from literature one of its most important theoretical tools, the concept of textuality, or the assumption that nonliterary and even nondiscursive cultural practices—indeed, even "culture" as a whole—can be "read" like literary texts.[29] On the other hand, for reasons both theoretical and institutional, cultural studies' interdisciplinary, contextualizing imperative has long been suspicious of—and indeed defined itself in opposition to—"traditional" literary studies, which it associates with a decontextualized New Critical idealism: "textual analysis in literary studies carries a history of convictions that texts are properly understood as wholly self-determined and independent objects as well as a bias about which kinds of texts are worthy of analysis. That burden of associations cannot be ignored."[30] The result of these contradictory attitudes toward literary textuality—both, in different ways, rooted in Williams' insistence that "we cannot separate literature and art from other kinds of social practice"—has been a tendency to read nonliterary texts *as* literary texts, and literary texts *through* nonliterary texts. The critical discourses surrounding a variety of cultural practices—film, advertising, design—have consequently been enriched through the application of "literary" reading techniques, while our understanding of literary texts has been enhanced by their politically oriented historical contextualization, and especially by their juxtaposition with other similarly historicized cultural practices. At the same time, however, owing in part to the politico-theoretical imperative to emphasize the similarities rather than the differences between literature and other cultural discourses, and in part to the negative associations of "traditional" literary studies, the study of literature's "specific features as [a] practice"—that is to say, of literary form as a cultural practice—has fallen into disfavor and neglect.[31]

❖ ❖ ❖ ❖ ❖

It is in this context—that of the roughly decade-long efflorescence of a politically oriented historical formalism and its subsequent effacement by a broader cultural studies paradigm—that new historicism emerged as both product and participant.[32] While the new historicists have been careful to distance themselves from a Marxism whose notions of history and causality they regard as dogmatic and totalizing,[33] when they do cite their materialist predecessors it is generally in the context of exactly the sorts of modifications to the traditional base/superstructure and reflectionist paradigms that laid the groundwork for the historical reconceptualization of form described above. In his 1989 "Professing the Renaissance," perhaps the most theoretically oriented discussion of new historicism by one of its early practitioners, Louis Montrose approvingly notes Althusser's description of ideology as an agent of subject formation (though he warns of its antihumanist implications); Williams' dynamic, conflictual model of ideology; and Jameson's complex, nonreflectionist construction of the relation between a text and its historical subtext.[34] Even when not directly acknowledged, the affiliation of new historicism with other materialist thought of the period is obvious, as evidenced by Montrose's opening characterization of the new methodology:

> There has recently emerged within Renaissance studies, as in Anglo-American literary studies generally, a renewed concern with the historical, social, and political conditions and consequences of literary production and reproduction: The writing and reading of texts, as well as the processes by which they are circulated and categorized, analyzed and taught, are being reconstrued as historically determined and determining modes of cultural work; apparently autonomous aesthetic and academic issues are being reunderstood as inextricably though complexly linked to other discourses and practices—such linkages constituting the social networks within which individual subjectivities and collective structures are mutually and continuously shaped. (15)

The twin premises of 1970s materialist literary criticism, literature's relative autonomy and its cultural productivity, are at the heart of new historicism's rejection not only of "vulgar" Marxist determinism but of New Critical transcendence and old historical reflectionism as well, as Montrose makes clear when he opposes models of literature "[a]s an autonomous aesthetic order . . . ; as a collection of inert discursive records of 'real events'; [and] as a superstructural reflexion of an economic base," to "[c]urrent practices [that] emphasize both the *relative* autonomy of specific discourses and their capacity to impact upon the social formation . . ." (23).

Given this context, we should not be surprised to find that new historicism's relation to questions of form is more complicated than its antiformalist rhetoric suggests. Even as they disavowed New Critical formalism, the early new historicists demonstrated marked affinities with the sort of historical formalism outlined above. Montrose's work in the early 1980s on Elizabethan pastoral and Stephen Orgel's 1975 book on the Stuart masque treat literary genres not as ahistorical archetypes or objects in a purely literary history, but as historically specific cultural practices involved in the shaping of subjects and the exercise of power.[35] Citing Williams' assertion in *Marxism and Literature* that "forms and conventions in art and literature [are] inalienable elements of a social material process," Montrose concludes that "[t]he historical study of Elizabethan pastoralism cannot confine its inquiry to matters of literary taxonomy and thematics, to what pastorals 'are' or what they 'mean'; it must also ask what pastorals *do,* and by what operations they perform their cultural work."[36] One might indeed argue that this historical formalism was as fundamental to early new historicism as its opposition to American academic formalism. The collection of essays for which Greenblatt coined the term "new historicism" was entitled *The Forms of Power and the Power of Forms in the Renaissance,* originally published as a special issue of the journal *Genre;* and in the same introduction in which he located new historicism's origins in its repudiation of New Critical idealist formalism, he concluded by asserting the importance to the new historical project of a formalism that understood literature's unique characteristics not as textually intrinsic and historically transcendent but as culturally produced and productive: "[distinctions] between artistic production and other kinds of social production. . . . do in fact exist, but they are not intrinsic to the texts; rather they are made up and redrawn by artists, audiences, and readers. These collective social constructions on the one hand define the range of aesthetic possibilities within a given representational mode and, on the other, link that mode to the complex network of institutions, practices, and beliefs that constitute the culture as a whole. In this light, the study of genre is an exploration of the poetics of culture" (6).

As new historicism solidified as a critical practice, however, developing a relatively consistent rhetoric and methodology, the importance of form began to diminish. The academic institutionalization of new historicism and cultural studies in the United States occurred at roughly the same time, and there was considerable cross-fertilization between the two in terms of both institutional prestige and theoretical focus, to the extent that both practitioners and critics of the former have come to regard it as a species or aspect of the latter.[37] Among other things, the two share a commitment to an interdisciplinary discourse analysis, breaking down the disciplinary boundaries that obscure the interaction of a full range of cultural discourses in the exercise of power. For new historicism, as for cultural studies, this has entailed the rejection of "traditional" literary studies, with its privileging of literature as a uniquely complex, transcendent, or reflective discourse, in favor of a more general notion of textuality that treats literature as one of many culturally productive discourses susceptible to critical analysis: Greenblatt has claimed that "[i]f there is any value to what has become known as 'new historicism,' it must be here, in an intensified willingness to read all of the textual traces of the past with the attention traditionally conferred only on literary texts."[38] While laudable both in intent and for the work it has produced, this interdiscursive focus, coupled with a desire to avoid the New Critical taint of formal study, has directed new historicism's attention away from literary form as an aspect of "the poetics of culture." Form remains a part of new historical rhetoric, but its focus on the deconstruction of essentialized boundaries between discourses has not produced a correspondent examination of the social construction and function of the formal markers of literature's difference from other discourses.[39] In "Professing the Renaissance," for example, Montrose cites the relative autonomy of literary genres and conventions as a potential source of ideological contestation (22), and notes the new historical "conviction that formal and historical concerns are not opposed but rather are inseparable"—a conviction that he acknowledges is "perhaps not yet adequately articulated or theorized" (17). Montrose's focus in the essay, though, is not on such a theorization but on the broader new historicist project of re-situating literary texts "not only in relation to other genres and modes of discourse but also in relationship to contemporaneous social institutions and non-discursive practices"—a construction in which literature as a whole becomes one discursive genre among others (17). Similarly, in "The Circulation of Social Energy," Greenblatt's earliest detailed effort to articulate his own theoretical practice, he claims that "sustained, scrupulous attention to formal and linguistic design will remain at the center of literary teaching and study. But . . . I propose something different: to look less at the presumed center of the literary domain than at its borders. . . . the half-hidden cultural transactions through which great works of art are empowered."[40] Consequently, though he lists among his interests the re-presentation of social materials in aesthetic form, his essay is far more concerned with the movement of extraliterary materials into and out of the literary domain than with the specific ways they are shaped by that domain. At the conclusion of the essay, which introduces *Shakespearean Negotiations,* Greenblatt notes almost as an afterthought that each of the four chapters that follow centers on a text from a different Shakespearean genre, and he quickly ascribes a social function to each genre, only immediately to concede that "the social energies I have detected in one genre may be found in equal measure in another" (20).

This ambivalent attitude toward form is reflected in the ensuing essays in *Shakespearean Negotiations,* which subordinate formal issues—if they are raised at all—to the dynamics of the by-now familiar "Greenblatt reading," which, often by means of a compelling anecdote, introduces a nonliterary cultural practice and proceeds to locate it in a literary or dramatic text; the goal is less to illuminate the meaning or function of the text itself than to demonstrate the functional continuity between different cultural discourses. Rather than criticizing these invariably insightful and provocative readings for not doing what they never claim to do, however, let us briefly consider an essay in which Greenblatt does explicitly emphasize issues of form—the 1983 "Murdering Peasants"—as the exception that proves the rule.[41] The essay—unusually for Greenblatt—draws its nonliterary material from within the traditional realm of the aesthetic: the sculptural genre of the victory column. Following a scrupulously historical analysis of the formal problems faced by Dürer in designing a hypothetical monument celebrating victory over a peasant uprising, Greenblatt offers a nuanced summary of the complex, potentially contradictory interaction of authorial intent, formal conventions, and historical subject matter:

the most important lesson to be learned from our discussion of Dürer's design is that intention and genre are as social, contingent, and ideological, as the historical situation they combine to represent. The genre of the monument is no more neutral and timeless than the Peasant's War, and Dürer's artistic intentions, as we have been able to reconstruct them, express a specific mode of engagement with the people and events to which his design refers. [But] [i]f intention, genre, and historical situation are all equally social and ideological, they by no means constitute a single socio-ideological "language." On the contrary, as Dürer's design suggests, they are, in effect, separate forces that may jostle, enter into alliance, or struggle fiercely with one another. (112)

These remarks point toward a genuine historical formalism. But when the essay turns to its literary materials—Sidney's "New" *Arcadia,* Spenser's *Faerie Queene,* and Shakespeare's *2 Henry VI*—its treatment of form is considerably less nuanced. The pastoral prose romance, heroic verse romance, and history play are all located within the largely unelaborated "heroic genre," and the discussion of the three texts is reduced to a single episode in each that addresses the dilemma faced by Dürer: how to represent an aristocratic victory over ignoble foes. The results, though offering a compelling analysis of class conflict, have much less to do with genre than with the interdiscursive analysis of an array of representational strategies for a particular social problem—the difference between heroic romance and history play, for example, is reduced to the supplanting of status relations with property relations ("Symbolic estate gives way to real estate"), an intriguing dichotomy that begs for—but receives no—elaboration (125). Even in an essay ostensibly devoted to the historicization of genre, the new historical reading subordinates literary form to interdisciplinarity.

As suggested earlier, when new historicism does expand the scope of its literary analysis beyond the historical contents and functions of individual texts, it tends to look not to genre or other formal conventions but to the category of literature itself as one cultural discourse among others—a category that is largely heuristic, existing primarily to be dissolved into the broader field of cultural practice, and thus usually left untheorized.[42] A similarly general aesthetic discursive category that has received considerably more historically specific and theoretically incisive attention from Renaissance new historicists—perhaps because of its more obviously social origins and effects—is theater, or the theatrical. But the sort of attention that theater as a cultural mode has received is indicative of new historicism's theoretical priorities. On the one hand, the Renaissance theater has received considerable attention as a material institution with its own physical space, social status, legal restrictions, and economic imperatives—much of the "circulation" discussed by Greenblatt in "The Circulation of Social Energy" concerns the material circumstances of theater's acquisition of scripts and properties and the means by which they were turned to profit. When this interest in theater as institution is extended to the interpretation of texts, it produces—in a neat reversal of the Renaissance commonplace concerning the subordination of aesthetic pleasure to the goal of moral improvement—a series of readings in which the economic profit accruing from aesthetic pleasure trumps ideological indoctrination as the social function of theater:

> The dramatist may have a palpable ideological purpose, generating anxiety, for example, to persuade women to submit to their husbands. . . . But in the public theater such purposes are subordinated to the overriding need to give pleasure. Anxiety takes its place alongside other means—erotic arousal, the excitement of spectacle, the joys of exquisite language, the satisfaction of curiosity about other peoples and places, and so forth—that the players employ to attract and satisfy their customers. The whole point of anxiety in the theater is to make it give such delight that the audience will pay for it again and again.[43]

In this way, despite the circulation of both material and ideological properties into the theater from the culture at large, Greenblatt's treatment of theater as institution uses its economic embeddedness to argue for its cultural autonomy.[44]

On the other hand, an essential component of new historicism's depiction of Renaissance England is its emphasis on what Jonathan Goldberg refers to as "the theatricality of culture."[45] This understanding of theatricality elevates it from an institutionally specific practice to the central ideological mechanism of early modern society, locating its effects in such diverse practices as royal self-display, public executions, and the self-fashioning of courtiers and others. For Greenblatt in particular, the pervasiveness of theatricality means not only that the theater is able to appropriate for its own use the fascination and prestige of other "theatrical" institutions like the church, but also that the pleasure an audience takes in the theater serves to reinforce the authority of a theatrically conceived dominant power structure. Discussing the scriptedness of the theatrical experience, Greenblatt contends:

> We could argue further that one of the ideological functions of the theater was precisely to create in its audience the sense that what seemed spontaneous or accidental was in fact fully plotted ahead of time by a playwright carefully calculating his effects, that behind experienced uncertainty there was design, whether the design of the human patriarchs—the fathers and rulers who unceasingly watched over the errant courses of their subjects—or the overarching design of the divine patriarch. The theater then would confirm the structure of human experience as proclaimed by those on top and would urge us to reconfirm this structure in our pleasure.[46]

This congruence of theatrical and royal power is at the heart of Greenblatt's most notorious articulation of his containment-based model of Renaissance culture, the conclusion of "Invisible Bullets," in which he argues that "[r]oyal power is manifested to its subjects as in a theater. . . . It is precisely because of the English form of absolutist theatricality that Shakespeare's drama, written for a theater subject to state censorship, can be so relentlessly subversive: the form itself, as a primary expression of Renaissance power, helps to contain the radical doubts it continually provokes."[47] Though Greenblatt allows that certain individual plays may escape the conservative implications of theatrical representation, given the new historicist account of the pervasiveness of theatricality in Renaissance culture it is perhaps not surprising that critics have taken Greenblatt's argument to be pessimistically monolithic.[48] And in at least one important sense, it is: for like cultural studies' use of textuality, the new historicist use of theatricality is essentially metaphorical, and its blanket application runs the risk of ignoring or obscuring differences as it emphasizes similarities. By setting aside the specificities of Renaissance theatrical practice in favor of a generalizable model of theatricality as self-conscious presentation to a largely passive and receptive audience, new historicism presents—or at least implies—an unjustifiably homogeneous version of Renaissance culture and at the same time further devalues the study of dramatic forms and conventions as culturally specific practices.

If this attempt to provide a historical basis for the theoretical deconstruction of the boundaries between Renaissance theater and culture relies on a selective account of Renaissance theatrical practice, a similar claim can be made of another new historical effort to deprivilege the literary: the pervasive, virtually foundational assertion that English Renaissance culture itself did not differentiate between "literary" and (other) political discourses but instead viewed them all as modes of cultural practice. In one of the earliest attempts to systematically characterize new historicism, Montrose offered this explanation of the method's popularity in Renaissance studies: "during the sixteenth and seventeenth centuries, the separation of 'Literature' and 'Art' from explicitly didactic and political discourses or from such disciplines as history or moral and natural philosophy was as yet incipient. . . . Because we now seem to be moving beyond this modern, essentialist orientation to 'Literature' [the "ideology of aesthetic disinterestedness"], we can begin to grasp it as an historical formation that had barely begun to emerge at the turn of the seventeenth century."[49] Among the most extended and revealing elaborations of this by-now commonplace premise is Greenblatt's recent essay, "What Is the History of Literature?" which, like Montrose, uses the contemporary demise of an essentialist model of literature to recover the functionalist model that preceded it: "I want to propose that, as the belletristic and national models slowly crumble about us, we look at some of the ways the term *literature* was used before either of those models was yet in place. What we immediately encounter is literature's implication in institutional structures, its deep functional utility."[50] Greenblatt first argues that before literature came to mean "creative writing" it stood for a more general notion of literacy which—as in the invocation of the "benefit of clergy"—served primarily to grant its possessors a degree of social power. He then turns to the "history of literature" called for in Francis Bacon's *Advancement of Learning*: after acknowledging that Bacon did have a conceptual category for "creative writing"—the Renaissance concept of "poesy"—he quickly subsumes that category into "a much larger whole encompassed by the term *literature,* a term whose modern equivalent would be *cultural poetics* in the sense of the sum of written discourses through which we apprehend and act upon the world . . ." (471). Not surprisingly, this Baconian history of literature is both cross-cultural and interdisciplinary ("with poetic inventions taking their place in relation to all other forms of discourse" [472]), and is clearly set apart from both "the display of taste" and the "close reading of works deliberately detached from extratextual or intertextual causality," which are the domain of (New?) "critics" rather than "historians" (473–74).

Compelling as this "discovery" of new historical principles in Renaissance texts may be, however, it is also based on a partial (in both senses) reading of early modern literary theory. Greenblatt and Montrose are certainly not wrong in insisting that the Renaissance counted literature among the didactic arts, viewing it not as a realm apart from, but as a powerful means of, cultural practice. But in their efforts to establish literature as one socially efficacious discourse among others, they downplay or ignore an equally fundamental aspect of Renaissance criticism: its careful delineation of the unique ways in which "poesy" performs its ideological suasion. The emphasis on similarity of ends over specificity and diversity of means is a new historical, not a Renaissance, trait: if Greenblatt's Bacon quickly passes over the formal and other conventional characteristics that set "poesy" apart from other discourses (figurative language and fictionalized content in Greenblatt's account), we need not look far afield to find in Sidney's *Apology for Poetry* a detailed account not only of the different means of persuasion used by poesy, history, and philosophy, but also of the distinct social functions performed by the various literary genres.[51] For at least some Renaissance thinkers and writers, an understanding of the formal features of literature that distinguished it from other discourses did not inhibit but on the contrary enabled an understanding of its social efficacy.

❖ ❖ ❖ ❖ ❖

Seen in this light, the call for a new historical formalism that is, finally, this essay's polemical goal is a recursive one, calling for critical progress by means of a return—to Greenblatt's early assertion that "the study of genre is an exploration of the poetics of culture"; to the work begun by the materialist formalists of the 1970s; and to the Renaissance conception of literary form as socially productive. The forms that such a critical practice might take are myriad—examples may be found in some of the essays in this volume[52]—and rather than prescribing or advocating a single method, I would like instead to offer a conceptual paradigm for thinking about the various roles that form may play in the historical study of literature—that of *mediation*. Mediation suggests not only the occupying of a middle position but also the forging of a relationship that need not be reduced to reflection, allowing instead for mutual influence and adjustment. In this sense, form not only provides the middle term (elided by new historical practice) between theatricality or literature "in general" and individual plays/texts, but also mediates two of the more vexed relationships in historical criticism, those between author and audience (or intention and reception) and between text and social context. The key to both mediations is the materialist insistence on the status of literary forms as social products shaped by specific historical circumstances to perform specific ideological tasks—on forms not simply as containers for extrinsic ideological content, but as practices with an ideological significance of their own. Whether she knows it or not, an author's choice of genres and conventions is an ideological choice among options provided by her audience, a choice that in turn provides that audience with an ideological context within which to interpret the text; even the decision to blend, alter, or reject conventions in the final disposition of the text's individual form is a choice freighted with ideological significance. If the task of a historical criticism is to reconstruct the conditions of a text's production, an understanding of the social functions of the forms available to its producers and consumers is essential.

Form may thus be said to mediate between text and social context as well as author and audience by providing a socially produced meaning or function—an ideology of form—to be reproduced, contested, or appropriated by the text. But form is not the only source of a text's ideological significance. The text also absorbs—through the process Greenblatt describes as "circulation"—ideologically charged aspects of the culture at large that become its raw material or subject matter. Moreover, the ideological charge(s) borne by that material need not match those of the text's form(s); and it is here that form performs its final and most complex mediation between text and context. When a text's form shapes and is in turn shaped by its raw material—when ideologies of form and content meet—the result will be a modification of both that is specific to the text itself, ranging from reinforcement to neutralization to potentially subversive contradiction. It is in this sense—that of form as mediation between a text's ideological raw materials and its eventual ideological effect, transforming social materials as they circulate into and out of the text—that a historical formalism can be most valuable to the new historical project. For while new historicism excels at mapping interdiscursive circulation, documenting the appropriation of materials from other discourses by literary or dramatic texts, it has been less successful at theorizing the *results* of that appropriation, the transformation visited upon extraliterary materials before they are recirculated by performance or publication to act upon the culture at large. When not linked to the enhancement of institutional or authorial prestige, the new historicist account of the relation between text and context has been what Alan Liu describes as "an intertextuality of culture without a functional philosophy or anti-philosophy" that—like the interdisciplinary application of "textuality" or "theatricality"—tends toward metaphorical rather than rigorously theoretical comparison.[53] The result, Liu argues, is new historicism's formalist treatment of culture as a network of interdiscursive connections based on likeness, a treatment that, lacking a more fully-developed methodology or "rhetoric" of text-context interaction, is unable to link new historicism's synchronic cultural model to a properly diachronic model of historical change.[54] A truly historical formalism, one which treated every text as a complex and unique interaction of historically specific formal and contextual ideologies, could prove just such a methodology by accounting for the literary text's relative autonomy from its informing discourses and rooting any consequent subversive potential not (as in the Marxist model) in postfacto ideological analysis but in audience expectation and its frustration or complication. A historical formalism is, in short, not a return to but a remedy for formalist essentialism, a theory of literature as both a measure and a means of historical change.

Notes

1. In *Resistant Structures: Particularity, Radicalism, and Renaissance Texts* (Berkeley: University of California Press, 1995), 67–68, Richard Strier offers a similar analysis of new historicism's titular duality, but asserts that the comparison with an older historical method is the more important meaning of the phrase. See also Kiernan Ryan's introduction to *New Historicism and Cultural Materialism: A Reader,* ed. Kiernan Ryan (London: Arnold, 1996), xiii-xiv.
2. Stephen Greenblatt, "Introduction" to a special issue, "The Forms of Power and the Power of Forms in the Renaissance," *Genre* 15, nos. 1, 2 (1982): 5. Further references in text.
3. Greenblatt, "Introduction," 6. In a telling passage in the introduction to a later collection of his own essays, Greenblatt personalizes—one might say Oedipalizes—his relation to New Criticism by embodying "the formalist

agenda" of the 1960s academy in the person of his graduate school professor William K. Wimsatt, who "seemed to be eight feet tall and to be the possessor of a set of absolute convictions, but I was anything but certain." *Learning to Curse: Essays in Early Modern Culture* (New York: Routledge, 1990), 1.

4. The phrases are Louis Montrose's, from "Professing the Renaissance: The Poetics and Politics of Culture," in *The New Historicism,* ed. H. Aram Veeser (New York: Routledge, 1989), 23. He employs them to underline one of new historicism's central claims and enabling premises, that literature "is the product of work and that it performs work in the process of being written, enacted, or read" (23).

5. From the descriptive note on the verso of the half-title page of books in the series. The series' general editor is new historicist *avant la lettre* Stephen Orgel, and its editorial board includes Jonathan Dollimore and Jonathan Goldberg.

6. John Brannigan, *New Historicism and Cultural Materialism* (New York: St. Martin's Press, 1998), 80–81. In the same paragraph, Brannigan refers to new historicism's success in "replacing the right-wing formalist orthodoxy with a historicizing and politicizing agenda...."

7. A partial exception may be found in Ryan, *New Historicism,* which contends that "[r]adical historicist criticism is undoubtedly the poorer for its reluctance to meet the complex demands of a text's diction and formal requirements..." (xviii).

8. The most nuanced and persuasive version of this argument of which I am aware is Alan Liu's "The Power of Formalism: The New Historicism," *ELH* 56 (1989): 721–771; for a variety of others, see Strier, *Resistant Structures,* 70–78; Ryan, *New Historicism,* xiii-xiv; Howard Felperin, "'Cultural Poetics' versus 'Cultural Materialism': The Two New Historicisms in Renaissance Studies," in *The Uses of the Canon* (Oxford: Clarendon Press, 1990), 154–55; Don E. Wayne, "Power, Politics, and the Shakespearean Text: Recent Criticism in England and the United States," in *Shakespeare Reproduced,* ed. Jean E. Howard and Marion F. O'Connor (New York: Methuen, 1987), 61; and Walter Cohen, "Political Criticism of Shakespeare," in Howard and O'Connor, *Shakespeare Reproduced,* 35–37. On the formalist connotations of the term "cultural poetics," see Brannigan, *New Historicism,* 83–84, 91–92; and Ryan, *New Historicism,* xiv. Greenblatt has refuted some of these charges against his own practice in "Resonance and Wonder" (*Learning to Curse,* 161–183). In "After the New Historicism" (*Alternative Shakespeares: Volume 2,* ed. Terence Hawkes [London: Routledge, 1996], 17–37), Steven Mullaney offers a qualified defense of Greenblatt while distinguishing his work from that of other new historicists more interested in resistance and historical change. While for the moment I am less interested in the accuracy than in the irony of these charges of "cultural formalism," I will return to them later to assess their relationship to new historicism's (non)treatment of literary form.

9. See for example, Lukács' *The Historical Novel* (London: Merlin Press, 1962), *The Meaning of Contemporary Realism* (London: Merlin Press, 1963), and *Studies in European Realism* (London: Hillway, 1950); and Goldmann's *The Hidden God* (London: Routledge & Kegan Paul, 1964) and *Towards a Sociology of the Novel* (London: Tavistock, 1975). For a useful summary of their work in relation to Marxist theories of literary form, see Terry Eagleton, *Marxism and Literary Criticism* (Berkeley: University of California Press, 1976), 27–34.
10. An extreme example of such an idealism is the Russian formalist doctrine that *all* literary form has a defamiliarizing function. While the stylistic means are historically variable, the defamiliarizing effect constitutes a definition of (true) literature, a goal to which literary content is entirely subordinated. On the value and limits of Russian formalism from a Marxist perspective, see Tony Bennett, *Marxism and Formalism* (London: Methuen, 1979), and Fredric Jameson, *The Prison-House of Language* (Princeton: Princeton University Press, 1972); see especially pp. 58–59 of the latter for the relation between the Russian formalist concept of *ostranenie* and Brecht's *Verfremdungseffekt.*
11. Louis Althusser, "Ideology and Ideological State Apparatuses," in *Lenin and Philosophy and Other Essays*, trans. Ben Brewster (New York: Monthly Review Press, 1971), 135. Further references in text. See also his argument that while ideology in general has no history (in the sense of being omnipresent and transhistorical—a not unproblematic assertion), individual ideologies and ideological apparatuses "have a history of their own (although it is determined in the last instance by the class struggle)" (160–161).
12. "The Ideological State Apparatuses are multiple, distinct, 'relatively autonomous' and capable of providing an objective field to contradictions which express, in forms which may be limited or extreme, the effects of the clashes between the capitalist class struggle and the proletarian class struggle . . ." (149). My intention here is not to try to adjudicate the vexed question of the conflict between the seemingly inescapable structural determinism of Althusser's treatment of "ideology in general" and his insistence on the possibility of resistance and change through conflicts within and for individual ideological apparatuses, but instead merely to describe some of the doors his work has opened for other critics.
13. "A Letter on Art in Reply to André Daspre," in Althusser, *Lenin and Philosophy,* 222. It should be noted that the "Letter on Art" is dated April 1966, three years prior to "Ideology and Ideological State Apparatuses."
14. The epithet is Eagleton's, from "Macherey and Marxist Literary Theory," in *Against the Grain: Essays 1975–1985* (London: Verso, 1986), 10. My discussion of Macherey's work is drawn from his *Theory of Literary Production,* trans. Geoffrey Wall (London: Routledge & Kegan Paul, 1978; first published in French by Librairie François Maspero, 1966), chapters 1–19.
15. Althusser, "Letter on Art," 222; Macherey, *Theory,* 46.
16. See, for example, Eagleton's critical summation in "Macherey and Marxist Literary Theory," 18–19. Without naming names, Greenblatt notes in his

defense of his own work against charges of political pessimism that "[i]n general I find dubious the assertion that certain rhetorical features in much-loved literary works constitute authentic acts of political liberation; the fact that this assertion is now heard from the left, where in my college days it was more often heard from the right, does not make it in most instances any less fatuous and presumptuous" ("Resonance and Wonder," 166).

17. Terry Eagleton, *Criticism and Ideology* (London: Verso, 1978; orig. pub. NLB, 1976), 64–69. Further references in text.

18. Though the form/content dichotomy is a convenient one, I should specify that by "content" here I mean not the ideological signification produced by the text (what Eagleton calls the unique "ideology of the text" [*Criticism*, 80]), but the aspects of the General Ideology that provide the text's subject matter.

19. Generally speaking, Althusser's influence on political and literary theory in the United States was both later and less profound than his impact in Britain, perhaps because of the difficult American relation to Marxism. Antony Easthope notes that in the 1960s and 1970s Britain came to post-structuralism through Althusser while America did so through Derrida (*British Post-Structuralism* [London: Routledge, 1988], xiii).

20. Fredric Jameson, *The Political Unconscious: Narrative as a Socially Symbolic Act* (Ithaca: Cornell University Press, 1981), 23–58. Further references in text.

21. "Magical Narratives: On the Dialectical Use of Genre Criticism," in Jameson, *The Political Unconscious*, 103–150.

22. The most likely objection to Jameson's model as the basis of a (non-Marxist) historical formalism is, of course, not the implications he fails to pursue but his insistence on a specifically Marxist version of history as the ultimate subtext of all literature. I would argue, however, that while that subtext is the foundational pretext of Jameson's argument, virtually all of his model of the relationship between history, form, and literature functions independently of its historical presuppositions—the value of his description of the ideology of form, for example, is not dependent on its attachment to the history of modes of production.

23. Williams designates his theory "cultural materialism" in the introduction to his *Marxism and Literature* (Oxford: Oxford University Press, 1977); my discussion of his ideas is drawn primarily from this volume. The "cultural materialism" that is generally considered the British cousin of American new historicism draws its name and considerable inspiration from Williams' theory, though the two are by no means identical; among the important borrowings of the former from the latter are an emphasis on the possibility of individual or collective agency in historical change and social resistance, and a sympathetic but selective relation to Marxism.

24. For the product/practice distinction, see Raymond Williams, "Base and Superstructure in Marxist Cultural Theory," in *Problems in Materialism and Culture* (London: Verso, 1980), 45–49. First published in 1973, the essay anticipates many of the issues elaborated in *Marxism and Literature*.

25. Williams, "Base and Superstructure," 44.
26. Antony Easthope notes that Williams' "either/or" construction of his preference for treating literature as practice rather than product risks collapsing "the continuing *relation* between the text as structure and the text as act of reading," with the latter effacing the former (*British Post-Structuralism*, 13–14). I believe that Williams escapes this hazard, but I will suggest below that many of his followers do not. See also Eagleton's similar concerns, cited in note 31 below.
27. See Williams, *Marxism and Literature*, 176: "conventions . . . can be identified by formal analysis but can be understood only by social analysis." Elsewhere, he calls for a sociology of literature that would include "the social history of literary forms, in their full particularity and variety but also in the complex of their relation with other formations," through which "changes of viewpoint, changes of known and knowable relationships, changes of actual and possible resolutions, could be directly demonstrated, as forms of literary organization, and then, just because they involved more than individual solutions, could be reasonably related to a real social history. . . ." (From "Literature and Sociology," in Williams, *Problems in Materialism and Culture*, 22, 26.)
28. Along with Richard Hoggart, Stuart Hall, and E. P. Thompson, Williams is generally considered one of the founding figures of cultural studies. For concise accounts of the field's origins and development, see the introductions to three useful cultural studies anthologies: Lawrence Grossberg, Cary Nelson, and Paula A. Treichler, eds., *Cultural Studies* (New York: Routledge, 1992); Simon During, ed., *The Cultural Studies Reader* (London: Routledge, 1993); and Jessica Munns and Gita Rajan, eds., *A Cultural Studies Reader: History, Theory, Practice*, (London: Longman, 1995).
29. In "The Subject of Literary and the Subject of Cultural Studies," Antony Easthope distinguishes between an old-fashioned base-superstructure model of cultural studies drawn from sociology and a preferred textualist model rooted in literary studies, which brings its interdisciplinary tools to bear on the central problematic of "the analysis of discursive or signifying practices." (In *Theory/Pedagogy/Politics*, ed. Donald Morton and Mas'ud Zavarzadeh [Urbana: University of Illinois Press, 1991], 34.) This cultural textualism is related but not identical to both the post-structuralist textuality characterized by the undecidable (and ahistorical) multiplicity of signification, and the new historicist "textuality of history," which insists that all access to history is mediated by texts (for the latter, see Montrose, "Professing the Renaissance," 20). In her "Introduction: History, Culture, and Text," Lynn Hunt discusses the role of textualism in cultural history and anthropology (especially the work of Clifford Geertz) and, citing Roger Chartier, underlines the essentially metaphoric nature of the concept, and the accompanying risk of overgeneralizing and ignoring significant differences between written and nonwritten practices. (In *The New Cultural History*, ed. Lynn Hunt [Berkeley: University of California Press, 1989]; see especially pages 12–17.)

30. Cary Nelson, Paula A. Treichler, and Lawrence Grossberg, "Cultural Studies: An Introduction," in Grossberg et al., *Cultural Studies*, 2. For a detailed discussion of cultural studies' efforts to differentiate itself from "traditional" literary study, see Easthope, "The Subject of Literary and the Subject of Cultural Studies."

31. I do not mean to suggest that the two methodologies—cultural studies and historical formalism—are theoretically incompatible; the problem is simply one of emphasis. When advocates of cultural studies argue for "close affinities between the way [one] reads a Shakespearean sonnet . . . and the way [one] 'reads' and understands events that take place in South Africa/Nicaragua/ [one's] social life," the emphasis on similarity rooted in the common cultural construction of all meaning, rather than on the different forms through which and functions for which that meaning is constructed, is entirely situational and polemical. (Masud Zavarzadeh and Donald Morton, "Theory Pedagogy Politics: The Crisis of 'The Subject' in the Humanities," in Morton and Zavarzadeh, *Theory/Pedagogy/Politics*, 7.) In his 1981 *Walter Benjamin, or, Towards a Revolutionary Criticism* (London: NLB), Eagleton approvingly notes—and credits to Williams—a shift in focus in Marxist cultural studies from "the analysis of an object named 'literature' to the social relations of cultural practice" but warns against the "fetishiz[ing]" of the latter, "a coy or cavalier disregard for the partial 'givenness' of a literary text licens[ing] a newly fashionable dissolution of products into processes" (97; see also the same volume's preface for Eagleton's situation of his own post–*Criticism and Ideology* work in the new cultural studies paradigm).

32. This is not, of course, the entirety of new historicism's remarkably diverse theoretical background but merely a largely unacknowledged context for its relation to issues of form. On new historicism's connections to an array of influences including Foucault, Geertzian anthropology, deconstruction, feminism, continental philosophy, and the American New Left, see Brannigan, *New Historicism*, and the essays in Veeser, *The New Historicism*, and Ryan, *New Historicism*, as well as the recent collection of essays, *Critical Self-Fashioning: Stephen Greenblatt and the New Historicism*, ed. Jürgen Pieters (Frankfurt am Main: Peter Lang, 1999).

33. Not surprisingly, as the foremost American Marxist of the era, Jameson is most often singled out for criticism. See Greenblatt, "Towards a Poetics of Culture," in Veeser, *The New Historicism*, 2–5; Montrose, "Professing the Renaissance," in Veeser, *The New Historicism*, 20; and Jonathan Goldberg, "The Politics of Renaissance Literature," *ELH* 49 (1982): 514–542, an early review essay on new historicism that compares it favorably to both Jameson's Marxism and old historicism. Further references to Montrose will be in text.

34. Montrose, "Professing the Renaissance," 16n3, 22, 23n15. See also Mullaney's discussion in "After the New Historicism" of Williams' influence on new historicism, in which he cites the latter's non-totalizing notion of hegemony, his break with Marxism's teleological historical model, and his rejec-

tion of the ultimate determinism of the economic (22–23). In the Introduction to *Learning to Curse* (2), Greenblatt cites his encounter with Williams at Cambridge as the enabling factor in his break from Wimsattian New Criticism, but he rarely acknowledges the specific nature of Williams' critical influence: the Cambridge story is the only reference to Williams in *Learning to Curse*, and Williams' name does not appear at all in the index of Greenblatt's *Shakespearean Negotiations: The Circulation of Social Energy in Renaissance England* (Berkeley: University of California Press, 1988).

35. See Louis Adrian Montrose, "'Eliza, Queene of Shepheardes,' and the Pastoral of Power," *English Literary Renaissance* 10 (1980): 153–82, and "Of Gentlemen and Shepherds: The Politics of Elizabethan Pastoral Form" *ELH* 50 (1983): 415–459; and Stephen Orgel, *The Illusion of Power: Political Theater in the English Renaissance* (Berkeley: University of California Press, 1975).

36. Montrose, "Of Gentlemen and Shepherds," 419, 416; cf. Williams, *Marxism and Literature*, 133.

37. Montrose ("Professing the Renaissance," 15) locates new historicism within cultural studies' emphasis on the reciprocity between language and the social, and Greenblatt ("Towards a Poetics of Culture," 12) refers to "the new historicism in cultural studies." Brannigan notes that cultural studies is "a discipline in which the new historicists are situated comfortably, and which indeed they have in many ways expanded" (33).

38. Introduction to Greenblatt, *Learning to Curse*, 14.

39. On this tendency, see Brook Thomas, "The New Historicism and the Privileging of Literature," *Annals of Scholarship* 4 (1987): 32–33; revised and reprinted in his *The New Historicism and Other Old-Fashioned Topics* (Princeton: Princeton University Press, 1991), ch. 6.

40. Stephen Greenblatt, "The Circulation of Social Energy," in Greenblatt, *Shakespearean Negotiations*, 4. Further references in text.

41. Stephen Greenblatt, "Murdering Peasants: Status, Genre, and the Representation of Rebellion," *Representations* 1 (1983), 1–29; reprinted in Greenblatt, *Learning to Curse*, 99–130. My in-text citations will be from the latter.

42. A partial—and frustrating—exception is Greenblatt's justification in "Resonance and Wonder" (169ff) of his primary interest in "imaginative literature" based on its capacity to provoke "wonder"—a term he illustrates with reference not to literature but to painting and other nondiscursive artifacts.

43. Stephen Greenblatt, "Martial Law in the Land of Cockaigne," in *Shakespearean Negotiations*, 134–35. See also Greenblatt's treatment of the theatrical appropriation and evacuation of religious ritual in "Shakespeare and the Exorcists," in the same volume, 94–128.

44. Though valuable for its extrapolation of what Eagleton calls "authorial ideology" to the theater's corporate mode of production, it is Greenblatt's focus on intent that renders this type of reading problematic by ignoring the "built-in" ideological implications of dramatic forms and conventions that may bypass authorial intent and still register with audiences. It also rests

upon entirely unsupported (and perhaps unsupportable) assumptions about the motives and priorities of Renaissance dramatists and other theatrical practitioners. On the politically conservative implications of this sort of reading and their connection to the conservatism of Greenblatt's synchronic "cultural formalism," see Stephen Cohen, "New Historicism and Genre: Towards a Historical Formalism," *REAL* 11 (1995): 408–411. Much of my treatment of new historicism in the present essay is a reconceptualization and recontextualization of this earlier work.

45. "The Politics of Renaissance Literature," 528.
46. "The Circulation of Social Energy," 19.
47. Stephen Greenblatt, "Invisible Bullets," in *Shakespearean Negotiations*, 65.
48. For Greenblatt's response to the critical reception of his essay—and to the tendency to conflate what he considers a distorted account of its argument with new historicism in general—see "Resonance and Wonder," 165–66. In "After the New Historicism," Mullaney echoes Greenblatt's defense of "Invisible Bullets" but proceeds to critique Greenblatt's ideological isolation of theater as a material institution as well as his oversimplification of both royal theatricality and theatrical royalism (26–33).
49. Louis Montrose, "Renaissance Literary Studies and the Subject of History," *English Literary Renaissance* 16 (1986): 12.
50. Stephen Greenblatt, "What Is the History of Literature?" *Critical Inquiry* 23 (1997): 462. Further references in text.
51. For a fuller consideration of Sidney's treatment of the social function of form, see Cohen, "New Historicism and Genre," 416–418.
52. Though not plentiful, valuable examples may be found elsewhere as well. In her 1990 *A Happier Eden: The Politics of Marriage in the Stuart Epithalamium* (Ithaca: Cornell University Press), Heather Dubrow calls for "a new formalism [that] can view aesthetic issues as related, not inimical, to history . . ." (268), and begins to meet her own challenge in that volume as well as her 1995 *Echoes of Desire: English Petrarchism and its Counterdiscourses* (Ithaca: Cornell University Press). Other extended considerations of the relations between history and form—each quite methodologically distinct from the others—include Franco Moretti, *Signs Taken for Wonders: Essays in the Sociology of Literary Forms*, trans. Susan Fischer, David Forgacs, and David Miller (London: Verso, 1983); Thomas O. Beebee, *The Ideology of Genre* (University Park: Pennsylvania State University Press, 1994); and Susan J. Wolfson, *Formal Charges: The Shaping of Poetry in British Romanticism* (Stanford: Stanford University Press, 1997). With the exception of Moretti's chapter on Renaissance tragedy (parts of which were printed earlier in the 1982 "Forms of Power and Power of Forms" issue of *Genre*), none of the three deals substantively with Renaissance literature.
53. Liu, "The Power of Formalism," 742–745; quotation from 744.
54. For Liu, even the new historical notion of subversion, absent a more adequate theory of historical change, merely replaces similarity with difference in what remains a fundamentally closed, formal system. Liu's solution is the

rejection of a formalist textualism in favor of a rhetorical model of text-as-action that insists on the historical agency of both producer and consumer—a version of Williams' cultural materialism. I would argue that a historical-formalist approach can provide such a model not by rejecting but by historicizing formalism, combining text-as-action (or practice) with text-as-product rather than allowing the former to efface the latter.

Shakespeare and the Composite Text

Douglas Bruster

Literary works of the English Renaissance tend to be unusually copious—thick, that is, with quotations of other texts, as well as with material from the world outside their pages.[1] Such copia, of course, has often attracted the attention of new historicism and other varieties of criticism interested in exploring the cultural contexts of Renaissance literature. In these critical modes, however, the literary and social materials of various texts are important not as sources of the texts in question but rather as potential sources for critical "thick descriptions" of those texts, descriptions that have become almost a separate literary genre in their own right. Obviously, the field has benefited a great deal from the cultural turn in literary study and from the thick descriptions that have accompanied this turn. But what often gets left out by thick description's interest in literary contexts is the relation between newer forms of criticism—criticism usefully gathered by the coinage "cultural historicism"[2]—and an older kind of formalist criticism that served as an unspoken, and perhaps unconscious, model for it: source study.

Much of what is currently practiced under the name of historicism and cultural criticism is actually a modified version of source study. For several decades now, this apparently old-fashioned mode of criticism has served as an unacknowledged model for these newer kinds of inquiry into English Renaissance literature and culture. Recognizing their relation to source study will help us understand some of their limitations, as well as some limitations traditionally attributed to source study. Only by understanding their shortcomings can we adapt these critical modes to account more fully for the composite nature of Renaissance literature. This is particularly true, I believe, in relation to plays from Shakespeare's era—plays whose "worldliness" often comes from the worlds of other books.

One reason for asking how sources relate to literary form and, by extension, to the practice of formalism in literary criticism is that source study is typically seen as a critical subgenre of its own. As an approach, source study seems unlike formalism in that it can be as interested in a work's prehistory as it is in that work's ultimate form. Conventional wisdom sometimes compounds this problem by associating formalism too closely with the ahistorical—defining it, that is, as the study of a frozen text, a work of literature that exists for us as a verbal object outside time. Few formalist inquiries actually embody this stereotype, of course: such topics as prosody, genre, metaphor, philology, and rhetoric have complex histories that often affect their appearance in literary works, and most critics respond to these histories when practicing formalist criticism.

The histories to which formalism attends reveal source study's affiliations with formalism. Just as a formalist study of a text might focus on the relation between elements of that work's form and prior instances of theory or practice relevant to the topic under examination—for example, a particular rhetorical trope in a text, previous instances of that trope, its apparent functions, and comments on its use and import—so does source study remind us that texts are fashioned, that they are fashioned with extant materials, and, further, that these materials have histories of their own. Source study is a formalism, then, not only through its interest in the parts which make up a textual whole, but also through its sensitivity to the histories of those parts.

The New Formalism

Yet if, in its attention to the elements of a literary text, source study *is* a variety of formalism, how can we hope to describe it as anything more than an antiquated practice? Whether called source study, *Quellenforschung* (*Quellenstudien*), or *le critique de génèse,* it remains one of the oldest modes of literary criticism. How might it be seen, then, as novel in any way? And what, for that matter, is so unprecedented about formalist study of literature today that it might justify such a collective label as "the new formalism"? We can start to address the question of source study's innovations by defining this larger critical genre.

New formalism could be defined as follows: a critical genre dedicated to examining the social, cultural, and historical aspects of literary form, and the function of form for those who produce and consume literary texts. The new formalism sees language and literary forms—from the single-lettered interjection "O" to the stanza, the epic battle, and epic itself—as socially, politically, and historically "thick." Instead of relying on literary texts primarily for anecdotes or synecdoches of the real, the new formalism seeks to understand texts—and their mediated relations to the external world—by scrutinizing the cultural work that forms do, the symbolic capital attached to specific forms, and the choices available to authors and others involved in the production of texts.

As it pertains to criticism of English Renaissance literature, the designation appears to have been coined by Heather Dubrow in the title of a special session at the December 1989 meeting of the Modern Language Association: "Toward the New Formalism: Formalist Approaches to Renaissance New Historicism and Feminism." The following year, in the conclusion to *A Happier Eden: The Politics of Marriage in the Stuart Epithalamium,* Dubrow noted both the ahistoricity of some new historicist and feminist criticism of the 1980s, as well as the marked lack of attention to language and form in these and other methodologies. Dubrow went on to argue that "the interplay between texts and their cultures can best be explicated through another kind of interplay, the dialogue between some of the questions posed by the new historicism and some of the methods employed by New Criticism, linguistics, and formalism."[3] Building on this observation about historicism's role in supplementing the concerns of formalist criticism, one could say that the new formalism is "new" not only in its expanded notice of the cultural valences of literary form, but also in its proximity to and qualification of the new historicism.

The late 1980s and the 1990s saw the publication of a number of formalist studies that, directly and indirectly, responded to the aformal directions of new historicism. In addition to Dubrow's book on epithalamia, studies that might be characterized as contributing to a new formalism include Annabel Patterson's *Pastoral and Ideology* (1987), Ann Baynes Coiro's *Robert Herrick's Hesperides and the Epigram Book Tradition* (1988), Joshua Scodel's *The English Poetic Epitaph* (1991), David Quint's *Epic and Empire* (1993), Mary Thomas Crane's *Framing Authority* (1993), Kevin Dunn's *Pretexts of Authority* (1994), Dubrow's *Echoes of Desire* (1995), Ann Moss' *Printed Commonplace-Books and the Structuring of Renaissance Thought* (1996), Judith Anderson's *Words That Matter* (1996), Patricia Parker's *Shakespeare from the Margins* (1996), Daniel Fischlin's *In Small Proportions* (1998), and Lynne Magnusson's *Shakespeare and Social Dialogue* (1999). To be sure, few if any of these authors announce a group identity with other formalists. Some might not welcome the identification of their work as "formalism" at all. But whether taking up words, tropes, figures, or genres, all helped renew a critical approach that had lagged in popularity, and most did so by stressing the social and political implications of literary form. Each of these studies understands form as possessing significant agency before, during, and after literary composition. Each sees form as not only a valid but an overwhelmingly compelling object of inquiry.

A variety of the new formalism has concerned itself with literary sources. In it, sources function in a more complex manner than previous criticism had allowed for. Robert Miola speaks to the changing assumptions behind this critical development when he notes that the traditional tendency, in source study, to "rely almost exclusively on verbal iteration as proof of influence" has given way to a model of source that is "plural rather than singular, encompassing and allowing for a wide range of possible interactions between sources, intermediaries, and texts."[4] Recent source studies that engage literary sources, and, by addressing the social and political implications of borrowing, ask us to revise our stereotypes of this practice, include Andrew Gurr's "Intertextuality at Windsor" (1987), Claire McEachern's "Fathering Himself: A Source Study of Shakespeare's Feminism" (1988), Miola's *Shakespeare and Classical Tragedy: The Influence of Seneca* (1992), his *Shakespeare and Classical Comedy: The Influence of Plautus and Terence* (1994), Eric Mallin's chapters on *Hamlet* and the plague, and on *Twelfth Night* and the Anjou affair, in his *Inscribing the Time: Shakespeare and the Ends of Elizabethan England* (1995), Frank Whigham's chapter on *Arden of Faversham* in *Seizures of the Will in Early Modern English Drama* (1996), Heather James' *Shakespeare's Troy: Drama, Politics, and the Translation of Empire* (1997), Richard Knowles' essay "Cordelia's Return" (1999), and Grace Tiffany's "Shakespeare's Dionysian Prince: Drama, Politics, and the 'Athenian' History Play" (1999).[5] Gurr represents the expanding definition of "source" in noting that the search for the sources of *The Merry Wives of Windsor* "becomes ... more complicated when it looks for echoes that are not specifically verbal, that are not overt, and that simply resonate the need of the two companies [playing in London in the mid- to late-1590s] to follow each other's fashion in playmaking. Subjects, plots, even the alignment in politics, religion or social questions begin to join the verbal parallels as examples of a writer's response to the intertextual activities of the time."[6]

The Sources of Culture

New formalist accounts of English Renaissance literature emphasize these social and political dimensions of form—dimensions, in Gurr's words, that are "not specifically verbal"—in large part because the field in general has embraced the cultural context of literary works. In this emphasis, such studies respond to the profound transformation of literary criticism since the late 1970s. Arguably the greatest disciplinary change during the twentieth century came in its last two decades, when—spurred by the new historicism, by feminist criticism, and by cultural materialism—a predominant concern with the structure and aesthetics of literary works gave way to a predominant interest in the relations of these works to the times, places, and persons who worked to produce them and for whom they were produced. During the 1980s and 1990s, criticism reproduced the trajectory that Raymond Williams described when he noted the change in the meaning of "culture" during his life: an earlier sense of culture as "high culture" (what Williams called "the teashop sense") was being replaced by our current sense of culture as "a whole way of life."[7] Formalist studies have merely responded to a growing conviction in the field that the "culture" of literary texts is less that of their literary heritage than that of their larger environment.

This conviction has produced a revolution in the objects of criticism, for we have moved from examining books toward examining culture. If before the 1980s books were often understood to be among the most significant products of their culture (indeed transcending their culture, in some instances), more recently we have embraced a notion of culture in which books are only one kind of object among many that should be scrutinized. Among the objects an expanded pattern of inquiry takes up are not only non-"literary" texts (such as, for instance, pamphlets and speeches), but items of material culture generally (such as embroidery and clocks), social practices (such as rituals and customs), and events (cases at law, social dramas). Obviously, this shift has had both supporters and detractors. Those who most strongly support it, for instance, point to the way this change in critical focus has opened up a host of cultural objects to our view, placing literature itself in a context richer than that afforded by a grand tradition of literary masterpieces. Those who find this critical revolution problematic sometimes note that these same literary masterpieces have an uncanny way of appearing in even the most politically "radical" research—that great literature provides the symbolic capital that underwrites such criticism—and that most critics are not well trained in the methodologies by which they seek to write cultural history.

This last reservation is worth exploring: not that this critical revolution has replaced the literary text with the "text" of culture, but that, in so doing, it has left largely unchanged the procedures by which the relevant text is analyzed. That is, in moving from literary text to culture *as* text, critics have generally retained the principles and methodology of literary analysis they were taught—which means, in most cases, the principles and methodology of formalism. What is too seldom observed in discussion of the changes in the field over the past few decades is that the new historicism, and much cultural inquiry generally, owes as great a debt to formalist criticism as the new formalism does to it.

To demonstrate this relation without forcing any single critic to be its exemplar, I would like to take the liberty of discussing an imaginary book. This addition to an academic publisher's booklist is titled *Pursued by a Bear: Representations of Russia in Early Modern England*. Although I have made up this title, it seems not at all inconceivable that a study like this may soon be written and published; certainly it sounds worth reading. Such a study might begin by noting the underacknowledged relations between Russia and early modern England. It would castigate scholars for having almost willfully overlooked these relations and chide those who *have* noticed them for not adequately differentiating the various peoples and subcultures of early modern Russia. This study would help make its case by examining strong commercial and political links between Russia and England at this time. It would quote relevant correspondence and pamphlets. Later chapters would survey literary representations of Russia. We could expect a chapter devoted to Russians in Shakespeare: *Love's Labor's Lost*, for instance, and *The Winter's Tale*. But the topic would also take one through many other plays (among them, *The Travels of the Three English Brothers*, *The Four Prentices of London*, and *The Loyal Subject*), as well as through prose fictions and poems. The study would conclude, of course, by suggesting that to neglect the importance of Russian themes and concerns to early modern England is to misapprehend English culture.

In place of "Russia" in this example we could supply any number of categories: from ethnic, national, and religious identities to social customs, body parts, and other physical objects. Many books and essays have followed the pattern I describe and have done so by employing various of the preceding categories. What I want to show with this hypothetical monograph is that, like much historicism and cultural inquiry today, it is essentially a source study. Instead of investigating, say, the sources of *Love's Labor's Lost*—in which "Russia" would be a contributing element, along with many others—this study takes the culture of early modern England as its text and argues that Russia is a significant and underacknowledged source of that text. Instead of taking a book as its central object, this study reads parts of books themselves as the sources of a larger cultural text. Critics have reversed the objects of the procedure, then, but have left the procedure intact.

Images of Source Study

The connections between source study and cultural inquiry are so seldom recognized because source study has acquired a negative reputation in the field. There is perhaps no better proof of this status, or lack thereof, than that offered recently by *The Norton Shakespeare*. Earlier editions of Shakespeare that sought to be "complete" in some way—here G. Blakemore Evans' *Riverside* and David Bevington's Harper-Collins edition come to mind—almost invariably included a section detailing Shakespeare's literary sources. Along with lists of characters, chronologies, first-line indexes to the poems, and selected critical bibliography, Shakespeare's sources were held to be as indispensable to a "complete works" as was a royal genealogy.

But although *The Norton Shakespeare* has a chart of the kings and queens of England, it omits a separate section on sources, preferring to mention them in passing in the editors' prefaces to the individual plays. In place of a section that might be called "Shakespeare's Sources" or "Shakespeare's Reading," the volume's general editor, Stephen Greenblatt, entertains readers with three imagined events that may have affected Shakespeare's later writing. These events are Shakespeare's possible attendance at, respectively, official ceremonies in which his father may have taken part; a royal Progress and parliamentary elections; and a Catholic exorcism.[8] That Greenblatt understands these fantasized primal scenes as *sources* of the plays is clear from the way that he introduces them:

> Even in ordinary mortals, the human imagination is a strange faculty; in Shakespeare, it seems to have been uncannily powerful, working its mysterious, transforming effects on everything he encountered. It is possible to study this power in his reworking of books by Raphael Holinshed, Plutarch, Ovid, Plautus, Seneca, and others. But books were clearly not the only objects of Shakespeare's attention; like most artists, he drew upon the whole range of his life experiences.[9]

By substituting these imaginary events for the lists of books, and excerpts from books, that other editions have traditionally provided for their readers under the heading of Shakespeare's "sources," Greenblatt illustrates the way in which historicism and cultural inquiry have expanded our notion of what counts as a possible source of literature. What Greenblatt summarizes as "the whole range of [Shakespeare's] life experiences" is most often defined not biographically but *culturally*. In addition to books, that is, things like weather, riots, marriages, diplomacy, the plague, cases at law, royal proclamations, economic fluctuations, trade disputes, social controversies, changes in fashion, religious conflicts, hangings, personalities, shipwrecks, wars, marital infidelities, and accents may be seen as contributing to a literary text.

None of these, of course, was unknown to traditional scholarship—to "old historicism"—which, if it is to be faulted, tended to go even further than Greenblatt in its speculative identification of the sources of Shakespeare's plays.[10] By "old historicism" here I am referring to a genre of criticism that seeks to identify the social material that has gone into the composition of literary texts. Instances of old historicism include John Dover Wilson's "Martin Marprelate and Shakespeare's Fluellen" (1912), Lilian Winstanley's *Hamlet and the Scottish Succession* (1921), Edith Rickert's "Political Propaganda and Satire in *A Midsummer Night's Dream*" (1923), Frances Yates' *A Study of "Love's Labour's Lost"* (1936), Henry Paul's *The Royal Play of "Macbeth"* (1950), E. C. Pettet's "*Coriolanus* and the Midlands

Insurrection of 1607" (1950), T. W. Baldwin's *On the Compositional Genetics of "The Comedy of Errors"* (1965), and B. N. De Luna's *Jonson's Romish Plot* (1967). These studies are alike in holding that the plays they examine directly incorporated identifiable figures and social events—from King James and social insurrections to the Gunpowder Plot—into their represented worlds. In this way, "old" and "new" historicisms share a conviction that literature is intensively worldly. Yet old historicism differs from its newer incarnation in that it never overlooked books as crucial, and interesting, sources of literary texts.

The Norton Shakespeare is not alone in finding literary sources unfashionable. The (new) New Arden editions of Shakespeare, as a recent commentator has observed, tend not to include significant examples of a play's literary sources. Reviewing the third series' *Antony and Cleopatra, King Henry V,* and *Titus Andronicus,* Barry Gaines points out that "No longer is a generous selection of source material included in appendixes; thus *Antony and Cleopatra* lacks excerpts from Plutarch, and *Henry V* lacks excerpts from Holinshed."[11] What makes the simultaneous exclusion of literary sources from these editions less than surprising is the reputation that traditional source study has come to possess with a new generation of editors. Even as source study provides the model for some of the most exciting kinds of cultural study practiced today, it is widely held to be an anachronistic mode of literary criticism.

Although a general sentiment about source study is that, in this anachronism, it remains bookish and irrelevant, there exist more pointed criticisms of it as a mode. These include the following, which we might introduce as *Reasons to Avoid Source Study:*

1. Some authors do not seem to use sources significantly
2. Authors always change the contexts of what they borrow
3. Authors make sources unnecessary precisely by using them
4. Source study distracts us from what is on the page in question
5. Source study, in its emphasis on books, doesn't allow us to treat social themes, such as gender, race, and social class
6. Source study is forensic, even prosecutory
7. The greater the influence on a text, the less visible is that influence in a text
8. Source study privileges those who have access to large libraries and archives

To respond to these claims, it may prove helpful to offer some of my own. I will start by saying that while various forms of expression, from painting and sculpture to dance and architecture, can be said to "quote" previous instances of their form, the verbal basis of literature makes it especially open to source study: when repeated across various texts, words and phrases can help identify more certainly which sources an author used. But even with literary works, source study is far from an exact science. Source study necessarily depends on the objects it examines; not every work of literature, or every genre, or every period of literary history, for instance, lends itself to an examination of sources. Source study tends to be a productive way to read plays of the English Renaissance because the authors of these plays were particularly aware of literary tradition and tended to read widely in the works of that tradition, as well as in the writings of their contemporaries. Dramatic works of this period were, in turn, profoundly heterogeneous, often containing within their pages a virtual microcosm of the cultural world they were written to please.

These claims are by no means original, and most are far from controversial. In themselves, however, they work to counter some of the criticisms listed above. For instance, the criticism that some authors do not make particularly significant use of sources (the first in the list above) does not apply to most Renaissance authors, and certainly not to most Renaissance playwrights. Dramatists of this period routinely looked to printed materials in their search for stories, characters, ideas, situations, words, and phrases. Making recourse to a wide range of source materials, they necessarily changed the contexts of what they borrowed. It is through this change of contexts that such authors made the sources more, rather than less, necessary to our understanding of their texts (the second and third criticism in the list above). In changing the contexts of these materials, the playwrights show us paths not taken and more lucidly foreground those ultimately decided upon.

The next two criticisms of source study—that it distracts us from what is on the page in question, and that, in its emphasis on books, it prevents us from treating social themes—would seem to cancel each other. One says, for instance, that "close reading" is the most desirable approach to a work of literature; the other, that a work's cultural and historical milieux are most important to its interpretation. Each of these criticisms speaks from the vantage of an effective mode of reading, and, although in potential opposition, these modes deserve to have their positions addressed. I would respond to the first criticism by admitting that source study indeed takes our attention away from what is on the page we read. It seems even the antithesis of close reading. Yet this diversion from the page or pages at hand need not be permanent or disabling. As was pointed out above, in adding other contexts to the texts, passages, and words in question, source study can enrich, rather than diminish, them. By providing these alternate contexts, source study can help us read more closely what is on the page.

The criticism that traditional source study prevents us from treating social themes is true only if one accepts two assertions: first, that traditional source study examined only books as sources; and second, that books themselves are not the repository of intensively social themes. This first assertion does not withstand much scrutiny, for, as I have pointed out, the "old" historicism routinely sought sources in the world surrounding the texts it took up, and recent instances of historicism and cultural criticism have drawn heavily on source study for some of their materials. The second assertion—that books do not contain social themes—cannot be assented to, logically, at the same time that one reads literature *for* these social themes. That is, if we see literature as incorporating and responding to its environment, we must also admit that when literary texts borrow from other texts, they are incorporating (in however mediated a way) elements from social environments that merit our attention. And while authors often borrow from older sources that do not seem to enclose a synchronic "truth" about the author's culture at the moment of the text's composition, borrowing is itself a social practice that can tell us a great deal about the older materials that help make up every culture, whether books of the Bible, passages from Ovid, ethnographic details from travel narratives, chronicles of the reigns of English monarchs, or Greek idylls. Source study thus helps us overcome the narrow synchronic window through which new historicism typically chooses to view literature's relation to the surrounding world.

The next two criticisms of source study—that it is forensic, even prosecutory in nature, and that the greater the influence, the less visible that influence is in a text—are perhaps among the most serious of those on the list. Each criticism has to do with problems of evidence and proof. It will help us evaluate their merit if we examine strong versions of these claims. I turn first, therefore, to G. W. Pigman III, who, in an essay titled "Neo-Latin Imitation of the Latin Classics," suggests that critics who sense they have found relations among texts (through imitations of models, quotations, and echoes) may well be noticing coincidental uses of language. Pigman goes on to elaborate this position:

> At first sight the proposition that neo-Latin imitations are more difficult to identify and interpret may well sound absurd, for a computer which had been fed the Roman poets and almost any collection of Renaissance neo-Latin verse could spit out line after Renaissance line with some phrase from an ancient poem. But actually, that is the heart of the problem: what do we do once we have our massive print-out of similar and identical phrases? It is impossible to believe that all of the repetitions are conscious, much less significant, and often a reader, deafened by the roar of the echo chamber, feels incapable of finding a signal in all that noise. I would hazard the guess that

a large proportion of the repetitions is due to coincidence and unconscious reminiscence—large enough, in any event, to raise doubts about "imitations" and "borrowings"[12]

What makes this passage relevant to our examination of source study is that it deals with difficulties of evidence relating to verbal recurrence. The problem, for Pigman, is that we have so much information that it can remain meaningless. His imaginary computer program overwhelms our senses: "spit out line after Renaissance line"; "deafened by the roar"; "all that noise." But although Pigman seems to base his reluctance here on an empirical issue—what can we know about literary relations, and on what evidence can we know it?—we are provided with merely his "guess" that the results of an experiment never conducted would leave us dubious about conscious appropriation of models.

The reluctance shown here is defensive, as though Pigman is anxious that a mechanical procedure (such as a computer program) might produce information that would exceed any single critic's control. Of course, his "massive print-out of similar and identical phrases" need not have been tied so closely to technology. Equally massive lists of possible sources exist for a variety of Renaissance authors, and these lists were produced long before the advent of computers. They are, as Pigman hints, intimidating lists. And this may be the larger cause of his anxiety: with prolific authors, source study is a humbling experience. Studying Shakespeare's sources, for example, requires a critic to read not only the works of Shakespeare, and works that Shakespeare may have read, but also the works of other critics who have published on the subject. This extensive course of study leaves us in a position where we are not guessing whether an undifferentiated print-out might be trustworthy. It means, instead, that we must proceed on a case-by-case basis in an attempt to ascertain the relation between a literary text and a possible source. Pigman is right to say that we need to be careful in this endeavor: two texts can indeed share a resemblance that does not derive from material contact. But this does not, and should not, preclude our noticing a resemblance that does.

In using the terms "imitation" and "model," Pigman takes us away from the core of source study, which is at heart a forensic practice—one that seeks material relations among texts and their specific sources. The more we move away from the specific, the more difficult it is to identify these relations with any precision. Hence the next criticism on our list: that the greatest influences *on* a text may not themselves appear *in* that text.[13] Like Pigman's reluctance, this one also involves questions of evidence and protocol: how are we to prove an influence, when the very word "influence" (from the Latin *influere,* "to flow in") suggests an amorphous fluidity? Here we can turn to

Laurence Lerner for a strong version of this potential criticism of source study. In an essay titled "Ovid and the Elizabethans," Lerner notes:

> There is one preliminary problem in discussing the presence of Ovid in sixteenth-century poetry: the difficulty of detecting it. If you absorbed Ovid, not perhaps with your mother's milk, but at any rate with your schoolmaster's rod, you—and your readers—might not know when you were using him.[14]

When Lerner identifies the critic's job with that of the detective ("the difficulty of *detecting* it"), he reveals a valid concern with the "how" of ascertaining literary relations. However, like Pigman's reservation, that of Lerner here risks jeopardizing a mode of criticism because it cannot produce perfect results. Surely all writers (critics included) are not always conscious of when they are using particular sources, or of when they are being influenced by an author or tradition. Lerner's recourse to metaphors of embodiment—taking in Ovid not "with your mother's milk, but . . . with your schoolmaster's rod"—aptly characterizes the way in which words, phrases, stories, even language itself, can seep into one's mind without one's awareness.

The unknown worries these two critics, both in terms of what an author does not know, and what critics do not discover. This situation is, I would argue, something that we not only must live with, but something that we can live with. To be sure, whether authors are conscious of what they do is sometimes important. We might take numerological structures in texts as a good example of this: much depends on whether an author appears to have consciously arranged a text in a numerologically significant manner. The calendrical structures of Spenser's *Epithalamion* are a familiar instance here.[15] But in many other cases, an author's consciousness of a particular source or textual formation does not seem as crucial. For instance, an author might reproduce Ovidian phrases or situations without realizing she was doing so, and what could be more important than her realization is the fact of reproduction itself. The fear that there may be textual borrowings and influences that, in Lerner's point of view, readers might not recognize is well-founded; there is always more about literary relations that we do not know than that we do. But, like Pigman's worry concerning unrelated resemblances, this should only be a spur to greater and more careful attention to questions of source.

The two criticisms just examined also display an uneasiness over scale: too many resemblances leading to potentially meaningless coincidence, and too great an acquaintance with a particular author, text, or tradition producing an unverifiable "influence" on an author and work. This concern brings us to our final criticism of source study, which is that it is made possible only by the large holdings of established libraries and archives. This is a more than trivial criticism, in part because it reveals that scholarship is a luxury obtained through access to books. We can see this potential disparity between the haves and have-nots of academic inquiry even in the price difference between, say, an inexpensive, pared-down, "thrift" edition of a Shakespeare play and an edition that includes copious notes, commentary, and appendices. Even in paperback, the latter—which, depending on the series, might include a section on the work's sources—could be expected to cost up to ten times what the former does. The differences in format in this example reflect a larger distinction between modes of reading—one in which the "text itself" is mainly sufficient, the other in which ancillary texts are indispensable to our understanding of the text. Until fairly recently, this distinction was pressed home to scholars lacking ready access to large libraries and archives. The situation has begun to change, of course, with the introduction of microfilmed texts and electronic databases, both of which can provide access to texts that once required extensive travel to consult. These changes, along with computerized search programs that help to identify verbal overlap among texts, mean that source study has become a more "open" critical mode.

Shakespeare and Source Study: Nashe and Henry V

I have argued, to this point, that source study is related in significant ways to historicism and cultural criticism. I have explored some of the charges commonly leveled against source study, giving reasons these criticisms should not prevent us from taking this mode seriously. In order to make a practical case for its usefulness, I would like to offer an example of source study. The paragraphs that follow address the relationship between the Chorus of Shakespeare's *Henry V* (1599) and Thomas Nashe's *The Unfortunate Traveller* (1594).

As the research of J. J. M. Tobin has demonstrated, Shakespeare almost certainly had various of Nashe's manuscripts and printed texts before him as he wrote many of his plays, using them for names, words, and phrases the way one would dip one's quill in fresh ink.[16] This borrowing stretches at least from *The Two Gentlemen of Verona* (1593) to *Macbeth* (1606) and includes such plays as *Titus Andronicus* (1594), *Love's Labor's Lost* (1595), *Romeo and Juliet* (1596), *1 Henry IV* (1597), *As You Like It* (1599), *Hamlet* (1601), *Measure for Measure* (1604), *Othello* (1604), and *King Lear* (1605). The texts from which Shakespeare borrowed range throughout Nashe's career, from *Pierce Penniless* (1592) and *Summer's Last Will and Testament* (1592), through *Christ's Tears over Jerusalem* (1593), *Have With You to Saffron-Walden* (1596), and *Lenten Stuffe* (1599). Tobin has identified an extremely close relation among certain passages in these two writers' texts; the overlap is so strong that it seems clear that Shakespeare routinely turned to Nashe's work for verbal *matériel*. That one writer borrowed from the other's manuscripts prior to publication, and did so over the course of many years, hints that the authors may have been on close terms as well.

The borrowing in question here occurs in the Chorus of *Henry V,* which, I will argue, was fashioned in part from material in Nashe's *The Unfortunate Traveller*. It is no exaggeration to call *The Unfortunate Traveller* one of the most important pieces of prose fiction in English before the rise of the novel. From one point of view a Menippean satire in its heterogeneity of incidents and materials, Nashe's story is, from another perspective, a remarkably copious "history" of the sixteenth century. Indeed, *The Unfortunate Traveller* remains a virtual encyclopedia of the Renaissance and Reformation in presenting figures both classical and contemporary, continental and domestic, and various centers of thought and activity. Having so much material to include, Nashe needs to maintain the audience's attention to the episodes at hand and to take them from one place and time to another, with no more than the authority of Jack Wilton, a roguish Vice figure, justifying the travel.

Jack's stories are thus cast as tales told to an interested but potentially unforgiving audience, one that needs its attention focused—particularly in the moments of transition between *The Unfortunate Traveller*'s episodes. Two instances of this focusing are given below. The first excerpts sentences from within a single paragraph; the second, several complete sentences a few pages later in the narrative. In these passages, Jack refers to Henry VIII's military campaign in the summer of 1513, a campaign in which the English king led an army across the Channel, captured the French cities of "Turney and Turwin," and returned victoriously to England. Jack tells his audience to follow his narrative with their imaginations:

> You must think in an Army . . .
> Well, suppose he was . . .
> Suppose out of the parings of a pair of false dice I appareled both him and my self
> . . .
> I must not place a volume in the precincts of a pamphlet: sleep an hour or two, and dream that Turney and Turwin is won, that the King is shipped again into England, and that I am close at hard meat at Windsor or at Hampton Court. What, will you in your indifferent opinions allow me for my travel no more signory over the Pages than I had before? yes, whether you will part with so much probable friendly suppose or no, I'll have it in spite of your hearts.[17]

Here "You must think"—a supposition of Jack's, rather than a command—quickly turns into imperative *suppose*s: "Well, suppose," "Suppose." Jack gains the authority for his narrative by taking it; he pleasantly commands his audience to imagine. By the second excerpt, he acknowledges that "probable friendly suppose" might not be given freely, yet assumes it anyway. Condensing over three months' worth of military action and travel into a sentence ("sleep . . . and dream that Turney and Turwin is won, that the King is shipped again into England"), he instructs his audience to suppose, by dreaming, two victories and a triumphant Henry VIII crossing the Channel back to England.

I believe that the passages here formed a material source for Shakespeare's well-known Chorus in *Henry V,* who delivers the Prologue and the Epilogue as well as the choric prefaces to Acts Two, Three, Four, and Five. Throughout the play, this Chorus begs the audience to be patient and imaginative while it apologizes for the inadequacies of the playhouse and its laborers, and for violating the unities of time and place: "Carry them here and there, / jumping o'er times, / Turning th' accomplishment of many years / Into an hour-glass" (Pro. 29–31).[18] It is worth observing that in the chronicle histories Shakespeare wrote before *The Unfortunate Traveller,* such dramatic "travel" had never been a problem. Critics, in fact, have long been puzzled as to why this play's choruses exist. As Samuel Johnson related, early on: "The lines given to the chorus have many admirers; but the truth is, that in them a little may be praised, and much must be forgiven; nor can it be easily discovered why the intelligence given by the chorus is more necessary in this play than in many others where it is omitted."[19] More recently, Anthony Brennan has held that "It is odd . . . that Shakespeare, who had already written many plays without resort to these old-fashioned devices, should employ a formal chorus in the play which brings to a close his preoccupation with the history of England."[20]

These positions represent a general uncertainty about why *Henry V* has a chorus at all. Read alongside Shakespeare's earlier chronicle histories, *Henry V* is indeed anomalous in using a presenter. But these positions do not acknowledge that Shakespeare had employed a chorus in *Romeo and Juliet,* some three years before *Henry V.* I have argued elsewhere that the Prologue and Chorus in *Romeo and Juliet* are "necessary" (in Johnson's words) from the demands of genre: what appears to be a romantic comedy—the son and daughter of rival houses meeting, falling in love, marrying, and thereby reconciling their parents—takes a tragic turn that might, without ample warning, shock its audience.[21] With *Henry V,* it is more difficult to say why Shakespeare felt it necessary to provide a chorus. Perhaps in this case, "necessity" is the wrong way to approach the problem. That is, what if we see Shakespeare not compelled by his materials to employ this Chorus, but enticed by them to do so? Holding opportunity rather than necessity to be central, what if we see Shakespeare writing this Chorus for *Henry V* not because he should, but because he could? In Nashe's work, Shakespeare found a device—that is, an author's apology for episodic leaps across time and space—and words on which he could capitalize to aesthetic effect in *Henry V.* As we will see, what may have been a choice motivated by aesthetics turns out to have implications of a political texture as well.

Having asked, in the Prologue, "Can this cockpit hold / The vasty fields of France? Or may we cram / Within this wooden O the very casques / That did affright the air at Agincourt?" (11–14), the Chorus precedes Act Three with the following:

> *Suppose* that you have seen
> The well-appointed king at Hampton pier
> Embark his royalty . . .
> . . . . .
> . . . *O, do but think*
> You stand upon the rivage and behold
> A city on th' inconstant billows dancing . . .
> . . . . .
> *Suppose* th' embassador from the French comes back
> . . . . .
> . . . Still be kind,
> And eche out our performance with your mind.
> (3.0.3–35; emphasis added)

Shakespeare appears to have turned Wilton's casual storytelling tools—"You must think," "Well, suppose," "Suppose"—into the Chorus' decidedly more formal directions: "Suppose," "O, do but think," "Suppose." The problem of space and time in Nashe occupies Shakespeare as well. Jack excuses his narrative compression by saying that "I must not place a volume in the precincts of a pamphlet," "precinct" from Latin *praecingere,* "to gird or encircle." Similarly, as we have seen, Shakespeare's Chorus worries about what may be crammed within the circle of the wooden O, about what a cockpit can hold.

Jack tells his audience to "sleep an hour or two, and dream that Turney and Turwin is won, that the King is shipped again into England, and that I am close at hard meat at Windsor or at Hampton Court." The dreaming imagination he asks for not only condenses events, but floats Henry and Jack home across the channel. Narrative *travail* and geographical *travel* join in a pun—"allow me for my travel"—no less central to Nashe's narrative than to its title. In Shakespeare, such condensed travel becomes important in passages like those above, and in lines like "Now we bear the King / Toward Callice; grant him there; there seen, / Heave him away upon your winged thoughts / Athwart the sea" (4.0.6–9). Nashe's passages seem to have provided many of the building blocks for Shakespeare's Chorus: Jack's acknowledgment of the smallness of his medium, his request for a dreamlike imagining by his audience, and his admission of their potential powers; the compression of time and space; the return of a triumphant King Henry across the Channel from France; and the imperative *supposes*. Shakespeare, I would offer, saw in Jack's otherwise minor remarks the basis for his Chorus.[22]

Perhaps the first thing to say about these two literary texts, and the passages I have quoted, is that any relationship between them must be alleged rather than proven. This holds for every instance of source study. We can "know," in the strong sense of that word, nothing further than that certain texts have resemblances and/or verbal overlap. Even when authors of imaginative literature cite their sources, or when we possess authors' personal copies of other writers' books (copies that sometimes annotate particular words and passages that occur in these authors' own writings), there is always room for skepticism about what seems a certain borrowing. If source study at times appears to present itself as a quasi-scientific mode of scholarship, its rhetoric must always remain in the suasive mode: "It seems probable, for X reason, that author Y borrowed from text Z." So strong do such probabilities seem in many cases that an author's "sources" harden into the appearance of fact. We might take Shakespeare's reliance on Holinshed's *Chronicles* for his history plays as an example of the latter; here the sentence structure given above is truncated to read " . . . author Y borowed from text Z," without the introductory "It seems probable, for X reason, that . . ." But in most cases, even when authors declare what their sources are, the question of source remains less fact than likelihood.

The dialogue between Shakespeare and Nashe here is telling, for the differences in their "voices" are significant. While Nashe notices what Shakespeare calls the issue "Of time, of numbers, and due course of things" (5.0.4), Nashe names it "travel" and sees it merely as a reason to make a transition. Shakespeare, on the other hand, uses it to justify the Chorus' recurrent and striking poetry. In doing so, he changes the tenor of the remarks in important ways. Nashe has Jack seem to relish the medium he works in, as the pun here on "Page"—coupled with similar puns throughout the work—goes to show. In contrast, Shakespeare's Chorus exaggerates the inadequacies of the playhouse to support poetic *occupatio*. Where Jack's storytelling is roguish and homely, Shakespeare's Chorus is lofty, even priggish in its continued apologies and obsequiousness. Where Jack is grounded in the cozening tradition of the cony-catching pamphlets of the early 1590s, the Chorus of *Henry V* has what Brennan has aptly described as a "priest-like" function.[23] In his edition of the play, Andrew Gurr refers to the Chorus as "coercive," and observes that instead of offering itself as a "humble servant" or representing a "humble author," it transfers the epithet "with some malignancy" by praying for the *audience's* "humble patience."[24]

If this act of borrowing comes as an assent or repetition with qualification—a kind of "Yes, but . . ."—that qualification speaks to the cultural and political positions of Shakespeare's Chorus. But before we consider what these positions are, perhaps it is advisable to begin by noticing what the borrowing does not do. It does not, for instance, contradict a critical tradition that places the Chorus (and, often, the play itself) alongside the epic.[25] Neither does it discount arguments that Shakespeare's concern with the issues of time and place here responds to Sidney's thoughts on these topics in the *Apology*.[26] It does not disprove a recent argument that Chapman's *Seven Books of the Iliads of Homer* (1598) provided material for both the Chorus and the play.[27] Nor, finally, does it prevent us from seeing the Chorus as a by-product of Essex's ambitions and activities in Ireland. But the borrowing from Nashe by Shakespeare here does tell us about a choice Shakespeare made.

This borrowing indicates, for instance, that he was aware of other possibilities for a chorus. Nashe's Jack is a strong presenter—a Pistol figure, almost, with narrative authority. We see Nashe's fondness for such a traditionalistic *homo gloriosus* in Will Summers in *Summer's Last Will and Testament*. Nashe endorses, that is, a boisterous and aggressive character who satisfies his and our appetites alike through his wit and linguistic facility. Shakespeare, on the other hand, confines his Pistol to the underplot and elevates the language and ideology of his presenter. Exposed to one model for such a figure—that of Jack Wilton—Shakespeare gives the choric words of his play to an anonymous, priest-like Chorus who apologizes in blank verse for the theater and its laborers' efforts. However much he is a part of the physical world of the playhouse, the Chorus puts himself above that world. The implications of this elevation become apparent when we realize that not only is this Chorus not from the tavern world of *Henry V,* he does not show that he knows this world exists. Indeed this sober Chorus never mentions or describes these lower orders and their environment—even when, as at the beginning of Act Two, the following scene takes place in just such an environment. The Chorus prepares us there for Southampton and the King, but we see instead the Eastcheap world. This Chorus has no language or time for Bardolph, Pistol, Quickly, or Nim; his is an idealizing, even aristocratic vision that does not include their world.

We can begin to see this as typical of Shakespeare when we note that Shakespeare often revised his sources so as to push agency and authority up the social ladder. In his revision of Plautine comedy, for example, aristocrats, not slaves, resolve his plays.[28] Something very similar occurs in this revision in *Henry V.* In writing his Chorus, Shakespeare appears to have drawn on Nashe but changed his presenter in important ways. One could offer many reasons for this, from the reigning tastes of Shakespeare's audiences and the abilities and traditions of the Lord Chamberlain's Men to the competing "pull" of other literary traditions and texts, such as Chapman's *Iliad* translation, and even Essex's ambitions in Ireland. It is also quite possible that we see in the changes some of Shakespeare's own political orientation: that part of Shakespeare that chose Hal over Falstaff, and Prospero over Caliban.

This said, I should point out that it is possible that the similarities in language, phrasing, and situation between *The Unfortunate Traveller* and *Henry V* are merely coincidental. They could be, that is, the product of two authors of roughly the same age, schooled in the same texts, writing for similar audiences at roughly the same time. This is a legitimate consideration, although I believe that, in the context of Shakespeare's use of Nashe's works in other of his plays, the similarities we have observed are much more likely to indicate a material relation between the two texts. Tobin has argued convincingly, for instance, that *The Unfortunate Traveller* provided material for Shakespeare in *Henry V,* Act Four, scenes 3–5, when Shakespeare was writing lines for both Pistol and Bourbon.[29]

Let us consider for a moment, though, what we may take away from this alignment of texts even if we do not believe there is a line of borrowing from one to the other. A comparison of the "presenters" in these two texts, regardless of our feelings about any material indebtedness, leaves us with almost the same findings that were suggested in the reading above. Even when it fails fully to persuade readers of a link between texts, that is, source study succeeds in putting similar things into temporary, and often productive, alignment. More than an arbitrary exercise in comparison and contrast, however, such an examination is based on likeness among objects—objects that, as we have seen, invariably disclose important differences as well.

When it succeeds in persuading readers of a material linkage of texts, source study enriches the narrative through which we understand the past. If a close comparison of *The Unfortunate Traveller* and *Henry V* would tell us some of the same things even if we had not noticed that Shakespeare borrowed from Nashe's text, the possibility that Shakespeare used this text gives us good reason to ask searching questions about differences between them— questions that might otherwise have floated above the works as contrived and extraneous, or not been asked at all. Knowing that Shakespeare made frequent recourse to Nashe identifies for us an important source of his raw materials. In this way source study can ground, in history, our queries and claims about what lies beyond the margins of Shakespeare's plays: by understanding writing as production, it allows us to concentrate on the material relations among texts; by understanding texts as made in time, it helps us explore the differences among them as historically contingent. By scrutinizing the sources of his plays, and how he transformed them, we can learn much about the choices Shakespeare had available to him and the political implications of the decisions he made.

Conclusion

The value of a source study concerned with the relations among books is that it allows us to trace the threads of ordinary borrowing, borrowing like that I have alleged between *Henry V* and *The Unfortunate Traveller*. As currently practiced, the new historicism would probably not take up such a moment for an essay on cultural poetics, for Shakespeare's borrowing in this passage seems only a matter of words—not social energy, power, or authority. Too, the borrowing here is much less provocative than the anecdotes that the new historicism typically chooses to engage. Neither would a vein of criticism interested in "high" literary relations be likely to expend much effort exploring the significance of such borrowing, for Nashe and his earthy narrative seem intrinsically "low," not part of the grand tradition such criticism typically studies.[30] Also working against our notice of this moment of borrowing is the fact that it is not deeply conflictive. Critics interested in divisive struggle between authors—struggle in which authors even devour their forbears—would find little of interest in this low-key, conversational act.[31] In contrast to these methodologies, a source study interested in the seemingly ordinary relations among books and authors provides a way of reading that helps elucidate the various positions of these books and authors in their time and culture, and over time as well.

Source study allows us to eavesdrop on literary "conversations." Such conversations may not always be a formal series of well-considered meditations on issues of high merit but, instead, a casual, sometimes chaotic mix of utterances that includes false starts, half-sentences, and wandering thoughts. Talk, that is, that resembles less the polished dialogue of *The Courtier* than it does the meandering remarks of Ben Jonson's *Conversations*. There is no reason to see authors as godlike makers in total control of their sources. The conversations they enter into with their source texts and authors are, much like our own conversations, less rational and controlled than we might wish. As Hans-Georg Gadamer has pointed out, our control over dialogue is partial, at best:

> We say that we "conduct" a conversation, but the more genuine a conversation is, the less its conduct lies within the will of either partner. Thus a genuine conversation is never the one that we wanted to conduct. Rather, it is generally more correct to say that we fall into conversation, or even that we become involved in it.[32]

The analogy to literature sticks, of course, on the word "genuine," for many literary works undergo a process of revision before they reach anything like their final form. Authors talk back to works: listen to them, respond to them, and perhaps listen again before responding once more. And surely parody, burlesque, *à clef* narratives, and topical stories depend on an intending, purposive author. Initially, then, nothing could seem less "genuine" than literature. But there is much about the role of accident in Gadamer's observation that holds true for literary conversation. Authors fall into conversations only partly in their control and conduct these conversations through and with texts made up of parts and forms of other texts. The larger historical and cultural conversations they become involved in are unavoidably literary situations—eras, schools, patronage and marketplace relations—not of their devising.

Since the cultural turn in literary studies, we have expanded our definition of the sources of literary texts to include these larger conversations. So rich are the plays of Shakespeare and his contemporaries that the entire world around them seems to have been actively engaged as a source of their heterogeneity. Although the epic is sometimes held to be the most capacious of all literary forms, plays composed for the theaters of Renaissance England are arguably even more varied in their makeup. Written, often, by diverse hands, for many actors, and for presentation in multiple venues, they are typically composed of a dazzling array of materials. In this, they deserve to be seen as thoroughly composite texts.

The new historicism has prompted us to see that social and cultural materials form a significant part of these plays—that these materials are "sources" of the plays, even as the plays themselves can be seen as sources of the larger cultural text that new historicism asks us to examine. It has been my contention that recent modes of criticism interested in the cultural aspects of these plays can benefit from a more studied consideration of the bookishness of these dramatic texts. Playwrights were, for the most part, voracious readers, and they drew significantly on printed matter in composing their plays. Although source study can seem an anachronistic mode of reading, it not only underlies much of what is currently practiced under the name of cultural criticism, but also offers us a powerful tool with which to examine the materials that make up every text. Source study that asks questions beyond the margins of texts can offer a solution to some of these shortcomings traditionally ascribed to it. Far from diverting our attention from these plays' relation to their environment, source study that acknowledges the profoundly composite nature of English Renaissance plays gives us deeper knowledge of the various ways these dramatic texts are positioned in their culture.

Notes

1. On what I am calling the "thickness" of Renaissance texts, see Linda Woodbridge, "Patchwork: Piecing the Early Modern Mind in England's First Century of Print Culture," *English Literary Renaissance* 23 (1993): 5–45. I have

discussed this phenomenon at more length in *Quoting Shakespeare: Form and Culture in Early Modern Drama* (Lincoln: University of Nebraska Press, 2000); see, especially, 13–51, 203–12.
2. On "cultural historicism," see Albert H. Tricomi. *Reading Tudor-Stuart Texts Through Cultural Historicism* (Gainesville: University Press of Florida, 1996).
3. Heather Dubrow, *A Happier Eden: The Politics of Marriage in the Stuart Epithalamium* (Ithaca: Cornell University Press, 1990), 266.
4. Robert S. Miola, "Othello *Furens,*" *Shakespeare Quarterly* 41 (1990): 49–64; 49. On the changing face of source study, see also Miola's "Shakespeare and His Sources: Observations on the Critical History of *Julius Caesar*," *Shakespeare Survey* 40 (1988): 69–76.
5. See Andrew Gurr, "Intertextuality at Windsor," *Shakespeare Quarterly* 38 (1987): 189–200; Claire McEachern, "Fathering Himself: A Source Study of Shakespeare's Feminism," *Shakespeare Quarterly* 39 (1988): 269–290; Robert S. Miola, *Shakespeare and Classical Tragedy: The Influence of Seneca* (Oxford: Oxford University Press, 1992) and *Shakespeare and Classical Comedy: The Influence of Plautus and Terence* (Oxford: Oxford University Press, 1994); Eric S. Mallin, *Inscribing the Time: Shakespeare and the End of Elizabethan England* (Berkeley: University of California Press, 1995); Frank Whigham, *Seizures of the Will in Early Modern English Drama* (Cambridge: Cambridge University Press, 1996), esp. 67–74; Heather James, *Shakespeare's Troy: Drama, Politics, and the Translation of Empire* (Cambridge: Cambridge University Press, 1997); Stephen J. Lynch, *Shakespearean Intertextuality: Studies in Selected Sources and Plays* (Westport, CT: Greenwood Press, 1998); Richard Knowles, "Cordelia's Return," *Shakespeare Quarterly* 50 (1999): 33–50; Grace Tiffany, "Shakespeare's Dionysian Prince: Drama, Politics, and the 'Athenian' History Play," *Renaissance Quarterly* 52 (1999): 366–83.
6. Gurr, "Intertextuality at Windsor," 189.
7. See Raymond Williams, *Keywords: A Vocabulary of Culture and Society,* rev. ed. (New York: Oxford University Press, 1985), 11–13.
8. *The Norton Shakespeare,* ed. Stephen Greenblatt (New York: Norton, 1997), 46–9.
9. *The Norton Shakespeare,* 46.
10. I have discussed the "old historicism" more extensively in "New Light on the Old Historicism: Shakespeare and the Forms of Historicist Criticism," in a special issue, "Shakespeare and History," *Literature and History,* third series, 5, no. 1 (1996): 1–18; see, especially, 2–6.
11. Barry Gaines, Review of John Wilders, ed., *Antony and Cleopatra, Shakespeare Quarterly* 50 (1999): 207.
12. G. W. Pigman III, "Neo-Latin Imitation of the Latin Classics," in *Latin Poetry and the Classical Tradition: Essays in Medieval and Renaissance Literature,* ed. Peter Goodman and Oswyn Murray, Oxford-Warburg Studies (Oxford: Clarendon Press, 1990), 199–210; 199, 200.

13. For a cogent articulation of this position, see the anonymous reader cited in Annabel Patterson, *Hermogenes and the Renaissance: Seven Ideas of Style* (Princeton: Princeton University Press, 1970), xi.
14. Laurence Lerner, "Ovid and the Elizabethans," in *Ovid Renewed: Ovidian Influences on Literature and Art from the Middle Ages to the Twentieth Century*, ed. Charles Martindale (Cambridge: Cambridge University Press, 1988), 121–135; 122.
15. On these structures, see A. Kent Hieatt, *Short Time's Endless Monument: The Symbolism of the Numbers in Spenser's "Epithalamion"* (New York: Columbia University Press, 1960); and Alastair Fowler, *Triumphal Forms: Structural Patterns in Elizabethan Poetry* (Cambridge: Cambridge University Press, 1970).
16. See, for example, J. J. M. Tobin, "*Hamlet* and *Christ's Teares over Jerusalem*," *The Aligarh Journal of English Studies* 6 (1981): 158–167; "Nashe and *The Two Gentlemen of Verona*," *Notes and Queries* 28 (1981): 122–123; "*Macbeth* and *Christ's Teares over Jerusalem*," *The Aligarh Journal of English Studies* 7 (1982): 72–78; "Nashe and *Richard II*," *American Notes & Queries* 24 (1985): 5–7; and "Nashe and Shakespeare: Some Further Borrowings," *Notes and Queries* 39 (1992): 309–320.
17. Thomas Nashe, *The Unfortunate Traveller*, in *The Works of Thomas Nashe*, ed. Ronald B. McKerrow (London: Sidgwick & Jackson, 1910), vol. 2: 217, 227.
18. All citations to Shakespeare here are to *The Riverside Shakespeare*, 2nd ed., ed. G. Blakemore Evans et al. (Boston: Houghton Mifflin, 1997).
19. Samuel Johnson, from his 1765 *Works of Shakespeare,* quoted in Michael Quinn, ed. *Shakespeare: "Henry V"* (London: Macmillan, 1969), 34.
20. Brennan, "That Within Which Passes Show: The Function of the Chorus in *Henry V*," *Philological Quarterly* 58 (1979): 40–52; 42. The opposite point of view was taken by Peter Alexander, who in *Shakespeare's Life and Art* (London: James Nisbit and Co., 1939) called the play "a thing of rags and patches, held together by the Choruses" (128).
21. See Douglas Bruster, "Teaching the Tragi-comedy of *Romeo and Juliet*," in *Approaches to Teaching Shakespeare's "Romeo and Juliet,"* ed. Maurice Hunt (New York: MLA, 2000), 59–68. The juxtaposition of comedy and tragedy in *Romeo and Juliet* "may explain why Shakespeare chose to emphasize, in his opening chorus, the tragic ending of the play: without this forewarning, audiences and readers unacquainted with the source story—and perhaps even those who knew it—could well resent the playwright for arbitrarily enforcing a cruel ending on the story's protagonists" (60).
22. A minor piece of supporting evidence might be taken from Gary Taylor's argument about the play's indebtedness to Nashe—and perhaps to *The Unfortunate Traveller*—for one of its unusual words. See Taylor, "Shakespeare's Leno: *Henry V*, IV.v.14.," *Notes and Queries*, new series, 26 (1979): 117–18.
23. "That Within Which Passes Show," p. 47.
24. Andrew Gurr, ed., *King Henry V* (Cambridge: Cambridge University Press, 1992), 6–16; 15.

25. On the epic tenor of the play—and especially, of the Chorus—see Albert H. Tolman, "The Epic Character of *Henry V*," *Modern Language Notes* 34 (1919): 7–16; John Dover Wilson, ed., *King Henry V,* The New Cambridge Shakespeare (Cambridge: Cambridge University Press, 1947); and Edward I. Berry, "'True Things and Mock'ries': Epic and History in *Henry V*," *JEGP* 78 (1979): 1–16.
26. See, for example, Alwin Thaler, *Shakespeare and Sir Philip Sidney: The Influence of "The Defense of Poesy"* (Cambridge: Harvard University Press, 1947), and J. H. Walter, ed., *Henry V,* The Arden Shakespeare (London: Methuen, 1954), xv-xvi.
27. See Gary Taylor, ed., *Henry V* (Oxford: Oxford University Press, 1994), 52–58.
28. See chapter 3 of *Quoting Shakespeare,* "The Agency of Quotation in Shakespearean Comedy," 88–116. An earlier version of this chapter was published as "Comedy and Control: Shakespeare and the Plautine Poeta," *Comparative Drama* 24 (1990): 217–31.
29. Tobin remarks on "the influence of Jack Wilton's adventure with the murdering rapist Esdras, whose forcing of Heraclide Shakespeare had already adopted for use as early as *Titus Andronicus*. The threatening of and forcing of Heraclide by Esdras and the rape of Jack Wilton's mistress by Bartol have provided material for Pistol's threatening of the captured French soldier and for Bourbon's imagining the fleeing soldiers as bawdy panders. The French soldier plays the role of the threatened Heraclide, with the brutally comic Pistol in the role of the bandit rapist Esdras." Tobin, "Nashe and Shakespeare: Some Further Borrowings," 315.
30. Here I am thinking about a tradition of scholarship best evidenced, perhaps, by Thomas Greene's *The Light in Troy: Imitation and Discovery in Renaissance Poetry* (New Haven: Yale University Press, 1982). Greene's influential book concentrates too exclusively, I believe, on prestigious authors and texts and fails to take into account the enormous range of reading and borrowing in the English Renaissance. Greene, for instance, mentions Nashe once in *The Light in Troy,* but only in a list of authors who inherited a *mundus* of "semiotic reserves" (20).
31. For the *locus classicus* of "conflict" theories of literary relations, see Harold Bloom's *The Anxiety of Influence: A Theory of Poetry* (New York: Oxford University Press, 1973); for criticism of Renaissance drama based on such a model, see Bruster, *Quoting Shakespeare,* 38–40, and n. 60, 221–22.
32. Hans-Georg Gadamer, *Truth and Method* (New York: Crossroad Publishing, 1991), 383.

The Politics of Aesthetics

Recuperating Formalism and the Country House Poem

Heather Dubrow

I

In the current critical climate, many scholars are far more comfortable detailing their sexual histories in print than confessing to an interest in literary form.[1] Indeed, in such circles the study of form is regarded as the irascible father who, unlike the obediently cheerful guests in the country house poems we will examine shortly, shows up uninvited at dinner parties at his children's newly and proudly built post-structuralist house. After insisting that they replace Gehry's dramatic entranceway of diagonal strips of sharp glass with some of those nice Corinthian columns, he attempts to dominate the dinner conversation with his unenlightening but unmistakably Enlightened pronouncements on Truth and Beauty despite—and more to the point because of—everyone else's desire to talk about those subjects once unmentionable at dinner parties, sex, religion, and, of course, above all politics.

Even more striking than the virulence formalism often evokes is the inconsistency and even illogicality that it engenders in any number of otherwise acute academics. Ralph Cohen has flagged the irony of post-structuralist critics who dismiss genre while nonetheless writing on it; similarly, as John Guillory observes, many Marxist critics assume the incompatibility of aesthetics with their enterprise despite considerable evidence to the contrary in the writings of Marx and some of his distinguished followers.[2] Such patterns are writ large in the paradoxical relationship between most of the critical practices in vogue at the end of the twentieth century and literary form: interest in that subject is variously demonized and demonstrated by people committed to the same methodologies, and sometimes by the same critic. Or discomfort with form may manifest itself in cursoriness; Stephen Greenblatt's trenchant introduction to a special issue of *Genre* entitled "The Forms of Power and the Power of Forms in the Renaissance," like that chiasmic title, might have been realized as forms embracing power but in fact can more accurately be described as putting power at the center and forms at the margins.[3] How and why, then, does formalism provoke such reactions in some of the best and the brightest of today's critics? And how should one's responses to this critical approach, which is variously and simultaneously an unwelcome and an honored guest in critical circles, shape interpretations of the subgenre that enacts and thematizes hospitality, the country house poem?

II

From certain perspectives the hostility to formalism is, like contemporaneous attacks on Freud, not only understandable but also overdetermined: in both its overt manifestations and its subterranean implications the study of form is antithetical to a host of values and practices currently celebrated in the academy. According to a widely accepted and often rehearsed narrative, the Enlightenment, responsible for the celebration of so many other politically suspect principles, witnessed the development of the Kantian concept of the aesthetic, which in its emphasis on a delight wholly unrelated to the conceptual, the moral, or to the material world outside the object of art not only denies but also disguises the relationship between art and the political. Hence, it has been argued, this determinedly apolitical version of the aesthetic impulse is itself complicitly political and ideological. In any event, the Kantian concept of the aesthetic is indisputably freighted with assumptions that further explain both its implications for the study of form and the contempt it attracts in many circles. Its frequent though not inevitable focus on the beauty of the object of art (philosophers continue to debate how natural beauty relates to aesthetics) helps to establish the singularity of high art, one of the targets of the post-structuralist attack on the aesthetic. Its emphasis on the subjective and immediate response to art plays up the individual; its suggestion that all will share that response when confronted with true beauty denies historical contingencies, social conditioning, and identity politics, while the very concept of beauty is determinedly essentialist in the sense of that term used by literary critics.[4] And its description of the rapture that beauty excites implicitly celebrates the power of art and the artist at a point when admiration, let alone excitement, are seen as suspect reactions to texts. The tensions resulting from these positions are evident in the defensiveness with which George Levine, the editor of the thought-provoking collection *Aesthetics and Ideology*, justifies the collection.[5]

An emphasis on form is rightly seen as central to this nexus of values, and hence also subject to the contempt and suspicion it evokes in so many contemporary critics. Kant, after all, insists in his *Critique of Judgment* that design is crucial to the aesthetic response; he distinguishes the true impression of beauty it provokes from the mere charm created by a particular color. Many of his heirs and assigns have pursued his focus on form. Hence both their analyses of formal characteristics and his are open to the accusation of, as it were, privileging privilege: the poet who spends hours polishing the rhyme scheme of his sestina is viewed as analogous to and even dependent on a society where some have the obligation to polish well-wrought urns for minimal wages and others the leisure to admire those vessels or the cultural capital to publish articles on them.

Yet these overviews of aesthetics in general and its pronouncements on form in particular oversimplify the texts they purport to summarize. Kant does devote most of his attention to the aesthetic response to a type of beauty that can be largely though not completely summarized in the terms outlined above; but he contrasts that so-called "free beauty" with what he terms "dependent beauty." The latter is indeed conceptual, based as it is on how a given object fits into a category. Thus Kant distinguishes the reaction to free beauty, which would involve responding to a beautiful object that happens to be a rose from that to dependent beauty, a response to a lovely American Beauty rose. To be sure, his discussion of this second category is brief, ambiguous. and, according to some students of his work, inconsistent.[6] But it introduces an aesthetic category that is, as we will see, germane to formalist inquiry in literature—and in so doing it warns literary critics and cultural historians against oversimplifying the Kantian aesthetic.

Moreover, even if one brackets the issue of dependent beauty, a reading of the *Critique of Judgement* and of the criticism it has provoked intensifies that warning, demonstrating that some generalizations that literary critics regularly proffer about Kant are more tendentious than they acknowledge. As subtle and learned a student of aesthetic theory as John Guillory at one point assumes that the concept of the aesthetic necessarily involves the disinterested and autonomous;[7] but, as I indicate below, students of Kant have persuasively called this into question. Others emphasize that Kant's category of free beauty, unlike that of dependent beauty, does not presuppose perfection;[8] thus the assumption that the author of the *Critique of Judgment* encourages the study of only well-wrought urns becomes debatable. The notion that Kant's concept of beauty is unrepresentational, uninstrumental, and amoral has been challenged by philosophers who find in it, as Donald W. Crawford does, the potentiality for cognitive or logical judgments, or who argue, as Noël Carroll does, that the moral and aesthetic dimensions of a work of art are connected because a negative judgment on the former may interfere with responses to the latter.[9] Carroll's argument thus reverses the often repeated assumption that the aesthetic performs the cultural work of concealing and hence rendering acceptable repressive social practices.

Several of the positions that literary critics often simply ascribe to Kant occur in less ambiguous form in later writers, notably Clive Bell and others associated with the position loosely known as "art for art's sake." Deeply indebted to Kant despite all his rejection of the Kantian concept of beauty, Bell pronounces, "To associate art with politics is always a mistake."[10] He too focuses on form, declaring that "significant form" is the one characteristic all works of art must share: "certain forms and relations of forms, stir our aesthetic emotions" (8). Bell proceeds to develop a conception of art for art's sake that renders overt and explicit the contempt for the so-called man in the street that is often latent in that type of aesthetic. More to our purposes now, the approach to form that is often associated with formalism in dismissive commentaries on it is unmistakable in Bell's clarion call for a form divorced from content; he takes the Futurists to task for attempting to convey ideas through their formal strategies. In associating such attitudes primarily with Kant rather than with texts like Bell's in which they so unambiguously appear, critics have advanced their agenda of linking the Enlightenment to politically suspect positions—but in so doing have compromised our understanding of that movement, which was more varied in its ideologies and its effects on our own than is sometimes acknowledged.

However one interprets the work of Kant and followers like Bell, subsequent philosophers and other theorists have offered a range of alternative models for the aesthetic, many of which invite an expanded sense of the potentialities of form. Theodor W. Adorno emphasizes the impossibility of separating form and content: "The unsolved antagonisms of reality return in artworks as immanent problems of form."[11] More recently, Arthur Danto and many others have argued for conceptual reactions to form.[12] The controversial relationship between aesthetics and ethics continues to be debated, with a number of theorists, such as Berys Gaut, maintaining that they are indeed connected, a position with obvious implications for the political and other instrumentality of texts.[13] Nor has the notion of form been confined to the smooth and perfect, that well-wrought urn: a number of other philosophers have developed conceptions of form that attribute aesthetic reactions in the strict and narrow sense of an apprehension of beauty to formal characteristics that in many circles would not generally be considered beautiful. Yuriko Saito, for example, talks about how and why certain types of Japanese aesthetic comprise a respect for forms ruined by age and unshapely by conventional standards.[14] Such arguments can fruitfully be adduced, as we will see, for phenomena ranging from slant rhyme to texts that struggle against generic norms.

Often the dismissal of formalism is connected not only to how the academy reads Kant but also to how it writes its own history. Gerald Graff has acutely identified repeated patterns through which established literary movements attempt to condemn the new kid on the block;[15] related patterns are evident in narratives of the development of literary criticism. I have argued elsewhere that Marxian models of ruptural change, as opposed to liberal paradigms of gradual shifts and incorporation, have long characterized many narratives about the development of the profession, appearing even in critics with no sympathy for radical critique.[16] In scripting this scenario, it is convenient to adduce formalism as a synecdochal representative of criticism before the 1970s. In addition, those favoring changes in critical methods are prone to cast such ruptural narratives in the comedic mode, while, not surprisingly, those viewing the metamorphoses as corruption favor tragic paradigms.[17] That is, according to this model, which has been deployed by successive generations of younger critics, the youthful and vigorous disdain the prevailing regime of rigid rules; they run off to a forest that is its antithesis (in recent versions of the narrative, laying in a supply of French currency before doing so). This comedic pattern may be discerned in the relationship between philologists and literary historians, literary historians and New Critics, old historicists and new historicists, and so on. When the monarch in that putative court of rigid rules is genre or form, the plot I'm outlining justifies seeing the study of literary types as inflexible and sterile, while the pre-existing attribution of those qualities to the analysis of genre activates and justifies the comedic narrative.

In many instances misprisions like these demonstrate the workings of demonization. Subtly studied by early modern critics in relation to Othering in political arenas, demonization also recurs within the academy, especially in personnel decisions, and for this reason alone deserves continued scrutiny. More to my purposes now, demonization, which not coincidentally often conceals its own agendas, typically operates through the related strategies of uncovering putative hidden characteristics in the Other and in that and other ways claiming to show an affiliation with what is already rejected. Witness the exposure of the devil's marks, which exemplifies both techniques, or, its latter-day analogues, the assertions that someone is really a formalist or a New Critic underneath and that scholars involved in cultural history "really belong in sociology departments" (an accusation that draws attention to the workings of distinction in the competitive rankings of fields).[18] Thus Alan Liu's incisive study of new historicism attacks it by claiming it is really a type of formalism.[19] Formalism is dismissed in just these ways when it is conflated with that laughing-stock of contemporary critical practice, New Criticism, a movement whose own complexity and variety are sometimes ignored in condescending generalizations. A similar process occurs in the connections between formalism and the Enlightenment and in the erosion of categories noted above.

Gender also figures in the academic misinterpretations of formalism, playing a role more subterranean, though no less significant, than that of other patterns posited here. Surely it is relevant that the formal as it is generally conceived has characteristics often gendered female and associated with a female subject position, though it is at once intriguing to speculate and impossible to determine to what extent formalism is demonized because it is feminized as opposed to vice versa.[20] Many philosophical descriptions of responses to form deploy the language of seduction: the formal transports, creates a rapture, and so on. And, of course, the formal is widely seen as nonconceptual, again invoking stereotypes about gender. Our professional dismissal of formalism coincided chronologically with the increasing presence and power of women in the profession. This was no accident—not because the female scholars in question typically practiced formalist criticism themselves (indeed, many women led the attacks on it that characterized the 1970s and 1980s), but rather because deflected resentment of highly visible female colleagues arguably intensified the rejection of the putatively feminized formal mode. Is it not possible as well that formalism's association with the fluid sexualities of Bloomsbury and of other writers associated with art for art's sake further encouraged the rejection of it in some quarters? Real men don't eat villanelles.

The demonization of formalism is particularly evident in discussions of a subject very germane to the country house poem tradition, generic norms. Indeed, genre has come to function as a prototype for form in the senses of prototypes explored by cognitive sciences, which helps to explain the immediate and almost visceral reactions the concept of genre can evoke. (This deployment of genre is all the more striking given that contemporary students of communications and rhetoric, as well certain literary critics, often stress function more than form when discussing generic types.) Despite the historicizing of literary kinds by many critics, generic norms are often represented as ahistorical, much as form is seen as divorced from material and political realities. Despite the work on genre and communication to which I will shortly turn, genre is sometimes seen as distinctly, even uniquely, literary: "Few concepts of literary criticism are quite as 'literary' as the concept of genre."[21] And, despite the way what the Renaissance terms *genera mista* or mixed genre challenges classification, genre is of course also associated with taxonomy, which, as Harriet Ritvo for one has trenchantly shown, can lend itself to racism; hence the attack on the concept of generic purity by Derrida and others.[22] The study of genre also lends itself to a comedic scenario similar to the one told about formalism: many still contrast the bad old days of a belief in generic norms (a literary decorum sometimes associated with the social decorum of suppressing argumentation) with the poststructuralist forest of formless forms. This narrative pivots on the largest and most telling misconception in discussions of genre, that strict rules were the norm until the advent of post-structuralism.[23] But it is clear that by both precept and example such regulations were often rejected. Witness even neoclassical pronouncements such as Johnson's comments on the unities in his *Preface to Shakespeare* and *Rambler* 125, and witness too the sixteen-line poems by George Meredith that he, like many later critics, labels "sonnets."

Attacks on the ideological agendas of generic analysis might also appear to be justified by texts like J. W. Lever's history of the sonnet; here the troubling connections between aesthetics and politics are apparent. In an influential and often incisive study originally published about ten years after the end of World War II and presumably written some years closer to that event, Lever delineates the differentiation of the English sonnet from its Italian models. In so doing, he deploys rhetoric that gestures toward the potential imbrication of discourses of liberalism, nationalism, and gender. "Tudor poets set out to make the Petrarchan sonnet their own.... The Tudor poets were indeed true pioneers both in form and content, breaking a virgin soil on which, in the fullness of days, the great Elizabethans were to raise their golden harvest."[24] Yet such passages hardly justify a blanket condemnation of genre studies, representing as they do only one of many potentialities for such work.

Indeed, as I have observed, since around 1980 the reductive oversimplifications of genre studies that I am analyzing have coexisted with repeated efforts to find new, or apparently new, ways of justifying the discussion of literary form. Academics committed to radical cultural critique variously (but usually not simultaneously) study form to reveal how it hides a conservative agenda, or, alternatively, how it reflects and even encourages social change.[25] Similarly, Thomas O. Beebee stresses the uneasy and often unresolved struggles among genres, thus exemplifying the drive to recuperate formalism for post-structuralism.[26] Formalism has also been made safe for cultural studies by tracing analogues to and even instances of literary types in "low" or popular culture, thus calling into question whether or not they are in fact literary.[27] Finally, the critical trend to reconceptualize texts as rhetorical rather than literary, hence building in assumptions about power, is another route toward discussing literary form without the putatively conservative assumptions associated with that enterprise. An early instance of this agenda, Jane Tompkins' reading of *Uncle Tom's Cabin* looks at techniques that might well be described in aesthetic terms, such as mirroring of episodes and other forms of repetition, in terms of their rhetorical instrumentality; the work on genre and rhetoric in the field of communications buttresses such enterprises.[28]

My own discussion of the current status of the formal, then, might appear itself to stage another comedic narrative: the potential fissures created by misreadings and misrepresentations can be prevented by approaching the texts in question more judiciously and by adopting the strategies for recuperating formalism that I have just listed. A reading of the country house poem does indeed demonstrate the feasibility of thus reconciling a discussion of form with contemporary literary concerns: they can dine at the same table. Yet comedy includes Marcade and Jacques, and an examination of country house poems also demonstrates the prices that can be exacted for that seemingly harmonious dinner party.

III

The country house poem offers an ideal test case for studying the potentialities and problems of formalist criticism. Engaging as it does with questions about orderly edifices, social and architectural, its own subject matter figures many issues we have been exploring; and its indisputable embeddedness in contemporary political and social tensions clearly invites an exploration of the relationship between literary forms and social formations. That exploration is, however, complicated by how this subgenre both invites and resists generalizations. The verbal echoes among some of the poems, most marked in the indebtedness of Carew's "To Saxham" to Jonson's "To Penshurst," may discourage an adequate acknowledgement of important distinctions. Obviously, Lanyer's fascinating "Description of Cooke-ham" is exceptional in this and other ways (and hence is treated more briefly than some other country house poems below). But even the texts more closely associated with the tradition established by "To Penshurst" manifest significant distinctions; for example, addressing such a poem to a brother, as Herrick does in "A Country Life: To his Brother, M. Thomas Herrick," is a very different act from writing about an aristocrat.[29]

Despite such distinctions, these poems are all rooted in the same rocky and mined soil, the tensions surrounding the responsibilities of landlords and the ownership of land and homes in early modern England.[30] In the early seventeenth century, the erection of ostentatious "prodigy houses" was bankrupting many of their owners, demonstrating the ethical ambivalences of that adjective. This extravagance diminished the owners' capacity, already threatened by other financial problems from which some members of the aristocracy were suffering, to offer hospitality and charity. In an intriguing though widely neglected treatise entitled *Christian Hospitalitie* (1632), Caleb Dalechamp attacks those whose expenditures on their houses preclude caring for guests. Condemning "The building and trimming of their houses: as if they were to live for ever in this World," he proceeds to demand, "What hospitalitie, trow ye, can be expected from those, that have turned great rents into great ruffs, and lands into laces?"[31] (Dalechamp, academics should note with care, soon moves on to the fifth point in his list of excessive charges: "The furnishing of their studies with books. For as too much reading weares the flesh, and wakeneth the bodie and brain: so the immoderate buying of books wastes a mans estate, and disables him from good works" [57]). More to our purposes now, early modern landlords, in addition to running up their Visa card charges in the ways Dalechamp catalogues, often spent long periods in London, thus neglecting social responsibilities at home, as James I passionately reminded them.

These social changes were complicated by a countervailing shift, the rise in hospitality as a distinctly middle-class ideal. Yet another reason Dalechamp's *Christian Hospitalitie* deserves attention is that it demonstrates this change in its condemnation of such traditional aristocratic pursuits as the keeping of horses and dogs and in its emphasis on hospitality as a duty enjoined on many members of the culture, not just the most elite.

Hospitality, as we will see, can transform a potentially transgressive invader into a guest whose behavior is regulated by social codes. Hence threats to hospitality, which coexisted with and arguably encouraged celebrations of it like Dalechamp's, intensified another impetus to the development of the country house poem, cultural fears about invasions of many types. Studied by Richard Helgerson and Linda Woodbridge, among many others, in terms of foreign powers, these anxieties also involved the domestic arena.[32] The permeable daub and wattle walls of many early modern homes troped their permeability in other respects—their vulnerability to the interrelated threats from burglars, from fire, from stepparents, from rivals in land disputes, and from would-be adulterers. Many contemporary documents speak to the fears surrounding such threats; it is telling, for example, that burglary was punished more severely than many other types of thievery. Demonstrating the interplay between literary form and cultural tensions, Puttenham lists as the first entry in his category of figures of disorder Hyperbaton, tellingly personified as the trespasser. And he proceeds to enumerate as his second figure parenthesis, or the Interruptor.

Through both content and form, country house poems negotiate the pressures I have been cataloguing, attempting in particular to control the relationship between inside and outside. Those who do not live in the house are welcomed within, guests at its table and in its vision; and the poor, rather than sneaking through the door to steal, receive charity at it:

> And though thy walls be of the countrey stone,
>   They'are rear'd with no mans ruine, no mans grone,

>   There's none, that dwell about them, wish them downe;
>   But all come in, the farmer, and the clowne.
>   ("To Penshurst," 43–48)[33]

If Dalechamp aptly glosses the tensions latent in such practices, equally germane are anthropological studies of hospitality, which stress that strangers are potential menaces who can and must be controlled through its laws.[34] Appearing repeatedly in classical discussions of hospitality, that assumption finds its early modern equivalent in the concluding lines of Carew's "To Saxham," which finesse the intense anxieties about burglary to which I referred: "And as for thieves, thy bounty's such / They cannot steale, thou giv'st so much" (57–58).[35] Here form mimes content as neatly as any place in this tradition. The final line opens on a phrase whose syntax might well lead us to believe that the thieves will become the primary grammatical subject. Yet much as semantically their subjectivity is compromised by the denial of the agency to do what makes them what they are ("They cannot steal" [58]), so grammatically by the end of the couplet the house itself steals from the would-be burglars the position of subject and the role of agent. From another perspective, the lines swerve between an implied version in which the thieves are the subject of an independent clause ("Thieves cannot steal because thy bounty's such") and an alternative that relegates them to a relative clause ("Thou giv'st so much that thieves cannot steal"). Indeed, the syntactical struggle between Saxham and its transgressors synecdochally stages the praxis of the subgenre. The formal closure that this final couplet effects in the poem, the closural potentiality of a couplet, and the syntactical containment and erasure in the privative "cannot" all enact the ways the house itself is sealed up, protected from thievery.

The regulated hospitality of country house poems is played out on many other formal levels as well: this subgenre invites certain potential rivals and enemies, in the form of other literary types, to dine at its table. Thus, as epistles addressed to the house rather than its owners, Carew's "To Saxham" and "To Penshurst" celebrate the friendly interaction between the house and potential guests that the poems celebrate while avoiding the sycophancy common in epistles directed to aristocrats. Similarly, many country house poems attempt to include, but in delimited and contained form, the acerbic notes of formal verse satire. Working out the relationship among these genres exemplifies the conceptual activity that should rightly be seen as part of the aesthetic experience in the expanded senses for which Carroll and others have argued.

Although country house poems generally negotiate tensions with the potentially threatening forces just beyond the pale by inviting them within, a pattern exemplified generically as we have seen, on occasion these texts also determinedly exclude would-be enemies. Genres, as many have observed, are typically relational in that they define themselves against other genres; in the country house poem, this relationality is often manifest in the significance of what is not written, the alternative genre toward which the text gestures. In particular, as James Grantham Turner and Raymond Williams, among others, have observed, it is by avoiding the realistic details of the georgic tradition to which they allude that these texts slide away from direct confrontation with social tensions.[36]

Hospitality is the mirror image of—and the devices we have been exploring the formal analogues to—the signature trait of the subgenre, the linguistic mannerism known as the negative formula. It deploys words of negation to deny the presence of something even while introducing it in the doorway of the poem, as it were. "Thou art not, *Penshurst*, built to envious show," Jonson famously observes, and in "To Saxham" Carew boasts, "Thou hast no porter at the door / T'examine or keep back the poor" (49–50). "Nor has the darknesse power to usher in / Feare to those sheets" ("A Country Life: To His Brother, M. Thomas Herrick," 39–40), Herrick writes in a cognate formulation that itself mimetically almost ushers in darkness and fear, yet fixes them at the threshold—much as the poor are firmly located at the doorway of Appleton House in a passage to which I will turn shortly.[37]

Not the least role of the couplets in country house poems is to trope these texts' vision of social harmony: the tenant and the lord rhyme with each other, as it were. These poems typically do not erase social distinctions but rather conceal their injustices by stressing harmony; Carew's "To My Friend G.N. From Wrest," for example, devotes six lines to detailing the differing dining arrangements for those of different ranks. Similarly, the couplet is based on uniting two words whose difference as well as similarity is emphasized through that union. Our pleasure in rhyme is indeed sensuous, immediate, and nonconceptual and hence an instance of an aesthetic experience in the narrow sense often cited by those literary critics who demonize it. Yet the rhymes in this tradition demonstrate the interaction between that type of aesthetic experience and the more capacious version that includes a ratiocinative element—or, to put it another way, they demonstrate how the sensuous pleasure of the rhyme may reinforce the political agenda it expresses in this case.

Moreover, the genre tropes the social conservatism to which it is committed through a version of literary conservatism. The respectful imitation that so often characterizes the members of the tribe of Ben has been cited to explain how closely several other poems echo "To Penshurst." Fair enough, yet the affinities between the work of Carew and Herrick on the one hand and their master on the other also serve to mime and endorse the orderly succession of generations that Jonson and other writers in the tradition stress; moreover, poems that laud the continuity of values and buildings themselves manifest a literary continuity. Arguably we might even read the final line of "To Saxham"—"They cannot steale, thou giv'st so much" (58)—as a gracious allusion to the relationship between the author and Jonson and thus, of course, also an apologia for what might otherwise have seemed to be stealing.

These poems also counter the threat of change and the fear that hospitality, like that originary country house Eden, is a lost ideal by speaking a grammar of present tenses. They deny the historical shifts that threaten their values by variously emphasizing stasis and a cyclical pattern of seasons. Witness the moment when Jonson boasts that the woods serve "seasoned deer." When I wrote on these poems some twenty years ago, I asserted that the phrase dovetails the raw and the cooked in more senses than one, turning the natural seasons into culinary seasoning and the inhabitants of the natural world into a willing feast for the human world; in so doing, it also suggests an orderly passage of time.[38] But it is as important, I now think, that the expression "seasoned deer" also negotiates temporality by denying it. Seasons, normally associated with the movement of time, and the act of seasoning move, as it were from the world of nouns and verbs to that of adjectives: "seasoned" negates seasons, suggesting as it does stasis, something that is always already present, much as hospitality is represented not as a temporary and imperiled ideal within the world of these houses but rather as a permanent practice.

Many of the patterns I have been exploring are crystallized in the troubled and troubling description of the poor in Marvell's "Upon Appleton House": "A Stately *Frontispice of Poor* / Adorns without [that is, outside] the open Door" (65–66).[39] This aestheticizing of the impoverished reminds one again why the concept of the aesthetic is so often distrusted. Marvell's language is—and should be—offensive to us, as it probably was to many of its original readers, but its strategies are telling. First, the poor are fixed in a carefully defined location, much as they are fixed in a present tense that erases both the past suffering that led them to approach the door and future potentialities for either insurrection or amelioration: in contrast to displaced and potentially displacing burglars and stepparents, the indigent are made to know their place and are firmly located in the proper relation to the house, at its door, rather than wandering as rogues and vagabonds do by definition and rather than invasively pushing their way in. Social place is established and represented through decisive spatial placement. The door is at once open, suggesting hospitality, and yet in a sense closed to them in that they remain at its boundary, suggesting the careful regulation and delimitation of the charity that is the analogue to hospitality. "Stately" (65) of course also suggests that the poor have acquired some of the values of the house; they

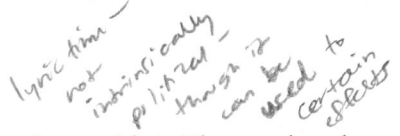

rhyme with it. The poor have been turned from a potential threat to the house into an adornment—and from agents into objects in several senses of the latter term, as their grammatical role in the prepositional phrase tacked on to "Stately *Frontispice*" (65) would indicate.

Yet to recognize that a range of formal strategies negotiates the ever-present threats associated with invasion and temporality is not to endorse the equation of form with conservative ideological agendas, whether in the instance of this literary type or of others. Country house poems also use formal and other devices to remind us of what cannot be contained. Discordant elements, cracks in a putatively well-wrought urn, interrupt the poems in question. In particular, when Jonson refers to his "gluttony" (68), a word that had in early modern England the same connotations it bears today, in a text celebrating moderation and order, his corpulent body both deflects and represents other types of excess that threaten the poem, notably flattery.[40] The social threat of sycophantic exaggeration is mirrored by its rhetorical counterpart, the use of hyperbole and copia, and by its structural analogue in these poems, lists such as the descriptions of the bounty of the house in "To Penshurst" or of the house's natural delights in Lanyer's "Description of Cookeham." A list is not necessarily excessive, of course; it may instead suggest order and control. Yet the lists in this subgenre, like the paratactic syntax that so often appears within them, often seem anticlosural, hence resembling gluttony more than a well-balanced diet. Much as Penshurst itself today strikes the viewer as indeed built for envious show, so Jonson's poem and cognate texts do not uniformly achieve the modesty they advocate. And, given the length of other country house poems and Marvell's own condemnation in a pivotal early stanza of "superfluously spread" (17) men and their "unproportion'd dwellings" (10), might not the ninety-seven stanzas of "Upon Appleton House" at the very least introduce uneasy questions? From one perspective, the poem's intellectual and moral complexity fully justifies its length; from another, its square footage raises doubts about the self-aggrandizement of the speaker and possibly the poet who characteristically attempts with only partial success to distance himself from his personas.

Similarly, if, as I suggested earlier, the control or exclusion of certain generic alternatives mimes the suppression of certain threats that wish to invade the house, so too the ghosts of other genres mime the discord that cannot be wholly excluded. While celebrating the irenic, poems in this genre are pulled toward the satiric in their description of less worthy houses; the genre's bitterness is partly but not completely contained by the negative formula.[41] Thus the tension between the drive to incorporate would-be enemies within and the impulse to wall them out is realized as well on the level of literary form. The decidedly postlapsarian bitterness of formal verse satire is an unwelcome guest that dines at the table, partly though not completely controlled by the laws of hospitality, when "To Penshurst" and "Upon Appleton House" describe the edifices they are rejecting; and in other texts in the genre it lurks by the gates, reminding us of its presence in the brief hints of acerbity that arise.

Gender generates other cracks in these urns. As Hugh Jenkins has emphasized, the women in these poems are at once emblems of their central values and potentially, at least, embodiments of what threatens and interrupts those values, not least the invasion of adultery.[42] In one of the most extraordinary passages in these extraordinary poems, Herrick assures his brother,

> Nor has the darknesse power to usher in
> Feare to those sheets, that know no sin.
> But still thy wife, by chast intentions led,
> Gives thee each night a Maidenhead.
> ("A Country Life: To His Brother, M. Thomas Herrick," 39–42)

The enjambment between lines 39 and 40 contrasts its own formal openness with the house, which excludes that would-be invader fear much as the female body within it excludes other invaders.[43] On one level the wife's body is simply the corporeal equivalent of the unchanging timelessness of her world, with her ever-renewed virginity providing a physiological analogue to the restoration of Eden that is the aim of these postlapsarian poems. Yet that virginity conflicts with the fruitfulness that is another value of the poems, and the urge for untouched purity is surely a product of the fear that the sheets could indeed know sin. And might not Jonson's characteristic reminder of limitations, "And if the high-swolne *Medway* faile thy dish" (31), deflect and express fears of a cognate failure, the miscarriage by a swollen female body? Liable to the blandishments of nuns and strangers, the bodies of the women in these poems are not necessarily impermeable, any more than their houses or their genre.

Thestylis' extraordinary interruption of Marvell's narrative in "Upon Appleton House," then, performs and figures what is present more implicitly in other country house poems: her breaking into and breaking up of narrativity, Marvell's version of hyperbaton, represents the ever-present possibility of an invasion of the poem and its genre by wandering, roguish values, alien literary types, and rival narratives and narrators:

> But bloody *Thestylis,* that waites
> To bring the moving Camp their Cates,
> Greedy as Kites has trust it up,
> And forthwith means on it to sup:

> When on another quick She lights,
> And cryes, he call'd us *Israelites;*
> But now, to make his saying true,
> Rails rain for Quails, for Manna Dew.
>
> (401–408)⁴⁴

Seizing the narrative much as she seizes the bird, Thestylis represents the ways a vision can be countered by gendered threats (tellingly, her counterpart in Virgil is not female) or simply by a critical alternative viewpoint. The genre is always deeply concerned with representation (notice, for example, the way the dream in Herrick's "A Country Life: To His Brother, M. Thomas Herrick" draws attention to the poem's own status as a representation); here, by breaking out of the narrative, Thestylis draws attention to its constructedness.

As the poem that Thestylis destabilizes reminds us, then, although texts that differ radically from earlier models of their genre are often described as markedly transgressive, in fact it is more precise to observe that they typically occupy an extreme position on the customary spectrum between close adherence to norms and wide divergence from them; most writing lies somewhere between those poles, often deviating sharply from certain norms while staying much closer to others. Indeed, the principal generic expectation of most readers of English literature, I suggest, is of a dynamic interplay between the ways a given text fits norms and the ways it deviates from them. Thus genre produces aesthetic effects, in the expanded senses of that concept, very like those of slant or off rhyme. Indeed, that prosodic technique not only illuminates genre but also provides a paradigm for reconciling certain poststructuralist reading strategies and the study of form: it encourages us to predict some measure of unpredictability, thus demonstrating how genre and many other types of form may achieve structure without rigidity or, to put it another way, instability without total amorphousness or formlessness.

IV

Kazuo Ishiguro's *The Remains of the Day,* winner of the 1989 Booker Prize, offers a coda to the problems we have been exploring, echoing many of the concerns in the country house poem—and their relationship to formalism. This extraordinary novel is narrated in the first person by the butler of Darlington Hall, Stevens (tellingly, we never learn his first name), who, in describing a journey he takes some years after the Second World War to see the former housekeeper, repeatedly interjects reminiscences about Darlington Hall in earlier years and reflections about his profession. Imitating not only the class accent but also the class mannerisms and values of his employer's culture, Stevens practices remarkable restraint and self-control. "I gave a small laugh," he reports at several junctures, varying this as well to "I gave a cough," with both formulations suggesting that even his emotions serve social ends ("gave") and that even the most apparently spontaneous emotional outbursts and physical reactions are planned.[45]

But the world Stevens represents and Stevens himself are under siege in the book: like the country house poem, the novel is narrated at the time of, and is in some senses about, the decline of the English country house. Lord Darlington, dangerously naive in his interpretation of nobility, aids the Nazis before the war and is vilified for doing so afterward. Thus the novel raises the question posed by one of Darlington's drunken guests: is this perfect English gentleman a perfect fool? Changes within Darlington Hall register larger social changes; if the ideal of communal dining had declined by the time of the country house poem, here the housekeeper, Miss Kenton, leaves not only Darlington but also the subject position of servant, and an American buys Darlington, his attempts to imitate a genuine English lord providing one of many instances of the book's concern with repetition and compulsive reenactments.

Again, like the country house poem, *The Remains of the Day* is preoccupied with place in both its geographical and social sense and with the connections between them. Simulacra, here represented by a butler and an American owner who imitate an English gentleman and in so doing gesture toward the possibility that Stevens is himself an imitation of a butler, involve a kind of displacement. Keenly conscious of his social place, the butler is concerned to keep everything and everyone about the house in its assigned position; not coincidentally, in several separate episodes tensions between Miss Kenton and Stevens pivot on displaced household objects. In making one of those objects a Chinaman, the Japanese-British author of this book signals the culture's concern with domesticating and, again, keeping in place the foreign.

And indeed, it is on hospitality, the regulated incorporation of the foreign, that the plot pivots, offering yet another connection with the country house poem. A dupe of the Germans, Lord Darlington invites to his home visitors he hopes will challenge the Versailles Treaty. But many of these guests are really invaders, violating the values of Darlington Hall and Lord Darlington in their manipulations of him. These visitors, entertained lavishly with every servant and every object in its assigned location, are out of place in the house. And Darlington tragically misunderstands his own social place and his capacities in attempting to negotiate with them.

As even this brief overview suggests, here, as in the country house poem, penetrating political and social observations are realized through formal strategies. In structuring the narrative around place, with each chapter named after a geographical locale, Ishiguro flags the problematics of position and displacement. Similarly, distortions in genre comment on distortions in values. This is, for example, on some level a novel of romantic quest, and in Stevens' journey toward a woman he believes has left her husband there is even an element of the rescue plot of romance. Yet the plots of these genres are deformed by Stevens' persuading himself that he is merely attempting to see whether Miss Kenton wishes to return as housekeeper. Thus generic changes register his habitual rejection of sexuality, a repulsion anticipated earlier when he refuses the flowers, those embodiments of fertility, that Miss Kenton attempts to bring to his room. In so doing Stevens becomes a synecdoche for the sterility of the dying culture he represents and celebrates. Similarly, Margaret Morganroth Gullette, in anatomizing the form she terms the midlife progress novel, distinguishes it from the midlife decline novel.[46] *The Remains of the Day* keeps reaching toward the midlife progress novel—it includes a spatial journey that figures a psychological one, the hope of romantic fulfillment, reevaluations of a career and a profession—but slipping into a decline novel, thus enacting generically the protagonist's and the culture's difficulty in moving up and away from the old country house culture to a saner social order.

Stevens' inability to acknowledge his reservations about Lord Darlington's political blunders is also realized formally in a type of narrativity that registers painful events indirectly, often by describing their consequences, rather than by recounting them directly. We learn about reactions to Stevens' father's fall before that event itself appears in the narrative, and, above all, the conclusion of the book enacts the butler's inability to acknowledge his own emotions (or, as Miss Kenton demands,"Why, Mr. Stevens, why, why, why, do you always have to *pretend?*" [154]). Stevens reports that a chance acquaintance responds to him with, "'Oh dear, mate. Here, you want a hankie?'" (243), without explicitly mentioning the extraordinary fact that he has started to weep. The erasure of that event from direct reportage stages the way not only Stevens but also his culture control and conceal emotion, positioning it safely outside the door.

Formal strategies of temporality also signal political analyses, as they do in different but cognate ways in the country house poem. Even to the extent of emphasizing a tense that seldom appears in this form in novelistic discourse ("and, at this moment, am sitting" [205]), the narrative is insistently located in the present, another connection with the country house poem. Yet geographically, as its chapter titles remind us, the book journeys west, toward the setting of the sun. And if the book is set in the present, it is imprisoned in the past. For when Stevens keeps interrupting his narrative for flashbacks, he formally enacts the novel's critique of Darlington's life and class: both attempt to move from present political complexities to an idealized past dangerously out of touch with those complexities. "The days when you could act out of your noble instincts are over," an American guest warns Darlington and other amateur diplomats (102). This urge to live in an ossified past is the temporal analogue to the spatial structure of the book: Stevens, now working for a new master and suffering grave though largely unacknowledged doubts about the political activities of his former one, undertakes a journey away from Darlington both geographically and psychologically, yet keeps pulling back to the values of that house.

V

Like *The Remains of the Day*, the country house poem is, then, hospitable to the critical approaches that recuperate formalism. Its ruptures and evasions, notably those connected with the appearance of Thestylis, offer yet more proof that the study of literary form can indeed be reconciled with poststructuralist paradigms. And, as we saw, some critics justify the study of genre by showing that social forms may mime and even encourage radical social change, while others justify it as a way of uncovering conservative social agendas; the country house poem demonstrates how and why the same form may do both, thus demonstrating as well the intimacy between form and content. Yet at the same time this literary type resists merely being cited as an apt instance of how form can serve the ends of the critical approaches that have flourished during the final decades of the twentieth century: aesthetic pleasure certainly serves political ends, but it functions in many other ways too, and to assume that those ways merely mystify its political workings is to flatten both the experience of writing these poems and that of reading them. One might perhaps make a case that Jonson's "painted partrich" (29) gestures toward the concerns about representation and misrepresentation that, as I have suggested, recur throughout the genre; but Jonson's primary pleasure in fashioning this adaptation of his classical source and ours in reading it lies in the sensual appeal and the cleverness of the image, and these levels should not be ignored. Similarly, whereas Marvell's final trope of the canoers culminates his references to inside and outside and all their political valences, the creation of a visually engaging and witty image is central to the aims and effects of the poem.

But even inviting in the formal only as a guest of the concerns of contemporary criticism is potentially dangerous for two reasons. First, rather than reconciling tensions it can temporarily mask them, allowing them to return in more virulent form. Students of the traditions of hospitality remind us that one reason for the imputed Arab habit of leaving one's host's home in the middle of the night is that once one had stepped over its boundaries, one was liable to attack.[47] Similarly, if we need to realize that the study of form can be reconciled with a commitment to, say, the study of ideology or gender, the position to which this essay is passionately committed, we need as well to confront and argue about tensions that will remain; the representation of the artist struggling with the complexities of a villanelle's rhyme, for example, implies an emphasis on authorial agency and autonomy that many critics would condemn, and these issues need to be fully addressed.

Second, reconciling form and contemporary criticism by turning the formal into a respectful guest, or perhaps more to the butler serving the guests, risks dangerous condescension. The guest-host relationship involves the walls of hierarchy as well as the open doors of conviviality; and the cheerful servants at country houses know their place and are firmly put in it by these texts ("He knowes, below, he shall finde plentie of meate" ["To Penshurst," 70]). Similarly, the assumption that formalism may once again become respectable simply because it can serve the needs of its host, historical and political criticism, relegates the formal to a secondary, supplementary role that neglects the depth and the range of its contributions to style and meaning. Critics who deplore the self-serving power plays of colonialism risk a colonialist appropriation of formalism if we defend it merely for its ability to provide raw material that can be manufactured into the goods of political analysis. Statecraft is one—and yet only one—of the central aims of literary craft; crafty manipulation one—and yet only one—of its central agendas.

Notes

1. I am indebted to Marshall Brown, Noël Carroll, Donald Rowe, and Susan Wolfson for extensive help with this essay.
2. Ralph Cohen, "Do Postmodern Genres Exist?" *Genre* 20 (1987): 241–257; John Guillory, *Cultural Capital: The Problem of Literary Canon Formation* (Chicago: University of Chicago Press, 1993), esp. 272–274.
3. Greenblatt, "Introduction," *Genre* 15 (1982): 3–6.
4. The term "essentialist" has a different significance in philosophy, suggesting that something is definable; in that sense the Kantian concept of beauty is not in fact essentialist.
5. See Levine's "Introduction: Reclaiming the Aesthetic," in *Aesthetics and Ideology*, ed. George Levine (New Brunswick: Rutgers University Press, 1994), 1–28.
6. On the problems of interpreting this concept, see, e.g., Donald W. Crawford, *Kant's Aesthetic Theory* (Madison: University of Wisconsin Press, 1974), 113–117.
7. Guillory, *Cultural Capital,* 327.
8. See, e.g., Robert Wicks, "Dependent Beauty as the Appreciation of Teleological Style," *Journal of Aesthetics and Art Criticism* 55 (1997): esp. 387–388.
9. See Crawford, *Kant's Aesthetic Theory,* esp. 31, 122–123; and two essays by Noël Carroll, "Moderate Moralism," *British Journal of Aesthetics* 36 (1996):

223–238; and "Moderate Moralism versus Moderate Autonomism," *British Journal of Aesthetics* 38 (1998): 419–424.
10. Clive Bell, *Art*, 2nd ed. (London: Chatto and Windus, 1949), 21. Subsequent references to this book will appear in parentheses in my text.
11. Theodor W. Adorno, *Aesthetic Theory*, ed. Gretel Adorno, Robert Hullot-Kentor, and Rolf Tiedemann, trans. Robert Hullot-Kentor (Minneapolis: University of Minnesota Press, 1997), 6.
12. Compare Arthur Danto's essay, "The Naked Truth," in *Aesthetics and Ethics: Essays at the Intersection*, ed. Jerrold Levinson (Cambridge: Cambridge University Press, 1998).
13. See, e.g., Berys Gaut, "The Ethical Criticism of Art," in Levinson, ed., *Aesthetics and Ethics*. The volume also contains a number of other valuable essays on the relationship between aesthetics and ethics.
14. Yuriko Saito, "The Japanese Aesthetics of Imperfection and Insufficiency," *Journal of Aesthetics and Art Criticism*, 55 (1997): 377–385.
15. Gerald Graff, *Professing Literature: An Institutional History* (Chicago: University of Chicago Press, 1987), 240–241.
16. See, e.g., my book *A Happier Eden: The Politics of Marriage in the Stuart Epithalamium* (Ithaca: Cornell University Press, 1990), esp. 265–266.
17. Compare Fredric Jameson's linkage of Marxism and romance in *The Political Unconscious: Narrative as a Socially Symbolic Act* (Ithaca: Cornell University Press, 1981), esp. 104–105.
18. In *Professing Literature*, Graff notes that new movements are often accused of merely replicating old ones (see esp. 1–15).
19. Alan Liu, "The Power of Formalism: The New Historicism," *ELH* 56 (1989): 721–771.
20. Certain philosophers argue that the beautiful is gendered female and the sublime male, a debate germane to but distinct from my argument. See, e.g., Paul Mattick, Jr., "Beautiful and Sublime: 'Gender Totemism' in the Constitution of Art," in *Feminism and Tradition in Aesthetics*, ed. Peggy Zeglin Brand and Carolyn Korsmeyer (University Park: Pennsylvania State University Press, 1995). On the relationship of gender and form, see also Susan J. Wolfson, *Formal Charges: The Shaping of Poetry in British Romanticism* (Stanford: Stanford University Press, 1997), esp. 149–161, 170–173.
21. Paul Hernadi, *Beyond Genre: New Directions in Literary Classification* (Ithaca: Cornell University Press, 1972), 1.
22. Harriet Ritvo, *The Platypus and the Mermaid and Other Figments of the Classifying Imagination* (Cambridge: Harvard University Press, 1997), esp. chap. 2.
23. For a related attack on this assumption, cf. Cohen, "Do Postmodern Genres Exist?"; his argument, however, focuses mainly on the eighteenth century.
24. J. W. Lever, *The Elizabethan Love Sonnet*, 2nd ed. (London: Methuen, 1966), 12, 13.
25. Fredric Jameson famously demonstrates the first of those approaches in *The Political Unconscious: Narrative as a Socially Symbolic Act* (Ithaca: Cornell University Press, 1981), chap. 2. For the second approach, see, e.g., the read-

ing of *Lycidas* in David Norbrook, *Poetry and Politics in the English Renaissance* (London: Routledge and Kegan Paul, 1984), esp. 282–285; Nigel Smith, *Literature and Revolution in England, 1640–1660* (New Haven: Yale University Press, 1994); Susan J. Wolfson, "'Romantic Ideology' and the Values of Aesthetic Form," in Levine, *Aesthetics and Ideology*.
26. Thomas O. Beebee, *The Ideology of Genre: A Comparative Study of Generic Instability* (University Park: Pennsylvania State University Press, 1994). The book also demonstrates Marxist approaches to genre.
27. See, e.g., Peter Rabinowitz, "'Reader, I Blew Him Away': Convention and Transgression in Sue Grafton," in *Famous Last Words: Changes in Gender and Narrative Closure*, ed. Alison Booth (Charlottesville: University Press of Virginia, 1993).
28. Jane Tompkins, *Sensational Designs: The Cultural Work of American Fiction 1790–1860* (New York: Oxford University Press, 1985), chap. 5. Many students of speech and communication have also investigated the rhetoricity of genre and genres; see, e.g., Carolyn R. Miller, "Genre as Social Action," *Quarterly Journal of Speech* 70 (1984): 151–167.
29. As its title suggests, Mary Ann C. McGuire's "The Cavalier Country-House Poem: Mutations on a Jonsonian Tradition" (*SEL* 19 [1979]: 93–108) posits a different though not incompatible distinction within the tradition.
30. On the erection of prodigy houses and the decline of hospitality, also see two important studies of the country house poem: G. R. Hibbard's article, "The Country-House Poem of the Seventeenth Century," *Journal of the Warburg and Courtauld Institutes* 19 (1956): 160–162; William A. McClung, *The Country House in English Renaissance Poetry* (Berkeley: University of California Press, 1977), esp. 18–35. For an argument connecting Jonson's "To Sir Robert Wroth" to a different historical issue, the relationship of local communities to the court, see Martin Elsky, "Microhistory and Cultural Geography: Ben Jonson's 'To Sir Robert Wroth' and the Absorption of Local Community in the Commonwealth," *Renaissance Quarterly* 53 (2000): 500–526.
31. Caleb Dalechamp, *Christian Hospitalitie* (London, 1632), 54. Subsequent citations from this book appear in my text.
32. These issues are discussed throughout two important recent studies: Richard Helgerson, *Adulterous Alliances: Home, State, and History in Early Modern European Drama and Painting* (Chicago: University of Chicago Press, 2000); and Linda Woodbridge, *Vagrancy, Homelessness, and English Renaissance Literature* (Urbana: University of Illinois Press, 2001). I am grateful to these authors for making their work available to me prior to publication. For a more detailed discussion of the domestic threats I cite, see my book *Shakespeare and Domestic Loss: Forms of Deprivation, Mourning, and Recuperation* (Cambridge: Cambridge University Press, 1999).
33. I cite *Ben Jonson*, ed. C. H. Herford and Percy and Evelyn Simpson, 11 vols. (Oxford: Clarendon, 1925–1952).
34. On theories of hospitality, see Ladislaus J. Bolchazy, *Hospitality in Early Rome: Livy's Concept of its Humanizing Force* (Chicago: Ares, 1977); Julian

Pitt-Rivers, *The Fate of Shechem; or, The Politics of Sex: Essays in the Anthropology of the Mediterranean* (Cambridge: Cambridge University Press, 1977), chap. 5.
35. I cite *The Poems of Thomas Carew,* ed. Rhodes Dunlap (Oxford: Clarendon, 1949).
36. James Turner, *The Politics of Landscape: Rural Scenery and Society in English Poetry 1630–1660* (Oxford: Basil Blackwell, 1979), 143–144; Raymond Williams, *The Country and the City* (London: Chatto and Windus, 1973), 27–34.
37. *The Poetical Works of Robert Herrick,* ed. L. C. Martin (Oxford: Clarendon Press, 1956); all citations are to this edition.
38. See my essay "The Country House Poem: A Study in Generic Development," *Genre* 12 (1979): 163.
39. Throughout this essay I cite *The Poems and Letters of Andrew Marvell,* ed. H. M. Margoliouth, 2nd ed., 2 vols. (Oxford: Clarendon, 1952).
40. *OED,* 1st ed., s.v. "gluttony."
41. I interpreted that containment more optimistically twenty years ago ("The Country-House Poem," esp. 161–162); but that was in another academic country.
42. Hugh Jenkins, "From Common Wealth to Commonwealth: The Alchemy of 'To Penshurst,'" *Clio* 25 (1995): 176–180. I am also indebted to Alexandra Block for useful suggestions about the female body in these poems.
43. I thank Susan J. Wolfson for drawing my attention to the significance of this enjambment.
44. For compatible but different interpretations of Thestylis, see Sarah Monette's essay, "Speaking and Silent Women in *Upon Appleton House,*" forthcoming in *SEL* (Winter 2002). I am also grateful to her and to other members of my English 961 class for stimulating discussions about the country house poem.
45. I cite Kazuo Ishiguro, *The Remains of the Day* (New York: Vintage, 1988). For instances of the phrases in question, see pp. 172, 177, and 209. Further page references will appear in parentheses within my text.
46. Margaret Morganroth Gullette, *Safe at Last in the Middle Years: The Invention of the Midlife Progress Novel: Saul Bellow, Margaret Drabble, Anne Tyler, John Updike* (Berkeley: University of California Press, 1988). On the relationship between the progress novel and midlife decline novels, see xx.
47. Pitt-Rivers, *The Fate of Shechem,* 108.

Marston's Gorge and the Question of Formalism

Joseph Loewenstein

> in the very temple of Delight
> Veiled Melancholy has her sovran shrine,
> Though seen of none save him whose strenuous tongue
> Can burst Joy's grape against his palate fine
>
> —Keats, "Ode on Melancholy"[1]

> Gnaw pesants on my scraps of poesie
>
> —Marston, "In Lectores prorsus indignos"[2]

To begin with some afterwords: in Shirley's *The Cardinal*, Antonio marvels over the Duchess, who seems to him as

> Serene, as I
> Have seen the morning rise upon the spring,
> No trouble in her breath, but such a wind
> As came to kiss and fan the smiling flowers.

Shirley wrote these lines in the aftermath of a period of tremendously skillful and tremendously critical cultural production. Over several decades verse drama had evolved technical norms of a very high standard, so that a fluent, flexible blank verse like that which breathes from Antonio was nearly the least a playgoer might expect; in fact, by 1641 an acceptably accomplished verse could register as mere shtick. "No trouble in her breath," says Antonio to Columbo, the play's Machiavel, "but such a wind / As came to kiss and fan the smiling flowers," and Columbo interrupts, flatly waving off this gentle description: "No poetry."[3] Shirley is writing in the aftermath of Shakespeare, Webster, and Fletcher, and he shows himself here to be quite perkily belated. Moreover—and this is probably more interesting than the mere fact of Columbo's little sneer, more interesting because closer to our own home—during the same versifying decades that prepared for this moment of efficient anaesthesia, both literary and popular culture had so elaborated and so polished a technology of demystification that Columbo's interruption could itself register as shtick. The interruption of an earlier moment was "More matter, with less art," but Gertrude, the shrewd amateur who spoke that phrase, was more committed to both moral and aesthetic connoisseurship; later, in what now seems a somewhat familiar aftermath, a *heimlich* moment of brilliant, if routinized critique, the tough-minded skeptic says merely, "No poetry."

The original version of this essay was written for a special session at the MLA convention entitled "Toward a New Formalism in Renaissance Studies." I was not confident that a new formalism had begun to take shape and, indeed, Mark Rasmussen betrayed an ambition to conjure formalism from its slumber, or its grave, when he asked, in his call for papers, "What might a self-conscious return to formal analysis look like in the wake of post-structuralism and the new historicism?" I was not sure that I shared this ambition, but what made me rise to the occasion was, in fact, a small pedagogical shock. I had been working on John Marston's odd revenge play, *Antonio's Revenge*, with a dozen unusually talented and ambitious English majors, and together we were finding it a fascinating piece of work. Almost endlessly involuted, the play converts the usual revenge-play despair of divine or royal justice into a sharp humiliation of the private sovereignties of stoicism, an unremitting assault on the Horatios of the late Elizabethan stage.[4] But what had struck me is that we made unusually interesting discoveries in the simple course of reading portions of the play aloud; it seemed to me that the solicitation to a new formalism would make an appropriate occasion to try to make sense of the odd sounds that we had been inspecting in the classroom.

That the study of poetry as an aesthetic practice solicitous of description and formal analysis has generally languished recently seems obvious enough, yet an anaesthesia like Columbo's is almost certainly not the last word on the fate of poetics. Burdened with a curious *embarras du succes*, historicist critics have been driven to under-theorized, fitful, and sometimes quite productive grapplings with the aesthetic, taking on such cultural supplements as—the list is heterogeneous—aura, symmetry, scale, formal tension, patina, translucency, and the catachretic. Even the concept of period style has undergone preliminary and perhaps halfhearted rehabilitation, under the auspices of Foucault, Deleuze, and even Greimas. The bandwagon of the aesthetic may be pulling out, and it may therefore seem less incautious now than it would have been, say, twenty years ago to attempt a cultural genetics of Marston's verse line as instanced, primarily, in *Antonio's Revenge*. But to treat that line, its rhythms and its lexicon, is (I hope) not merely to be modish but to address what I take to be an interesting object of properly historical reflection, for Marston's verse was taken to be egregious in his own day: my purpose is to account for that egregiousness by imagining the cultural poetics of the throat in revenge tragedy, in the War of the Theatres, and in the political struggle over satire at the end of the century.

We might begin by facing the historical fact that verse manner *could* manifest itself as egregious: the existence of a thriving early modern culture of prosodic connoisseurship has been amply documented, though generally forgotten. For example, the assembled ideologues whose reported conversation frames the poems of the early Elizabethan *Mirror for Magistrates* devote a considerable portion of their commentary to metrical issues, particularly to matters of metrical decorum, and the evidence of metrical interest actually increases after the first edition of the *Mirror,* as the author-*cum*-editor-*cum*-publisher, William Baldwin, reflects on the interests of his readers and refines his own sense of mission. (On this evidence, the verse line is as much a nationalist instrument as is, say, the chronicle or the map.) In the course of the next decades, during which time this central monument to Inns of Court literary nationalism steadily expanded, Spenser and Harvey made an elaborate bid for public notice by publishing a series of their familiar letters, at least half of which are devoted to matters of specifically prosodic connoisseurship. And Puttenham's account of poetics as an analogue of courtiership confirms that lines were fashioned in accordance with a rhetoric specified as homologous to that governing the fashioning of selves. Indeed, for Puttenham, versifying presents itself—in its rhetoric *and* its rhythms—as a calculable form of behavior. It is therefore at least a little odd that the most recent systematic attempt to assess the contribution of versification to early modern dramaturgy, and so to provide a detailed articulation of the prosodic within some larger semantic system, some more embracing cultural practice, is now twenty years old.[5] And it is particularly disappointing that so little has been done to follow up on Derek Attridge's study, published nearly thirty years ago, of the attempt to write Elizabethan verse in classical meters.[6] Specialized as it is, Attridge's work deserves a hard second look. One of the core projects of recent cultural historiography has been to examine the various ways in which the most intimate properties and aptitudes of organic life—sexuality, consumption, vision—are subjected to discipline, and it should be clear that the broad and gently contested disciplining of the phonetic that took place as various features of classical prosody were imposed upon vernacular verbal practice should find a significant place in that historiography. The culture of prosodic system building and connoisseurship conferred special opacities on language use; it contributed to the standardization of orthography, the literalization of the word; and it was a means by which the *habitus* of the schoolroom persisted within adult culture (making the reading of poetry at once exceptionally *rigorous* and, I suspect, remarkably infantilizing, or at least "juvenating").[7] English prosodic theory and theoretically attuned practice must therefore figure in that total history of creative unfreedom in which we seem so irresistibly and so productively engaged.

Marston recommends himself as an object of scrutiny for two reasons, the simpler and less interesting of them being that from the beginning of his career he testifies explicitly to an unsettled sense of his own prosodic identity. His first poem, an epyllion on Pygmalion, no doubt circulated independently in manuscript, but when it was first printed, in 1598, a short collection of *Satyres* was appended to it, the first of which is entitled "The authour in prayse of his *precedent* Poem." Like Jonson, with whom he was entangled for years in toils of envious criticism, Marston appears addicted to defensive self-inspection; and the compulsion to self-criticism often makes him quite brilliantly alert to his own idiosyncratic technique, as he is in this early poem, in which he describes the mercenary strut of his own stanzas, which stanzas, he says, "March rich bedight in warlike equipage":

> Glittering in dawbed lac'd accoustrements,
> And pleasing sutes of loves habiliments.
> Yet puffie as Dutch hose they are within,
> Faint, and white liver'd, as our gallants bin;
> Patch't like a beggars cloake, and run as sweet
> As doth a tumbrell in the paved street.
>
> (20–26)

We are dealing here with the period-specific aesthetics of the "fantastical," here specified as the sartorial manner of the military braggart in love: the characteristic features of the fantastical are a composite and awkward glitter crusting over a failing interior structure.[8] Here Marston invokes the fantastical as, among other things, a dubiously tasteful fashion-aesthetic of the line. But Marston's concluding evocation of the awkward movement of his stanzas—they "run as sweet / As doth a tumbrell in the paved street"—offers more than a prosodic description, more even than an imitative description. The key term, tumbrel, means "dung-cart," and the term makes a modal affiliation, pinpointing the generic eccentricity of *Pygmalion's Image*, its decisive swerve toward an excrementality specifically associated not with epyllion (or with metamorphosis in general) but with satire. The tendency to satire, the aptitude for verbal danger, is entirely consistent with Marston's habit of listening to himself in order to gauge his effect on an imagined audience. At the end of this short poem, Marston likens this self-inspection to the "Popelings discipline," the strategic masochism of penance: I "censure my selfe," he tells us, "fore others me deride / And scoffe at me, as if I had deni'd / Or thought my Poem good" (37, 39–41). Let us say, then, that the case of Marston offers special opportunities to the cultural historian of prosody. In him the prosodic sensitivities fostered by the Elizabethan schoolroom are supplemented by the satirist's especially nervous aptitudes of the socialized ear. More of this shortly.

As for the other, more interesting reason why Marston recommends himself to the historian of prosody, the students in my seminar recognized it immediately; it's that his verse is unspeakable. Not unspeakably amateurish or unspeakably crude, but—often, though not always—simply unspeakable.[9] Since this at least sounds like the sort of tinnily grandiose dictum one might find in Saintsbury or in Swinburne's essays on Elizabethan dramatists, there's certainly nothing post - post-structuralist or neohistoricist about it. I do, however, want to distinguish my assessment from that of Swinburne, who, it turns out, is a good deal more concerned with the merely semantic than with the prosodic when he describes Marston's verse manner as "perpetually, indefatigably, and fatiguingly strenuous" and not perpetually, but "too often vehemently, emphatically, and laboriously clumsy."[10] Swinburne is here having a poet's fun approximating the unmistakable thunk of Marston's most Marstonian rhythms; he is having a *scholar*-poet's fun in his choice of epithets, for *strenuous* is a word that Marston introduced to the language, and while Marston's fellow satirist, Joseph Hall, is responsible for having coined *clumsy,* Marston quickly appropriated it and made it very much his own. In Marston's verse both terms register as ingeniously onomatopoeic, as deeply self-exemplifying coinages. Here, for example, is the Prologue of *Antonio's Revenge:*

> The rawish dank of clumsy winter ramps
> The fluent summer's vein; and drizzling sleet
> Chilleth the wan bleak cheek of the numb'd earth,
> While snarling gusts nibble the juiceless leaves
> From the nak'd shudd'ring branch, and pills the skin
> From off the soft and delicate aspects.

This is deliberately and perfectly clumsy, both in the sense that the term rapidly acquired and in the etymological sense (from Icelandic) of "benumbed with cold," though it also takes some color from the dialect term *clum,* meaning silent, clammed up—for the verse is thickened to throat-stopping clumps. I said it is deliberately clumsy, for somatic dysfunction is the name of this play's game:

> But if a breast
> Nail'd to th'earth with grief, if any heart
> Pierc'd through with anguish, pant within this ring,
> If there be any blood whose heat is chok'd
> And stifled with true sense of misery,
> If ought of these strains fill this consort up,
> Th'arrive most welcome.

This last is merely hilarious, the idea of a consort, a chamber orchestra, of voices silenced by anguish.[11] To the macabre levity of the figure, Marston will conjoin a more hackneyed topos, giving it his own special clumsy weight. The verse will make one or two feints toward ease but will recur in theme and cadence to its earlier unspeakable stagger:

> O that our power
> Could lackey or keep wing with our desires,
> That with unused peise of style and sense
> We might weigh massy in judicious scale
> —Yet here's the prop that doth support our hopes:
> When our scenes falter, or invention halts,
> Your favor will give crutches to our faults.[12]

A skeptical reader unfamiliar with *Antonio's Revenge* may suspect that the struggle of enunciation demanded in these lines is only momentary, perhaps some special effect dictated for the prologue. But consider the opening lines of the play proper, when Piero enters, smeared with the blood, a torch in one hand and poiniard in the other, and shouting

> Ho, Gaspar Strotzo, bind Feliche's trunk
> Unto the panting side of Mellida
> 'Tis yet dead night, yet all the earth is clutch'd
> In the dull leaden hand of snoring sleep.
>
> (1.1.1–4)

It makes the Browning of *Sordello* sound like the Tennyson of "The Lotos Eaters." The historical problem is to ascertain how such sounds registered to an Elizabethan. Marston, for one, seems to have found these textures so taking that he used them again to close the scene:

> Strotzo, to bed; snort in securest sleep;
> For see, the dapple-grey coursers of the morn
> Beat up the light with their bright silver hooves
> And chase it through the sky.
>
> (1.1.106–9)

To allege spondaic slowing seems a prosodist's bland cliché here, for it hardly does justice to the piling consonants, to the jammed-up liquids and clustered dentals, or to the way articulation gets mired in uvular quicksand.[13] This is as much Piero's idiom as it was the Prologue's. He eggs Strotzo on to precipitous flattery, and as soon as the sycophant speaks, he rebukes him for interrupting: "Stroke not the head of infant speech / Till it be fully born" (1.1.39–40). There is Marston, right there in the fantasy of speech-stopping speech, of infant speech, inarticulate, silent. Which explains Strotzo's baffled, self-silencing response: "How now? Fut, I'll not smother your speech" (1.1.42).[14]

Nor is this a dialect exclusive to villainy and gloomy prologue, for the hero, Antonio, enters, his throat stuffed with this same unspeakable language:

> Darkness is fled; look, infant morn hath drawn
> Bright silver curtains 'bout the couch of night . . .

—perhaps a bit more palatable, but almost a parody of an *aubade*, nonetheless—

> look, infant morn hath drawn
> Bright silver curtains 'bout the couch of night;
> And now Aurora's horse trots azure rings.
> (1.2.65–7)

Although I have taken these examples from the first act of *Antonio's Revenge*, Marston wrote such verse throughout his career, and I want to account for this prosodic eccentricity. One such accounting has already been implied—that here and everywhere Marston's prosody is profoundly influenced by a satiric proclivity. I believe this to be more than mere redescription, for Marston's identification with satire was unusual in both its intensity and its specificity. I can't give a full account of that identification, but it begins in 1598 with poems charging Joseph Hall, then the pre-eminent writer of nondramatic satire, with indecent literary assault, and proceeds to satiric comedies attacking Jonson, then the pre-eminent master of that form.[15] (You can already see how easily such a poet could move to writing revenge plays, since his literary career was shaped, from the outset, by imitative aggression.) In the initial attack on Hall, Marston works with a set of modal clichés, railing against Hall's railing against literary culture. And you can hear how Marston finds his own cramping voice even as he protests Hall's:

> must . . . some shameless Satyrist
> with odious and opprobrius termes insist

> To blast so high resolv'd intention
> with a malignant vile detraction?
> So have I seene a curre dogge in the streete
> Pisse gainst the fairest posts he still could meete.
>
> (115–20)

The poem is called "Reactio," the fourth of his *Certaine Satyres;* Marston here portrays Hall as a "stinking Scavenger" (11) filling "his dungy tumbrel" (13) and, as our ears tell us and the documentary record confirms, Marston's portrait of Hall soon became a self-portrait. By this I mean not only that Marston's contemporaries began to describe him in the terms he had used of Hall, so that in *The Second Return from Parnassus* he is taxed with "lifting up [his] legge and pissing against the world" (267–8).[16] This became Marston's own voice print, for even a sympathetic reader could feel that Marston's satiric assaults were uncannily redounding upon him. Thus, in *Skialetheia*, a manuscript poem that surveys the literary scene in London in 1598, Edward Guilpin, apparently a close friend of Marston, writes that

> The double volum'd *Satyre* praised is,
> And lik'd of divers for his Rods in pisse,
> Yet other-some, who would his credite crack
> Have clap'd *Reactioes* Action on his back.
>
> (E1v)

That the satirist is somehow doomed to satire may seem a romantic myth, but the myth dogs Marston. His fourth satire acknowledges the possibility that contemporary satire might constitute an assault on the literary per se— "What Satyre!" he exclaims, "sucke the soule from Poesie / And leave him spritles?" (99–100)—but Marston claims for himself an almost magical immunity to the effects of working in the form. He therefore opens his next volume, *The Scourge of Villainie*, with a poem addressed to Detraction itself:

> I heare expose, to thy all-taynting breath
> The issue of my braine, snarle, raile, barke, bite,
> Know that my spirit scornes *Detractions* spight.
>
> (4–6)

The assertion of lofty superiority to the form in which Marston works seems to me to be far more hopeful than confident. This is one of the more anxious vocation-poems I know, since it imagines and defends self-esteem against the considerable cost of satiric practice:

> A cankered verdit of malignant Hate
> Shall nere provoke me, worse my selfe to deeme.

Marston's Gorge and the Question of Formalism 97

> Spight of despight, and rancors villainie,
> I am my selfe, so is my poesie
>
> (21–24)

This begins Marston's long and thwarted courtship of Stoic *apatheia*—a posture of ethical poise that sustains particular humiliation in *Antonio's Revenge:* he dedicated the second edition of *The Scourge of Villainie,* which was published within weeks of the first, "To his most esteemed, and best beloved Selfe." His readers would have none of it, would refuse to recognize a self-assured and *super*-satiric Marston. But his failed and perhaps disingenuous campaign to project an apathetic persona is less interesting than his claim that a fixed and untainted core self was linked to—and could be discerned in—a fixed and untainted poetic manner: "I am my selfe, so is my poesie." (This, I think, warrants an aside: Marston here issues a fairly straightforward invitation to criticism—that the historical study of the self should presumably entail a historical study of the self as styled self. But to continue:) Elsewhere in *The Scourge of Villainie,* Marston claims that he must force himself to write satire and calls upon Melancholy to assist him in overcoming a nearly physical indisposition to the form:

> Ingenuous Melancholy, I implore
> Thy grave assistance, take thy gloomie seate,
> Inthrone thee in my blood; Let me intreate
> Stay his quick jocond skips, and force him runne
> A sadde pac'd course, until my whips be done.

Marston reverts here to the old poetic myth of stylistic and modal option, the idea that, each time he or she writes, even the merely competent poet will adopt the lexicon and particular prosodic manner specific to one of the more or less discrete literary modes or genres. That Marston figures modal practice as somatic, as seated in the blood, somewhat compromises the claim that, with application and effort, he can set aside one manner and adopt another. "I can quit anytime," he tells us, and the versification almost enacts the myth:

> *Daphne,* unclip thine armes from my sad brow,
> Black Cypress crowne me whilst I up do plow
> The hidden entrails of ranke villainie.
> Tearing the vaile from damn'd Impietie.
>   Quake guzell dogs, that live on putrid slime,
> Skud from the lashes of my yerking rime.
>
>   ("Proemium in librum primum," 10–20)

Although there is appreciable variation in the shift from jocund blood to putrid slime, we can hardly credit the claim to stylistic voluntarism. The verse never seemed jocund, and there is a gasping fanfare to "whilst I up do plow": Marston is plainly, if paradoxically, uncomfortable until his pen is plowing "the hidden entrails of ranke villanie."[17]

The reader need not take my word for this. As I have already said, his contemporaries would have none of the fiction of Marston the merely optional satirist. They suspected him of a compulsive passion for verbal violence.[18] In *The Whipping of the Satyre* (1601), John Weever [?] likens Marston to a dog who has finally broken his chain, "But with his collar almost choked first, / And with full mouth, or rather foul-mouth'd speach / He war'd at all" (B7v). Note that this glosses the prosody as well as the affect; note too that both prosody and affect are said nearly to choke the indiscriminately warring dog. Ingram has discerned that the site of Marstonian satire is, above all, the throat—often, specifically the satirist's throat.[19]

That, in Marston's case, verse-manner is demonstrably more somatic than optional goes a long way toward making my original case—that we really should pay attention to prosody when we undertake a total history of early modern creative unfreedom. But the Marston chapter of this macrohistory would have more to do than to remark Marston's odd susceptibility to merely modal constraints; a full account of the somatics of Marston's style would have to recall the tongue-tying, or rather the throttling, of satire in June of 1599, shortly after Marston's first two volumes of satire appeared. By order of the Bishop of London those volumes were called in and burnt at Stationers Hall, burnt, as had been customary for heretical books, by the common hangman. Book burning is not, of course, an effective method of eliminating books from circulation but is, rather, metonymic, a substitution of books for authors deemed heretical. If we often identify books and authors—speaking, as we do, of "a Virgil" or "a Shakespeare" when we mean a book of Virgil's poems or Shakespeare's plays—book burning fiercely confirms that casual identification with the special emphases of violence. The book burnings that ensued from the Bishop's Ban on satire would thus have answered to Marston's worst fears, simply by suturing satire to the satirist. (I might say in passing that Elizabethans were quite aware that one of the functions of judicial and penal procedures was to *confirm* the criminality of the suspect or convict.) So the book burnings of 1599 marked Marston as somehow constitutively satirical. To pursue the logic of this event a step farther, we would have to recall that heretics undergo burning, rather than beheading or hanging, as an efficient means of linking capital punishment with ritual purgation, which is to say that burning pathologizes heresy and that book burning construes the book thus purged as an illness, as both a symptom and an agent of contagion. To anticipate my conclusion, then, the Order Against Satire not only identified satire and satirist; it also adumbrated Ben Jonson's critique of Marston by pathologizing the satirist.

Theater historians should recall with some amusement that while the Bishop's Order inhibited nondramatic satire, it stimulated dramatic satire, launching theatrical practice along the very particular path of style and attitude that we experience as typically "Jacobean." In Marston's particular case, the Order drove him from page to stage and inspired him to switch competitors, from Hall to Jonson.[20] And although he experimented with other forms, with dramatic satire, romantic comedy, and revenge play, he could not surrender the clotted line: if the throat is the site of Marstonian satire it is even more the irritable scene of Marstonian revenge tragedy. The immediate narrowing of Marston's imagination is almost ridiculous. Within a couple of months of the Bishop's Order of Conflagration Marston finished his first play, *Antonio and Mellida*, which begins with the recollection of a ghastly shipwreck:

> when, lo, the sea grew mad,
> His bowels rumbling with wind passion.
> Straight swarthy darkness popp'd out Phoebus' eye,
> And blurr'd the jocund face of bright-cheek'd day,
> Whilst crudl'd fogs masked even darkness' brow;
> Heaven bade's good night, and the rocks groan'd
> At the intestine uproar of the main.
> Now gusty flaws struck up the very heels
> Of our mainmast, whilst the keen lightning shot
> Through the black bowels of the quaking air.
> Straight chops a wave, and in his slifter'd paunch
> Down falls our ship, and there he breaks his neck,
> Which in an instant up was belk'd again.[21]

I quoted at length in order to get to the belch, which I'm afraid also became Marston's dramatic signature.[22] The indigestion would recur in less than a year, for the Piero of *Antonio's Revenge* claims to have "burn'd in inward swelt'ring hate, / And fester'd rankling malice in my breast"—note that "fester'd" is transitive; that is, practically willful—and this indigestion is not to be relieved "till I might belk revenge upon his eyes." (This develops his earlier satiric idea of utterance as tumbrel, by the way, for that term for dung cart was commonly used, by metaphoric extension, to describe the gorge on the brink of eructation.)[23]

Antonio's Revenge is a play of hideous digestion. As the corpses begin to pile up, the ghost of the hero's father arises to speak the exhortation, "Graves, eat your dead again," but the rising of the ghost demonstrates that this meal cannot be kept down.[24] Because the villainous Piero is said to have "suck'd / The steam of reeking gore" (2.1.19–20) the heroic Antonio vows to "suck red vengeance / Out of Piero's wounds" (3.1.129–30). As part of his plot Piero tricks Strotzo into offering a confession, and he can only describe guilt as dyspepsia:

> Thy honest stomach that could not digest
> The crudities of murder; but surcharg'd,
> Vomit'st them up in Christian piety.[25]

As in *Coriolanus,* the rhetoric of which Marston seems almost certainly to have influenced, the throat is the special locus of violence, for the play proceeds from an initial poisoning, and its concluding vengeance begins when Antonio rips out Piero's tongue. In the meantime, Piero murders his accomplice, and even the stage direction gags: "Piero comes from his chair, snatchet the cords end, and Castilio aideth him; both strangle *Strotzo.*"[26] This play's version of the avenger's *Vindicta mihi,* can therefore hardly surprise us: "Now pell-mell! Thus the hand of heaven chokes / The throat of murder."[27]

Vomit, breath, and unspeakable verse compete for places within that narrowing throat. Even verbal modality sticks in the craw, for when Antonio's mourning mother says, "Choke breath and life," the sentence is lodged between imperative and indicative.[28] Marston keeps the clotted frustration of speech constantly before us. Early in the play that frustration becomes the casual object of Piero's violence: "I could eat / Thy fumbling throat for thy lagg'd censure" (1.1.79–80), he says to his inarticulate accomplice. And he gets as good as he gives from the furious avenger. When Piero impugns the heroine as part of the cover-up for the murder of Feliche, Antonio scorns him, "Dog I will make thee eat thy vomit up, / Which thou hast belk't 'gainst taintless Mellida," whereupon, in weird defiance, Piero challenges him to go ahead and *make* him eat his vomit: "Ram't quickly down"—an obscenely pure Marstonian construction—"Ram't quickly down that it may not rise up / T'embraid my thoughts. Behold my stomach's—" and here the syntax of the printed speech breaks off and the line appears to stop.[29] It only seems metrically defective on the page, however, for Piero presumably makes up the last foot by spitting or perhaps belching: "Behold my stomach's [ ]." Stress in this most Marstonian foot is infantile, corporeal, and inarticulate, a mere eruption of the glottis.[30]

A few years later, *The Malcontent* began to free itself of the glottal style. A sententiousness that Marston would have disdained in the late nineties confers a flattened fluency on the verse:

> The heart's disquiet is revenge most deep:
> He that gets blood, the life of flesh but spills,
> But he that breaks heart's peace, the dear soul kills.—

> Well, this disguise doth yet afford me that
> Which kings do seldom hear, or great men use—
> Free speech; and though my state's usurp'd,
> Yet this affected strain gives me a tongue
> As fetterless as is an emperor's.
>
> (1.3.155–62)

There is better, more fetterless and far more various utterance in this play. (Remorse can speak with especially affecting pathos and power.)³¹ But one does not need to listen very closely to hear, in Mendoza's taunting commiseration, how much of Marston's earlier manner lingers, conferring interest as if by its very persistence:

> Why, what cold phlegm could choose,
> Knowing a lord so honest, virtuous,
> So boundless-loving, bounteous, fair-shap'd sweet,
> To be contemn'd, abus'd, defam'd made cuckold?
> Heart! I hate all women for't: sweet sheets, wax lights, antique
>   bedposts, cambric smocks, villainous curtains, arras pic-
>   tures, oil'd hinges, and all the tongue-tied lascivious wit-
>   nesses of great creatures' wantonness! What salvation can
>   you expect?
>
> (1.7.34–42)

The oral manner of the earlier plays is considerably muted here, but the mythos of those plays is only slightly tempered.³² Mendoza concludes this same scene with the odd undertaking, "As bears shape young, so I'll form my device, / Which grown proves horrid: vengeance makes men wise" (1.7.77–8), and the eccentricity of the *sententia* is far less startling than the simile, which gives the beast-lore concerning bears an eerily idiosyncratic twist. That the shape of bear cubs is left to the mouthing of their mothers is usually applied to invoke the power of nurture, of humanist pedagogy, and emphasis falls on the willful production of identities, but here the horror of the mature beast seems at once inevitable ("which grown proves horrid") and the very aim of mouth-work. It is Marston's old myth: the tongue is potent; its power is specifically horrid; the tongue's intentions are predetermined, inevitable, a knot of cruel nature.

❦ ❦ ❦ ❦ ❦

Having recognized that the verse of *The Malcontent* is less intractable than that of the Antonio plays, I should probably concede at last that even the verse of *Antonio's Revenge* was not, technically, unspeakable. But it's worth remembering who spoke these lines. Marston wrote for the boys' companies, and one wants to keep in mind the particular pleasures that their performances afforded. When Lyly started writing for them more than a decade earlier, their specialty was mellifluousness (these actors were recruited from troupes of choristers) and classicism; but by the late nineties they were doing a repertoire mixing the major plays of the adult companies with up-to-the minute dramatic satire, often quite ribald satire—and no doubt their appeal in both sorts of plays was comparable.[33] One went to see youngsters—not *so* young; many of them were in their mid-teens—behave cheekily in the satires and that sense of cheek must have at least tinged their performances of, say, *The Spanish Tragedy:* there would have been some "camp" appeal, the same sort of arch impudence that one finds in the Ovidian poems of this same cultural moment. I think Marston's verse is pitched to that taste, whether consciously or unconsciously; the fun would be to make those boys put their pretty mouths around these lines.[34] I'm not suggesting that this is pure camp; only that "unspeakability" would have its place in the overall aesthetic.

To acknowledge the aesthetic archness will do two things for us. First, it gives us a particular context for the Jacobean idiom of revenge drama. The comic tincture to which Eliot was so usefully sensitive is being invented here—generally, in the circulation of tragedy through performance by the children's companies and, particularly, in Marston's mischievous exaggeration of the peculiar tonalities that the boys could confer. Let's say that Marston found the perfect use for his pathologically narrowed verbal disposition in his work for the children's companies. The other thing that we gain by facing up to the campiness of all this is that it enables us to explain the extravagance of Jonson's response: he, too, wrote for the boys, and he, too, exploited their impudence, but he hated most things that threatened the idea of gravity—unless he were himself rigorously controlling the device of threat—and he would have hated the trick of making these youngsters perform this kind of overwrought, blood-spattered drama.

As most theater historians recall, Jonson and Marston staged their falling-out publicly in the late nineties. In *Histriomastix,* Marston offered a respectful portrait of Jonson in the character of Chrisoganus. He was treading on thin ice, for Jonson was deeply jealous of self-representation, and he would have found Marston's depiction annoyingly blurred, for however Jonsonian were Chrisoganus' attacks on popular taste, he speaks in an entirely Marstonian disgestive idiom:

> Write on, crie on, yawle to the common sort
> Of thick-skin'd auditours: such rotten stuffs,
> More fit to fill the paunch of Esquiline,
> Then feed the hearings of judiciall eares,

Yee shades tryumphe, while foggy Ignorance
Clouds bright *Apollos* beauty.[35]

Revenge was swift. Within months of *Histriomastix* and *Antonio's Revenge*, Jonson staged an attack on the glottal style in the conclusion of *Poetaster*, his most systematic (and I think most underestimated) defense of poesy. The two poetasters of the title are Crispinus and Demetrius, carefully twinned renderings of Marston and Dekker. Demetrius-Dekker is a plagiarist—Jonson is our first great analyst of plagiarism—Demetrius-Dekker is a plagiarist, which is to say that Demetrius is a poet of pure optionality, his self fully disarticulated from the poems that pass as his. Crispinus, on the other hand, is a complex and far less trivial alternative, for *his* literary manner seems to be a matter of unregulated body chemistry. He "bespawls"—a Marstonian coinage; it means "to cover with saliva"—"bespawls / The conscious time with humorous foam."[36] Demetrius is punished, by the logic of *contrapasso*, by having a double vizard clamped to his face, whereas Crispinus-Marston is given a literary purgative and spends the last scene of the play actually vomiting up those terms that Jonson found most egregious: *retrograde, reciprocal, incubus, magnificate, glibbery, lubrical*—note that we are dealing with dactyls, notoriously difficult to assimilate to English blank verse; but there are also the characteristically clotted and snarling *defunct, spurious, snotteries, clutched, chilblained, clumsy*—of course, *clumsy*; Crispinus nearly chokes on it—*barmy froth, quaking custard, snarling gusts* (from the prologue to *Antonio's Revenge*), *fatuate, puffy, inflate, turgidous, ventositous*—and from this, the language of dyspepsia, we move into a sequence of ghastly coinages—*oblatrant, furibund, prorumped, strenuous*, and finally, *obstupefact*.[37] Now the logic of Jonson's scene is fairly complex. That this vocabulary can be vomited suggests that the terms are undigested—not precisely plagiarized, of course, since many of them are coinages, but imperfectly integrated. On the other hand, the alimentary tracking of the vocabulary registers that the destiny of Marstonian vocabulary, its career, aims toward an identification of self and poetic manner, and to this extent is more or less Jonsonian—Jonson recognizes a fellow traveler in Marston. They had collaborated, after this falling-out they would collaborate again.[38] But there is no gainsaying Jonson's shrewd cruelty here. He knew Marston well and had keenly sensed his nervous fear that in him the satirist's mood and manner was involuntary. With niggardly compassion, Jonson here assures his colleague that the yerking line is not quite a genetic fatality, is merely a lexical disease infecting stomach, mouth, and glottis.[39]

Both men seem to have taken the somatic construction of prosody quite seriously. Editors have noticed that many of the words that Crispinus vomits appear nowhere in the Marston corpus and they therefore plausibly surmise that Marston purged them from his texts when he revised his plays and poems—as he seems carefully to have done—for publication. Jonson's fictive purgative thus had real effects, effects more specific than that general stylistic therapy at work in *The Malcontent*. Now editors have also noticed that the Folio version of *Poetaster* introduces a number of changes to the lexicon vomited into the basin of the quarto. It thus seems that as Marston wrote new plays and revised old ones, Jonson fudged and updated his colleague's medical record. Having once acquiesced to Jonson's fantasy, Marston licensed his amateur physician to continue in practice. My best explanation for this uncanny collusion is that it enabled Marston to probe a serious uncertainty, the question of the degree to which language use can be voluntary, whether it is a disease that's in the flesh or the product of deliberation, whether a prosody is also an identity.[40]

The idea of a rhythmic or textural identity is usually allowed only to a few late romantic poets, to Keats, Browning, Hopkins, or, say, Stevens, but this particular idea of the "poetical character" has nearly dropped out of critical notice. Even our most exuberant prosodist, John Hollander, all but evades the matter, save in an intricate and important essay on Spenser's undersong.[41] He there describes how a topos, the fragment of a myth, and an early and probably inadvertent cadence, all conjoined into a single trope, are made to appear Spenser's essential mark, his secret signal to and of himself as a supernaturalist maker. For Spenser the swerve to alexandrine, the glancing awareness of where the muses have been, and the idea of verse attuned to the fall of often particular water became a trope of self. To put it this way may seem both right and mystifying: that is, to single out a particular prosodic feature—Spenser's alexandrine, say, or his habit of linking quatrains by means of chaining cross-rhyme—to speak of literary production at this level has come to seem merely crotchety, a crude obtrusion of the procedures of reviewing or classification upon the domain of "real" criticism. My point is that in the case of Marston, the poetical character is spectacular and nearly pathological, as if it were written back on the body itself. Hollander would have it that Spenser simply found his signature in certain felicitous lapses of the pen or failures of prosodic regularity; I'm saying that, in Marston's case, what he had nervously claimed as a merely optional manner became—partly through the effects of censorship and partly because of a parasitical or at least debilitating therapy from Marston's Dr. Jonson—a lump in his throat. An extreme case, I realize, but one that exposes prosody as a clinical project and fluency as a form of hygiene.

I want to conclude by suggesting that there will be some ancillary benefits to reviving and, more important, reincarnating the historical criticism of verse as such. Although the body has dominated criticism in recent years, most literary scholars will concede that we haven't yet succeeded in articulating a nuanced vocabulary for zoned, corporeal affect, much less for the meanings mapped onto the body. The best work on the body on the Renaissance stage—by Peter Stallybrass, Stephen Orgel, and Gail Paster, among others—can't be excepted from these reservations.[42] But to take what is, I think, a very fine leading case, Paster's theatrical body is genital and anal, the body as almost everywhere eroticized. One could imagine that the mouth, tongue, and throat might "naturally" be included in this specifically erogenous mapping of the body. Certainly that is the case in *Twelfth Night*, when Orsino takes the measure of Cesario's vocal apparatus, observing that "Diana's lip / Is not more smooth and rubious; thy small pipe"—Cesario's throat, that is—"Is as the maiden's organ, shrill and sound, / And all is semblative a woman's part" (1.4.30–3). But I wonder if it's not the case that sometimes a throat is just a throat.

To make this reservation stick, of course, one might wish to subject Marston's verbal habits to sustained psychoanalytical analysis. But, by the same token, the body articulated by psychoanalysis would need to be measured against the body articulated by Renaissance anatomists, and, especially, by Renaissance schoolmasters and music teachers—by John Hart, Charles Butler, and John Brinsley, by William Bathe and Robert Dowland.[43] Of course, these disciplinarians of the throat and their (admittedly) very few modern historians would need to concede that the body and its parts will often take their meaning from the various erotic cathexes. That is certainly the case, for example, in Spenser, yet a serious criticism of Spenser would have to admit that the body is also, and crucially, the occasion and instrument of balance, that it is, just as crucially, the condition of our visibility—of our visibility not only to the scopophiliac but to the historian, the censor, and perhaps the skeptic. Body and body parts will speak to us of more than desire, of more even than hunger, or weariness.[44] In Marston's plays, the throat takes its meanings from Marston's uncanny awareness that the throat has a triple function as a conduit of breath, of food (and its reflux), and of language: all three flows are felt to crowd each other, thus binding versification to a gasping, tortuous, and deeply organic life.

Bruce Smith has recently completed a study that would overlap the project of taking the early modern body on the terms of early modern theorists (among others), and indeed it is to Smith that we can turn for signs of a New Extra-Erotic Corporalism in Renaissance Studies.[45] His study *The Acoustic World of Early Modern England* is more attuned to acculturated aptitudes of the ear than to the closely related disciplines of the mouth, but it reminds us once again of how alert the early modern English were to the bodiliness of the verbal.[46] Smith quotes Jonson's sustained comparison (in *Discoveries*) of verbal style to the body itself and makes note of Bacon's interest in constructing a laboratory for the taxonomy of sounds and in describing the physiology of both speech production and hearing.[47]

The task of taking Marston's verse seriously was particularly easy, course, since his dramatic verse and his figurations of speech are so egregious. His verbal personality is, in every sense of the word, gross, which is why Jonson could lampoon him so easily. That Jonson was just a little bit embarrassed about taking aim at such an easy target is implied by the self-exhortation he attributes to Crispinus: "Ramp up my genius, be not retrograde / But boldly nominate a spade a spade" (5.3.275–76). Jonson is right, of course: an historical criticism carefully addressed to "voice," and specifically to prosodic and lexical manner, would eventually be obliged to proceed more subtly, picking more delicate objects of scrutiny, but perhaps it makes sense to begin simply, by calling a spade a spade, a throat a throat, a throttled prosody difficult, nearly unspeakable—this as an attempt to advance a properly historical formalism.

Notes

1. Miriam Allott, ed., *The Poems of John Keats* (London: Longman, 1970).
2. Arnold Davenport, ed., *The Poems of John Marston* (Liverpool: Liverpool University Press, 1961). All references to Marston's poems are to this edition.
3. James Shirley, *The Cardinal*, ed. E. M. Yearling (Manchester: Manchester University Press, 1986), 2.1.117–21.
4. In the introduction to his edition of *Antonio and Mellida* (cited below, note 21), G. K. Hunter recalls Lamb's (and might have recalled Swinburne's) orientation to the beautifully rendered moments of nobility in Marston, noting that Lamb found Marston unable to sustain these moments: "but I would argue that the play is not intended to sustain them; in the betrayal lies the art. . . . What Marston is interested in is not the way that one attitude forms itself out of another, but how one collapses to reveal the unexpected coexistence of another" (xiv).
5. Coburn Freer, *The Poetics of Jacobean Drama* (Baltimore: Johns Hopkins University Press, 1981); Freer assembles a large body of evidence reminding us that stress, pause, tone contour, and pace were recognized matters of professional theatrical concern (41–46). Not only did dramatists remark when a fellow did not stand upon points, but so did audiences and other actors; apparently, players could expect to be coached by playwrights in elocution and heckled by those who disapproved of the results. See also O. B. Hardison's *Prosody and Purpose in the English Renaissance* (Baltimore: Johns Hopkins University Press, 1989), which is extremely useful in enlarging the historiography of technique offered by Attridge (see note 6 following), but which is somewhat unsystematic in its treatment of dramatic poetry.

6. Derek Attridge, *Well-weighed Syllables: Elizabethan Verse in Classical Metres* (Cambridge: Cambridge University Press, 1974).
7. Attridge concludes that educated Elizabethans would have felt that Latin verse should be read with speech stresses but would have practiced a method of reading ictus as stress as a way of clarifying the quantitative system. (He infers that a talented schoolboy would then convert the stressed ictus to a quantitative reading and might even try to keep that going in tension with a speech-stressed reading.) There are frequent Jacobean comments about foolish schoolboys who treat ictus as the proper guide to pronounced stress. Erasmus and his followers keep an idea that ictus has to do with pitch before many schoolmasters, though there was an attempt at the turn of the century to scour this out. We could say that Latin voice production was an area both of discipline and theoretical contest.

 We may say more. The force of authority in licensing counter-intuitive substitutions was very strong, and substitution would have been a chief site of the sense of the arbitrary force of regulation, which is to say that prosodic speaking would also seem a site of perversely inexplicable impositions. (See John Bird's *Grounds of Grammar* [Oxford, 1639], with its explicit discussion of "Authority.") There is a strong analogy here in the rift that opens between practical and speculative music, another swamp of tyrannically counterintuitive theory in which the boy actors of Marston's early plays would have been steeped.
8. For the related "puffed," a favorite word, see *Antonio and Mellida*, 1.1.56.
9. My difficulty in transcribing the quotations for this essay is surely a relevant datum. Since I don't touch-type, I must constantly shift my gaze between page, keyboard, and screen, and although I can usually carry a line or two of verse in my head unaltered from one moment to the next, as I worked I kept getting Marston wrong, for I persistently edited and smoothed, trying to relieve the pressure on my mind's throat.
10. Edmund Gosse and Thomas James Wise, eds., *The Complete Works of Algernon Charles Swinburne,* 20 vols. (London: Heinemann, 1926), 11:354. Swinburne, who alleges that Marston's piece in Chester's volume "may perhaps claim the singular distinction of being more incomprehensible, more crabbed, more preposterous, and more inexplicable than any other copy of verses . . . in which Marston has the honour to stand next to Shakespeare" (371), will later praise him for the "healthy disgust" of his satiric manner (377). Swinburne describes Marston's verbal manner best, I think, when he charges that "he sets himself to bring to perfection the qualities of crabbed turgidity and barbarous bombast with which nature had but too richly endowed him, mingling these among many better gifts with so cunning a hand and so malignant a liberality as wellnigh to stifle the good seed of which yet she had not been sparing" (12:141). This gets things almost exactly right, which is why it is so dismaying that Swinburne believed himself to be describing, not Marston here, but Chapman—as would have been clear had I sustained the quotation, for Swinburne immediately focuses his

attention on a characteristic "obscurity," which is not Marston's, but Chapman's, middle name.

11. And cf. Piero's "this brain hath chok'd / The organ of his breast" (1.1.14–15).
12. John Marston, *Antonio's Revenge*, ed. G. K. Hunter (Lincoln: University of Nebraska Press, 1965), Prologue 1–6 and 21–33.
13. And cf. Antonio's mother's self-pitying "And poor Maria must appear ungrac'd / Of the bright fulgor of gloss'd majesty" (1.2.7–8). A longer version of this essay would be obliged to extend the discussion of Hall's influence on Marston's prosodic thinking at precisely this juncture. In *Virigidemarium* (1597), Hall sneers at bad playwrights who have so poor an instinct for English prosody that they 1) attempt quantitative writing for the stage and 2) choose spondaic over dactylic movement for dramatic speech. Marston's early plays seem specifically to flout Hall's latter stricture.
14. Cf. the parallel situation in *The Malcontent*, when the usurper Pietro threatens the subordinate collaborator who controls him: "A mischiefe fill thy throate, thou fowle jaw'd slave"; John Marston, *The Malcontent*, ed. M. L. Wine (Lincoln: University of Nebraska Press, 1964), 1.7.1.
15. T. F. Wharton has many useful things to say about the tactics of Marston's contentions in *The Critical Fall and Rise of John Marston* (Columbia: Camden House, 1994), 5ff.
16. *The Three Parnassus Plays*, ed. J. B. Leishman (London: Nicholson, 1949).
17. The question of optional satire will take us to the core of Marston's oeuvre, certainly to the core of his most famous play. The central device of *The Malcontent* is the hero's *masquerade* as a satirist, which seems to me to act on Marston's fundamental but paradoxical wish as an artist—to be undetermined by the satiric mode (to have broken its chain, as it were) and to arrogate determining authority to satire. Altofronto (nominally) stands above satire; disguised as Malevole he humiliates his usurping brother and recovers his dukedom by mere expressive bile. By its very mildness, *The Tempest* reforms this fantasy; Jonson, bitterly, had attempted to purge it.
18. A Ruffian in his stile . . .
   He quaffes a cup of Frenchmans Helicon,
   Then royster doyster in his oylie tearmes,
   Cutts, thrusts, and foines at whomsoever he meets,
   And strewes about Ram-ally meditations.
   (*Second Return from Parnassus*, 269, 270–74)
19. See *Antonio's Revenge*, 4.1.5, with its classist reference to the "rheum of censure."
20. Not that Hall was surrendered entirely, as witness the Marstonian spondee: see note 13 above.
21. John Marston, *Antonio and Mellida*, ed. G. K. Hunter (Lincoln: University of Nebraska Press, 1965), 1.1.208–20.
22. It is difficult to resist quoting Marston, if only for the purpose of registering his astonishingly shifted spectrum of utterance. The noble Andrugio might be expected to speak Marston's most poised and dignified verse; here is his

evocation of a Venetian dawn: "Is not yon gleam the shuddering morn that flakes, / With silver tincture, the east verge of heaven?"

For the Marston of *Antonio and Mellida* aggression is almost inevitably oral, but idiosyncratically so. Of pride, Feliche observes,

> O she's ominous
> Enticeth princes to devour heaven
> Swallow omnipotence, outstare dread fate,
> Subdue eternity in giant thought,
> Heaves up the heart with swelling puff'd conceit
> Till their souls burst with venom'd arrogance
>
> (1.1.51–6)

The idiom persists in the somewhat "healthier" verse of *The Malcontent*. There, the witness to a suicide reports having

> view'd his body fall and souse
> Into the foamy main. O, then I saw
> That which methinks I see: it was the duke,
> Whom straight the nicer-stomach'd sea
> Belch'd up ...
>
> (4.3.44–8)

It is a false account; the Duke is fabricating the story of his own death; and Marston has perhaps recurred to rhythms and terms he has, with effort, outgrown, in order to render the inauthenticity of the utterance.

23. This moment ought to alert us to the nasty undermeanings of Kent's angry clause in *King Lear*, "whil'st I can vent clamor from my throat." Compare 3.1.5. and 1.2.125, where the earth "belks" the "ghost of a misshapen simile."

24. 3.2.95; see also the reference to grief's stomach at 2.2.3, as well as passages at 4.1.42, 5.2.33, and especially, 5.3.52. But indigestion is not the sole somatic subtext: a kind of cholera rages at the death of Andrugio (2.1.243).

25. 2.2.205–7; earlier in the same scene, Antonio similarly expresses an impatience with an exhortation to patience: "That grief is wanton-sick / Whose stomach can digest and brook the diet / Of stale, ill-relish'd counsel" (2.2.2–4).

26. 4.1.189 s.d.; and cf. 2.2.197.

27. 5.3.108–9; this responds quite directly to Piero's curse on Andrugio's corpse, "Oblivion choke the passage of thy fame" (2.1.3).

28. 1.2.248; Antonio's stoic friend, Pandulpho, is obliged to reflect in his turn that "men of hope are crush'd / Good are suppress'd by base desertless clods, / That stifle gasping virtue" (1.2.304–6).

29. 1.2.204–7; 207 ends with a colon in Q (sig. B4v). This device may be compared with that in *Every Man Out of His Humour*, in which successive pulls on a pipe of tobacco are rendered as dashes in the printed text.

30. See also 4.1.5. One might wish to bring this moment into some sort of relationship with the wonderfully hypermetrical line at 4.1.208 with its great phrase "ding'd down."
31. See Pietro at 2.3.55–77 and Aurelia at 4.5.31–50.
32. The early manner is not always effectively muted; see note 22 above.
33. The ribaldry, though, didn't become a real specialty until a few years later, in the next century. Others have remarked rather differently on the specific effect of boys' performance on this play and its predecessor, *Antonio and Mellida;* see Hunter's edition of the later play, xvi-xvii, in which he judiciously responds to arguments by Anthony Caputi and R. A. Foakes.
34. Marston would contrive related addresses to this taste, as when, in *Antonio and Mellida,* Antonio disguises himself as an Amazon in order to keep company with Mellida.
35. H. Harvey Wood, ed., *The Plays of John Marston,* 3 vols. (Edinburgh: Oliver & Boyd, 1934–39) 3:273–74.
36. Ben Jonson, *Poetaster,* ed. Tom Cain (Manchester: Manchester University Press, 1995), 5.3.281–2. Even leisure is effortful for Crispinus. Invited to tour Albius' garden, he prefers to sit still, assuring his host, with a draw on the core Marstonian lexicon, "I am most strenuously well, I thank you, sir" (2.1.13).
37. "Barmy-froth" is from *Scourge* (Davenport, *Poems,* 96), which already shows Marston discovering his idiom, provoked by the challenge of series:

> Castilios, Cyprians, court-boyes, spanish blocks,
> Ribanded eares, granado-netherstocks
> Fidlers, Scriveners, pedlers, tynkering knaves,
> Base blew-coats, tapsters, brod-cloth-minded slaves.

38. These two were under each other's skin, which may explain why critics have been so uncertain about the tone of Marston's representation of Jonson, as Chrisoganus, in *Histriomastix.* When Marston's Chrisoganus employs the familiar digestive idiom in his insult to popular taste—"Write on, crie on, yawle to the common sort"—he is reprising the sentiments of Marston's own assault on popular taste, the poem "*In Lectores prorsus indignos*": it is no more insulting to Jonson—and no less—than Marston's *self*-representation in *The Scourge of Villainie.* Contrapasso is always responsive, but Jonson's seems especially so, since he sees it as a Marstonian form of punishment: see *Antonio's Revenge,* 3.1.140, "I'll force him feed on life / Till he shall loathe it." It bears recalling that two or three years later Marston dedicated *The Malcontent* to Jonson.
39. Jonson is playing a very old trick in this scene. Marston had relied heavily on the modal topoi of satire, which figure satire as punitive or purgative—and in either case, as a physical irritant. Jonson's game is to take Marston "at his word," but he plays the game with much more than mechanical attention.
40. Freer concludes his study of the poetics of Jacobean drama with the hypothesis that "by a kind of displacement, verse may have assumed some of

the role of physical activity" (205), but he is hard put to show how prosodic features compete with the inventive violence of Jacobean stage action. Jonson corroborates, and parodies, Freer's hypothesis.

41. John Hollander, "Spenser's Undersong," in *Cannibals, Witches, and Divorce: Estranging the Renaissance*, ed. Marjorie Garber, *Selected Papers from the English Institute*, n.s. 11 (Baltimore: Johns Hopkins University Press, 1985), 1–20.

42. Peter Stallybrass, "Transvestism and the 'Body Beneath': Speculating on the Boy Actor," in *Erotic Politics: Desire on the Renaissance Stage*, ed. Susan Zimmerman (London: Routledge, 1992); Stephen Orgel, *Impersonations: The Performance of Gender in Shakespeare's England* (Cambridge: Cambridge University Press, 1996); Gail Kern Paster, *The Body Embarrassed: Drama and the Disciplines of Shame in Early Modern England* (Ithaca: Cornell University Press, 1993). Jeff Masten, "Is the Fundament a Grave?" in *The Body in Parts: Fantasies of Corporeality in Early Modern Europe*, ed. David Hillman and Carla Mazzio (New York: Routledge, 1997), 129–46, may be excepted from these reservations.

43. Hart indicates a desire to methodize orthography according to rigorously discriminated phonetics; Butler, who was also a music theorist, has the same goal, and the eccentricity of his orthography betrays both radicalism and a disciplinarian's temperament. The drive to construct a phonetic orthography suggests an attempt to make writing a science of the voice. Butler may be the key figure, since he also wrote a number of rhetorics that attend very closely to the pronunciation of spoken Latin and of Latin verse. He was especially interested in breaking down the phonetics of verse, carefully discriminating pitch contour, speech accent, and quantity as competing components of rhythm.

It is worth noting that Elizabethan and Jacobean writers on music will sometimes linger nearly as much over the time system as over matters of counterpoint. (Morley spends most of the first book of *A Plain and Easy Introduction to Practical Music* on time notation, whereas he has only a sentence on temperament.) This suggests that music presents itself very much as an art of pure regulation (and, perhaps, specifically breath control) rather than of practical euphony. Of special interest to the historian of prosody is Ornithoparchus' emphasis in the *Micrologus* (1517, translated by John Dowland in 1609) on the problem of reconciling speech stress and musical accent.

Early modern treatises on practical music are generally pertinent to the study of Marstonian verse not because of any emphasis on voice production—a matter left to music masters—but because of the heavy theoretical overlay that dogs attempts to popularize the craft of composition. To some extent this is a mere residue of academic music pedagogy—certainly that residue is thick in Butler's *Principles of Musick in Singing and Setting* (1636)—but it is plain and remarkable that, in a era of great advances in practical pedagogy, training in music composition and singing did not shed a dense overlay of theoretical jargon and principle. The arts of descant are not roughed out and then left to the elaboration of a cultivated practitioner; rather, the whole range of permissible intervals is subjected to minute analytic scrutiny, from which a vast body of rules proliferates. Students were taught that to compose and to improvise was to scruple, to know and name and choose. Sound production, then, was to be a deeply inhibited form of beautification.

44. For a related and far more sustained account of the extra-erotic early modern body, see Michael Carl Schoenfeldt, *Bodies and Selves in Early Modern England: Physiology and Inwardness in Spenser, Shakespeare, Herbert, and Milton* (Cambridge: Cambridge University Press, 1999).

45. One may also turn to Schoenfeldt, *Bodies and Selves,* and to the fine collection of Hillman and Mazzio, *The Body in Parts;* the latter contains several extra-erotic analyses of the body and some extremely salutary investigations of how the body is parcellized according to a range of figurative practices for a range of rhetorical ends. The investigation I am proposing would involve a focus at once slightly different and more inclusive, one that would take in the culturally conditioned ways in which body parts and bodily systems are put into practice.

46. Bruce Smith, *The Acoustic World of Early Modern England: Attending to the O-Factor* (Chicago: University of Chicago Press, 1999).

47. Smith, *Acoustic World,* 49 and 96–101.

Part II

Renewing the Literary

Learning from the New Criticism

The Example of Shakespeare's Sonnets

Paul Alpers

Writing about the changes in Renaissance and early modern literary studies, Leah Marcus says: "Pace T. S. Eliot and the New Critics, the lyric has lost its centrality in seventeenth-century studies and been replaced by less elitist genres such as the drama."[1] The elitism to which she objects has less to do with the status of lyric poetry in the sixteenth and seventeenth centuries than with its status in modern criticism. It is certainly the case that modernist criticism privileged lyric poetry and that, for both the New Critics in this country and the *Scrutiny* group in England, poetry mattered because it implicitly resisted the forces of democracy, industrialism, and technology. Since the 1960s, there has been a widespread reaction against the values and procedures of modernist criticism, which are frequently stigmatized as formalist. Some of the main forms of current interest in Renaissance lyric—such as the attention to poetry as courtly display and maneuvering and to manuscript circulation among various coteries—are consciously antiformalist. Hence Marcus says, "It is arguable that the new work on the cultural construction of the lyric will stimulate a revival of critical and pedagogical interest in the genre, but the lyric will not be the same transcendent, serenely aloof artifact it was for earlier generations of scholars."[2] Putting the case this way simply reinscribes the problem. It brings out how much today's historicizing interests are motivated by antagonism to yesterday's New Criticism. Such prejudging of the claims of lyric makes it impossible to reconceive sixteenth and seventeenth century poems in a way that recognizes their distinctiveness.

If a formalist account of Renaissance lyric is to be fruitful and convincing now, it cannot simply revive the terms and protocols of modernist criticism. At the same time, I think it important that we work *through* the modernist account of poetry instead of setting it up as an antagonist, because so far as Renaissance poetry is concerned, no coherent view of lyric has come along to replace it. This situation is made very clear by Chaviva Hosek's and Patricia Parker's excellent collection, *Lyric Poetry: Beyond New Criticism*.[3] Most of the essays in this volume provide a coherent post-New Critical, predominantly deconstructive, account of lyric poetry. These essays concern canonical poets, both French and English, of the nineteenth and twentieth centuries. The volume also includes four essays on lyric poetry of the English Renaissance. The concerns of these four essays and their modes of interpretation not only have nothing to do with the essays on Romantic and modern poetry, they have very little to do with each other.[4] I therefore think we need to return to the critical tradition that once gave us our bearings on Renaissance lyric and still haunts our accounts of it. Accordingly, this essay examines the difficulties modernist criticism has had in dealing with Shakespeare's Sonnets—not, however, in order to disavow this criticism and its endeavors, but rather to show that it has been capable of self-adjustment and that it can still provide resources for formalist analysis.[5]

In 1938, the year after he came to Kenyon College and the year before the founding of *Kenyon Review*, John Crowe Ransom published an essay called "Shakespeare at Sonnets." It begins with the puckish seriousness that is one of his most attractive qualities as a writer:

> One may be well disposed to the New Deal, and not relish the attitude of giving comfort to the enemy by criticizing Mr. Roosevelt publicly, yet in a qualified company do it freely. The same thing applies in the matter of the poet Shakespeare.... I will not hold back from throwing a few stones at Shakespeare, aiming them as accurately as I can at the vulnerable parts.[6]

Ransom singles out two targets. He thinks many of the sonnets fail to work within the structure dictated by their rhyme scheme. He is unhappy with sonnets that are not like 73 ("That time of year thou mayst in me behold"), with its three equally weighted quatrains. In addition, he is unhappy with the kind of writing he finds in many of the sonnets, like 33:

> Full many a glorious morning have I seen
> Flatter the mountain tops with sovereign eye,
> Kissing with golden face the meadows green,
> Gilding pale streams with heavenly alchemy ...[7]

He complains that "this sun is weakly imagined; rather, it may be said to be only felt, a loose cluster of images as obscure as they are pleasant." He calls this "an associationist poetry," claiming that there is a "failure of objectivity."

He understands why readers value lines like these. "The pretty words have pleasing if indefinite associations; and . . . the associations tend rather to cohere than to repel each other." But these words "do not cohere into a logical or definitive object"; rather, the feeling of coherence comes from the meter.[8] He rephrases this objection by drawing a distinction which, as we shall see, is one of the foundations of his criticism. "*Logically,*" he says, "this is a poetry of wonderful imprecision, and the only precision it has is metrical, therefore *adventitious.*"[9]

Ransom's critique of Sonnet 33 is, in effect, that it fails to live up to the principle stated in the introduction to Cleanth Brooks and Robert Penn Warren's New Critical textbook, *Understanding Poetry:* "A poem should always be treated as an organic system of relationships, and the poetic quality should never be understood as inhering in one or more factors taken in isolation."[10] Another great modern critic, Yvor Winters, gives us an alternative way of understanding the difficulty Ransom feels. The year after Ransom's essay, Winters published a radically innovative series of essays on sixteenth-century poetry, in which he raises a question about Shakespeare's Sonnets.[11] These poems, he says, have a powerful suggestiveness, and in that power lies a danger. Suggestiveness can arise from meanings of words that are, strictly speaking, irrelevant to the subject or the dramatic situation of the poem in which they occur. When this happens, feeling is separated from any motive that has been convincingly presented. Winters too feels the danger of loose, imprecise associations, and we can use his key term to state Ransom's uneasiness about the Sonnets. If structure, meter, imagery, and diction go their separate ways and are not closely interrelated, then we cannot feel that as elements of the poem they are sufficiently *motivated.*

Ransom, Winters, and Brooks wrote extensively about each other's criticism. They shared enough in their fundamental views of poetry and its importance that they could disagree fruitfully with each other. What is curious is that Ransom's main criticism of both Winters and Brooks concerns the assumption about poetic unity that seems to underlie his own criticism of Shakespeare's Sonnets. He expresses this criticism in terms he used throughout his career. He maintained that in considering a poem, one had to distinguish and be aware of logic and structure, on the one hand, and, on the other, what he called "texture." In *The New Criticism,* the book that gave this school or movement its name, he calls Winters "the logical critic" and praises him as "the critic who is best at pouncing upon the structure of a poem."[12] But he objects to Winters' requirement that all elements of a poem—meter, figurative language, the connotations of words—be motivated by the moral intention that the structure conveys. Ransom argues that Winters denies too much of what happens locally in a poem, what he calls its "texture." In Ransom's view, the various local elements, like meter and metaphor, take on a life of their own; they enhance the poem not by being subordinate to logic or structure but by increasing the poem's overall density, the way it suggests an engagement with the particularities and complexities of real experience. Ransom was willing to speak of a poem's texture as "a tissue of irrelevance"—a phrase that prompted a vigorous critique by Winters.[13]

In discussing Brooks, Ransom invokes the structure-texture dichotomy in another way. One of Brooks' principles, in maintaining that every aspect of a poem is essential to its wholeness and achieved effect, was that it is illegitimate to represent a poem by a prose paraphrase. He had good reason for this, insofar as he was opposing the classroom practice of discussing "what a poem says" as if it were separate from its poetic usages and devices. But when in his most influential book, *The Well Wrought Urn,* he speaks of "the heresy of paraphrase," the religious metaphor reveals a certain mystification of the poem's organic wholeness.[14] This is the point Ransom made in his admiring discussion of the book. If poetry has important human uses, he says, and if it is to make its way in the world, we have to recognize that a poem has "two kinds of meaning." "One is the ostensible argument, which we can render by paraphrase, and which is entirely useful and reputable. The other is the tissue of meaning [compare his usual term, "texture"] which resists rendering."[15]

In the thirties and forties there were surprisingly few essays that spoke of Shakespeare's Sonnets with discerning admiration. Plenty of critics sang their praises, of course. But few *New* critics did. Unlike the lyrics of Donne and other seventeenth-century poets, the Sonnets were not spoken of as exemplary poems, in a sense they were not trusted, by the critics who practiced the searching, specific verbal analysis that Ransom and his colleagues most valued.[16] The curious thing is that Ransom, who wrote the most notorious attack on the Sonnets, seems to have been in the best position to understand their workings. Kenneth Burke began a review of *The New Criticism* with the following observations:

> An ideal procedure for a critic . . . would be . . . to say: "I shall here propose a set of key terms for the consideration of the work of art. Other sets of terms also yield results, but not the results I am after. I shall show what resources of illumination and evaluation I have discovered in my terms. I shall show the kind of problems they solve . . ."[17]

I would say that the terms "structure" and "texture" are precisely the ones that can address the problems Ransom identified in Shakespeare's Sonnets. Burke suggests why, when he discusses the pairing of these two terms:

> Usually, a dialectic of this sort treats the details of a work as consistent with some unitary generating principle or "idea." The novel twist in Mr. Ransom's

terminology derives from the fact that he stresses the *divergent* nature of the details.... The great virtue of this terminology is in its ability to keep us fully aware of the fact that a good poem is not just one steady over-all concentration, but a constant succession of minor concentrations, each with some stylistic virtue of its own. Each incidental metaphor, for instance, is then perceived as a kind of poem in miniature, capable of being savored for itself, like the individual sonnets of a sonnet sequence.[18]

The New Critical breakthrough in analyzing the Sonnets came when a critic saw that one could understand the way they work by, in effect, turning Ransom right side up. This critic was Stephen Booth, who published a book on the Sonnets in 1964 and, ten years later, an edition with an exhaustive commentary.[19] A few examples will show his strengths and principles. The first is his comment on the beginning of Sonnet 33:

> Full many a glorious morning have I seen
> Flatter the mountain tops with sovereign eye,
> Kissing with golden face the meadows green,
> Gilding pale streams with heav'nly alchemy,
> Anon permit the basest clouds to ride
> With ugly rack on his celestial face ...

Ransom had objected that the precision of meter and verse here is an isolated accomplishment that covers up looseness in the imagery. Booth shows that meter and verse do significant work. He points out two occurrences of double syntax in these lines. Line 1—"Full many a glorious morning have I seen"—seems a complete sentence in itself, and this is true no matter how the line is punctuated, because the line of verse as such is felt to be independent.[20] In Ransom's terms, this effect is due to precision of meter. But the next line makes us reconceive the syntax of the sentence: we now understand the object of "have I seen" to be not simply the morning but its action of flattering the mountain tops. This newly understood sentence again seems complete at the end of line 4—not only because of the syntax but also because the verse, the completion of the quatrain, gives a strong sense of closure. But the first line of the second quatrain once more reverses our understanding of the grammar: it does not begin a new sentence, as we expected, but continues the sentence we thought had been completed in the first quatrain.

Now this is the kind of thing to which Ransom objected. He would say that overriding the division between quatrains contradicts the Shakespearean sonnet form, and he could back up this judgment with a grammatical analysis. (Grammatical comments occur throughout Ransom's criticism, probably because of his training in classical languages.) What he or Winters might point out here is a certain slipperiness of syntax. "Permit" in line 5 is parallel to "flatter" in line 2; they are the two main verbs in the long clause that is the object of "have seen," which is the main verb of the whole sentence. But the sentence in prose would have to read: "I have seen many a morning flatter the mountains and then (or but then) permit the clouds to ride." If lines 3 and 4 are omitted, the sentence as Shakespeare wrote it does not feel right. The reason we accept it is that the participles "kissing" and "gilding," which control lines 3 and 4, look both backward and forward. They can be linked syntactically not only with "flatter" but also, when it occurs, with "permit."

Booth justifies this shiftiness in the following terms: "The mutability of syntactic identities acts as a stylistic metaphor for the unexpected inconstancy the poem talks about: the reader's syntactic experience is to his expectations about sentences as sudden changes in weather or in a beloved's mood are to the non-literary situations described." This is the kind of argument that Booth and I learned from our New Critical elders. It seeks to show that the main theme of the sonnet motivates its poetic devices and that the poem is therefore unified even in its smallest details. But in fact this is not the line Booth usually takes in pointing out syntactic doubleness and instability. His fundamental argument about the Sonnets and his fundamental explanation of their poetic richness is that they contain many different kinds of ordering, and that these exist and come into play independently of each other. They are valuable because of the activity they promote in the mind of the reader. The lines may seem simple or obvious—Booth indeed thinks this is usually the case—but, he argues, a lot is going on in our minds even if we are not aware of it. Whether or not we notice double or unstable syntax, it increases our feeling that what we are reading is rich and powerful. A similar enriching effect comes from the various sound patterns that saturate the Sonnets.

Booth's long commentary on Sonnet 116 is meant to show what he calls "the special grandeur of the best sonnets."[21] His analysis involves something very much like Ransom's distinction between structure and texture. Early in his "general note" on the poem, he says, "Sonnet 116 has simple clear content; indeed . . . it is one of the few Shakespeare sonnets that can be paraphrased without brutality." He sums up his account in the following terms:

> Sonnet 116 is overlaid with relationships established in patterning factors that do not pertain to or impinge upon the logic and syntax of the particular authoritative statement it makes. The most obvious of them, of course, are the formal iambic pentameter rhythmic pattern and the sonnet rhyme scheme. This sonnet, however, also contains patterns of a kind that falls between the ideational structure (what the poem says) and the substantively irrelevant phonetic patterns of the sonnet form: patterns established by the relationship

of the meanings of its words—in this case meanings that are irrelevant to, and do not color, the particular sentences in which they appear here but which do pertain generally to the topic about which the sentences isolate particular truths in particular frames of reference.

As an example of Boothian analysis, consider what he says about lines 5 and 6:

> O no, it is an ever-fixèd mark
> That looks on tempests and is never shaken.

Booth's particular interest is in the way line 6 complicates the simple metaphor of love as "an ever fixèd mark"—that is, a sea-mark, a beacon or lighthouse. How, he asks, do we understand this line? He gives three answers. 1) The overall sense, prompted by "ever-fixèd," is that "looks on" is synonymous to "endures," "persists in the face of." 2) It makes sense to say a beacon "looks," both because of its appearance at night and because the Elizabethans thought that the eyes see by emitting rays which reflect off the objects seen. 3) "A tiny distant flame that withstands . . . a tempest is [a] fitting emblem of steadfastness." Booth sums up this analysis in the following way:

> None of that is poetically remarkable. What is remarkable is that the logic in which *looks on* indicates "persists," the logic in which a seamark is eye-like and can be considered capable of looking, and the logic in which a feeble but constant flame is emblematic of steadfastness are independent of one another; each supports the assertion without reference to its relation to the other two.

This analysis suggests that Ransom saw accurately enough how the Sonnets work poetically. But it took Booth to show—and it was a major achievement—that seeing how they work should lead you to admire them. Why does Booth value such poetry? Throughout his discussion of 116, he is concerned with the way the sonnet's broad, paraphrasable assertion is given particularity and concreteness. This is a characteristic modernist concern, which we have already seen in Ransom's emphasis on the competing claims of logic and texture. Hence Booth praises line 6 by saying, in the sentence following the ones I have just quoted: "The statement [that true love is steadfast] gets all the validity of the seamark's concreteness but remains mystic and wonderful, made as resistant to comprehension as available to it." It is these final phrases that show where Booth parts company with Ransom and Winters and they with him. We need not merely imagine Winters' indignant snort, because he put it in print. Speaking of the same quatrain, he says, "Shakespeare contents himself here with a vague feeling of the mysterious and supernatural, and the feeling is very vague indeed."[22] The point we have reached, where Booth sees clearly what Ransom saw dimly, is also a point of serious disagreement. We therefore need to return to Ransom and ask why, if he describes the Sonnets pretty accurately, he is made uneasy by them.

After criticizing the Sonnets for uncertain structure and loose, Romantic diction, Ransom asks whether Shakespeare works successfully in another style. He cites Sonnet 87 ("Farewell, thou art too dear for my possessing") with approval for the way it employs a legal figure, the cancellation of a bond, to represent the human situation, the lover's renouncing his claim to the beloved. "Three times," Ransom says, "in as many quatrains, the lover makes an exploration within the field of the figure." This leads him to a central definition: "The impulse to metaphysical poetry, I shall assume, consists in committing the feelings in the case—those of unrequited love for example—to their determination within the elected figure."[23] But Shakespeare is declared unable or unwilling to write poetry on these terms. Weighing him in the balance with Donne, Ransom finds him wanting. Sonnet 55 ("Not marble nor the gilded monuments") is said to be "strong" but "not quite intelligent enough to be metaphysical."[24] (Ransom said he was going to throw some stones!) By comparison, the "controlled yet exuberant use of the imagination" in a poem by Donne is said to be "an intellectual feat."[25]

We are on familiar New Critical ground in all this. Allen Tate, Ransom's closest intellectual companion, calls "Shakespeare at Sonnets" "a remarkable essay" and particularly approves the description just quoted of metaphysical poetry. "That is to say," Tate explains, "in metaphysical poetry the logical order is explicit; it must be coherent; the imagery by which it is sensuously embodied must have at least the appearance of logical determinism."[26] Considerations like these make poetic style a central issue, and concentration on style and technique was often productive for modernist critics. It enabled them to treat poems as poems and to pay specific, analytic attention to observable features like diction, imagery, and verse form. More broadly, by focusing on style they were able to encourage their readers to reconsider their tastes and expectations in poetry, to see the strength and interest of kinds of poetry that might at first seem "unpoetical." But concern with style sometimes has the effect of displacing or obscuring what is at stake for these critics. Why, after all, should we particularly value poetry that commits feelings to their determination within the elected figure?

One of the impressive things about "Shakespeare at Sonnets" is that Ransom provides an answer to this question. He begins by asking "what are feelings?" and continues as follows:

> I am sure I do not know, but I will suppose for the present they are calls to action, and always want to realize their destiny, which is to turn into actions

and vanish. I will suppose also, and this is from experience, that we find ourselves sometimes possessed of powerful feelings and yet cannot quite tell what actions they want of us; or find ourselves even learning to enjoy the pangs of feelings, in the conceited consciousness they are our very own.[27]

In both its philosophical grounding and its attractive, quirky candor, this is characteristic Ransom. It leads him to the fundamental distinction between the two models of poetry he has brought to bear on Shakespeare's Sonnets:

> Lovers (and other persons too) often have feelings which cannot take, and do not seek, their natural outlet in physical actions.... Then they find appropriate actions through imagination, in intellectual constructions. These lovers at their best are poets. These poets at their best perform complete actions, very likely by means of metaphysical poems. So, on the one hand, there is an associationist poetry, a half-way action providing many charming resting-places for the feelings to agitate themselves; and, on the other hand, there is a metaphysical poetry, which elects its line of action and goes straight through to the completion of the cycle and the extinction of the feelings.[28]

The basis of the stylistic distinction is ethical. The associationist poet indulges his feelings; he is what New Critics stigmatized as sentimental. The metaphysical poet deals properly with his feelings; he is what New Critics called mature. As the old saying goes, the style is the man. By spelling out his ethical conception of poetic style, Ransom makes clear that what is at issue for him, in criticizing the Sonnets, is their character as first-person expression.

Modernist critics resisted saying that lyric poetry is self-expression, because that idea, for them, came trailing clouds of Romantic vagueness. But neither the various ways in which modern poets sought to make their poems "impersonal" or "objective" nor the various ways in which critics sought to treat poems as verbal artifacts or as objects of analysis meant that subjectivity had been banished from the lyric. Jonathan Culler has argued that the modern conception of lyric—and we should remember how many important modern critics were themselves poets—is that a poem "describe[s] the movement of a consciousness attempting to come to terms with fundamental aspects of the human condition, as embodied in the situation confronting it."[29] "To interpret a poem as a lyric, by this model," says Culler, "is to attempt to identify with an act of consciousness on the part of a constructed speaker."[30] A *constructed* speaker, because not identical with the poet himself or herself; this was the reaction against the Romantic heritage. But because the drama of consciousness involves matters of tone and attitude within a represented situation, modernist critics characteristically "posit a speaker to whom they can be attributed."[31] Hence the dogma, in New

Critical classrooms, that the "I," the first person, of a lyric poem be referred to as "the speaker," and not Keats or Dickinson or Yeats or whoever the poet happens to be.

In the case of Shakespeare it was particularly urgent to get away from treating the Sonnets as the poet's self-expression. During the nineteenth century, this assumption had led to a vast amount of biographical speculation. Who was Mr. W. H.? Who was the rival poet? Who was the Dark Lady? The fruitless answers to these questions are entombed in the Variorum edition of Hyder Rollins, who patiently showed how little substance any of them had. The great literary account of the motives and deceptions of this way of thinking about the Sonnets is Oscar Wilde's brilliant fantasia, "The Portrait of Mr. W. H." As Wilde's story shows, the nineteenth-century search for biographical clues was not a matter of dry-as-dust scholarship. It went hand in hand with thinking about the Sonnets as intimate revelations, as if they were the poet's diary. The watchword for this interest appears in Wordsworth's "Scorn not the Sonnet": "With this key Shakespeare unlocked his heart." Modern critics should have had no difficulty in objecting to the useless speculations and sentimental hankerings of the nineteenth-century tradition. They could have shown that the Sonnets were good in modernist terms—that they were tougher, more ironic, and more complex than readers had been led to believe. But as Ransom's essay shows, the Sonnets did not meet modernist expectations, and the fundamental reason is that the constructed speaker in these poems is not what modernist critics valued as a dramatic speaker—that is, one who has a continuous, observable presence in the poem and whose tone of voice and whose rhetoric (for example, the way he stays within the elected figure) shows his awareness of the situation in which the poem places him and the coherence of his attitude toward it.

Modernist uneasiness with the Sonnets was not only felt on this side of the Atlantic. A few years before Ransom's essay, L. C. Knights, one of the main contributors to *Scrutiny*, wrote a long, intelligent, and ambivalent essay about them. Knights' discussion of Sonnet 35 shows what troubles a good modernist critic in these poems and what he looks to find in them:

> No more be grieved at that which thou hast done:
> Roses have thorns, and silver fountains mud,
> Clouds and eclipses stain both moon and sun,
> And loathsome canker lives in sweetest bud.
> All men make faults, and even I in this,
> Authorizing thy trespass with compare,
> Myself corrupting salving thy amiss,
> Excusing thy sins more than thy sins are.[32]

The first quatrain, in Knights' view, exemplifies the kind of conventional Elizabethan poetizing that Shakespeare was learning to write his way out of. In this earlier style, the imagery and the various devices of sound "seem to exist as objects of attention in themselves rather than as the medium of a compulsive force working from within."[33] Hence "the play upon the letters *s* and *l* is mainly musical and decorative." But the next quatrain is entirely different. It reveals "a painful complexity of feeling," which emerges most decisively in line 7. In a nice bit of modernist analysis, Knights points out that the line has two meanings. If "myself" is the object of "corrupting," the line means "I corrupt myself when I find excuses for you." If "myself" is the agent of corrupting, the line means "I'm afraid I myself make you worse by excusing your faults."[34] The colloquial "I'm afraid" that begins this paraphrase shows that Knights wants to enhance the speaker's dramatic presence, and this same critical motive leads to his comment on the alliteration in this quatrain. Here it is no longer "musical and decorative" but "functional": "with the change of tone and direction the alliterative *s* becomes a hiss of half-impotent venom." Where the first quatrain exemplifies the "formal and incantatory mode" of many of the sonnets, the second quatrain shows "the use of speech movement and idiom to obtain a further command of tone."[35]

I agree that the second quatrain is the most remarkable part of the poem, but I myself do not hear that "hiss of half-impotent venom." Knights *has* to hear it, because he can only assign complexity of feeling to a dramatically conceived speaker. If you have learned from Booth, you will say that what is operative in line 7 is a *pattern* of sound and that it organizes the words very interestingly: the *s* sound links the words "myself," "salving," and "amiss" and thus sustains the double meaning Knights identified. In Boothian terms, the line is complex not as the conceived utterance of a dramatic speaker but because of the meanings of the words in themselves—not only the single words "corrupting" and "salving," which clash at the center of the line, but also the double grammar, which sets the action of corrupting in two different lights. Seen this way, the line is motivated less by a dramatic situation than by its being an instance of the general truth, "All men make faults," which has a related double meaning ("All men have faults," and "All men create faults"). Once we are freed from having to hear a dramatic voice, we can see that alliteration is equally "functional" in a line that Knights dismisses: "And loathsome canker lives in sweetest bud." Here the *l* and *s* sounds of "loathsome" reappear in "lives" and "sweetest" and thus support the sense of contradiction in discovering how loveliness can be tainted. I have called these readings Boothian. They are not, however, Booth's own readings of Sonnet 35, because it happens that he really dislikes this poem. And he dislikes it precisely because he feels the speaker's presence all too directly. He says the poem "evokes responses contrary to those its rhetorical gestures seem designed to elicit," and his summary comment concludes as follows: "All in all, the manner of this poem is that of a long-suffering and relentlessly selfless wife. The facts the poem reports should make the speaker seem admirable in a reader's eyes; the speaker's manner, however, gives conviction to the idea that he is worthy of the contempt he says he deserves."

The dramatic speaker of lyric may appear, at this point in time, to be simply a modernist dogma. So it is important to recognize how, in practice, the presence or absence of such speakers is discerned. The critics from whom we can still learn begin where any criticism should—from the words on the page and the power and complexity they are felt to have. Knights does not look for "the speaker" in Sonnet 35 and suddenly discover him in the second quatrain. He recognizes that the quatrain registers complexity of feeling, and he attributes this to a conceived dramatic speaker. Ransom's difficulties with the Sonnets come not from failing to recognize their rhetorical workings but from feeling unable to conceive them as motivated by a serious first person whose language has worked turbulent feelings through to a point of understanding. Booth observed what Ransom did and said, "This is precisely why the poems are so good." But in order to do this, he turned his back on the speaker, whether real or constructed. He turned his attention to the reader and asked how the reader's mind can coherently take in all that is going on in these poems. This meant treating them, with all their patterns of sound and meaning, as if they were simply there, like natural objects, rather than as if they were motivated utterances. In thus resolving the modernist strictures, Booth freed the Sonnets for the admiring attention of a generation of readers. But as Paul de Man's formulation has it, any powerful critical insight has an attendant blindness. Booth's blindness was to the character of the first-person speaker of the Sonnets. To his modernist masters and predecessors, he said, in effect, you are looking in the wrong direction and for the wrong thing. But as his own burst of irritation at Sonnet 35 shows, we cannot ignore or marginalize the "I" of these poems, whether we call him Shakespeare or "the speaker." I therefore want to turn to one more example of a modernist objection to a passage in the Sonnets and see how we can develop a different way of conceiving its relation to first-person self-representation and utterance.

Twenty-five years after "Shakespeare at Sonnets," Yvor Winters found himself agreeing that Ransom's stones were hurled at appropriate targets. After accusing Shakespeare, as Ransom did, of "seldom tak[ing] the sonnet form with any real seriousness," and after observing, with Knights, Shakespeare's weakness for clichés in these poems, Winters turns to his most serious charge—that Shakespeare uses words "for some vague connotative value, with little regard for exact denotation."[36] His main example is from Sonnet 116:

> O no, it is an ever-fixèd mark
> That looks on tempests and is never shaken;
> It is the star to every wand'ring bark,
> Whose worth's unknown, although his height be taken.

The difficulty here [Winters says] resides in the word *worth*. The fixed star, which guides the mariner, is compared to true love, which guides the lover. The mariner, by taking the height of the star, can estimate his position at sea, despite the fact that he knows nothing of the star's "worth." . . . The lover, by fixing his mind on the concept of true love, similarly can guide himself in his personal life. But what does *worth*, as distinct from height, mean in this second connection? For the lover can scarcely guide himself by a concept of true love, he can scarcely indeed have a concept of true love, unless he has some idea of the worth of true love. The comparison blurs at this point, and with it the meaning. . . . There is simply no such separation between the two functions of true love as there is between the two functions of the star, yet the comparison is made in such a way as to indicate a separation.[37]

Winters' critical demands often seem narrowly focused, but they are always forceful and intelligent, and I think we should be able to answer this critique. One possible answer is given by Arthur Mizener, in the most effective contemporary response to Ransom's essay; he says that "the characteristic feature of Shakespeare's kind of poetry at its best is a soft focus."[38] This sounds like what Booth was later to argue about the Sonnets, and one is not surprised to learn that Mizener's essay is one that Booth especially admires.

But Booth's commentary on "worth" is rather unsatisfactory. He says the word "is imprecisely used in this line; its general sense is dictated by context." Let us recall that in discussing the sea-mark image, Booth was precise and analytic about each of its elements: it is only their combination that makes the image "mysterious and wonderful." But he offers no such account of "worth"—only the suggestion that "Shakespeare may have chosen the word in order to play on 'worth' meaning 'high value.'" He then switches our attention back to the star's height—precisely the maneuver Winters criticized, on the grounds that the line insists on a distinction between "worth" and "height." Booth's implicit response to Winters is clear enough—that the line is good for the reasons Winters thinks it bad—but in this case, the claim is more a matter of critical faith than critical demonstration. This difficulty appears in Booth's account, because he shares with Winters a fundamental assumption about this poem—that it is a definition of love, as it certainly seems to be, and that its speaker, the one who defines love, therefore has a coherent identity.

Neither Winters nor Booth takes into account the strong element of rhetorical assertion in the sonnet, for which I think the most precise term is "asseveration"—an emphatic or solemn affirmation or declaration. Consider the difference between "O no, it is an ever-fixèd mark" and possible alternatives, like "Love rather is an ever-fixèd mark" or "But true love is an ever-fixèd mark." What I want to explore here is the way this asseverative rhetoric affects the speaker's presence in the poem and his relation to its images. To begin, let us ask what "O no, it is an ever-fixèd mark" means—for even without punctuation, it is grammatically complete and complete as a line of verse. Most editors, like Booth, define "mark" as a sea-mark,[39] but *OED* shows that the word has a wider range of meanings, several of which can come into play here. As a target or as a post marking the end of a race, "mark" suggests one's goal. As an object that guides a traveler—any traveler, on land or sea—it adds the idea of always knowing where one is. In all cases, "mark" seems to be something external to the speaker, something he knows with complete confidence as his aim, his goal, his guide. It is only in the next line that the mark becomes a sea-mark. But something more than making the image more specific happens in this line. Because of the rhetorical energy of both lines, their asseverative force, one feels not simply that the image of the sea-mark is personified, as Booth says, but that the speaker identifies himself with it: he identifies with what "looks on tempests and is never shaken." This speaker does not simply know what love is as an external ideal; the rhetoric and image of line 6 claim that he embodies it.

Now consider the speaker's self-identification in the next two lines. Where do we locate him in line 7, "It is the star to every wand'ring bark"? (We note that this line too is grammatically complete.) Because of his identification with the mark "that looks on tempests and is never shaken" and the general sense that he exemplifies what love is, one tends to identify the speaker with the star—all the more so because "*every* wand'ring bark" suggests the ordinary lovers from whom he seems to claim to stand apart. There is a strong suggestion of what Julius Caesar more directly boasts, in lines cited here by most editors: "I am constant as the northern star, / Of whose true-fix'd and resting quality / There is no fellow in the firmament" (3.1.60–2). But the next line shifts the speaker's identification. To say, "Whose worth's unknown, although his height be taken" associates him not with the star but with the wandering ships, who, in a familiar Petrarchan image, represent the ordinary human experience of love. These shifting identifications on the part of the speaker are what I think really trouble Winters and, by implication, Ransom. For it is not a matter of figuring out what the worth of an actual star might be. It is that everything up to this point suggests that the speaker *does* know the worth of the love the star represents.

How can the speaker of this poem allow his metaphor to undo him in this way? One possible answer is given in the opening lines of a sonnet by Shakespeare's contemporary, Michael Drayton:

> As other men, so I myself do muse
> Why in this sort I wrest invention so,
> And why these giddy metaphors I use,
> Leaving the path the greater part do go.
> I will resolve you. I am lunatic . . . [40]

Why should we not say the same of the speaker of Sonnet 116? The poem's extravagance is apparent throughout and nowhere more than in the final couplet: "If this be error and upon me proved, / I never writ and no man ever loved." Booth calls this ridiculous when taken literally, and it prompts another editor (John Kerrigan) to speak of the "vulnerability of this clamorously negative assertion." (Other editors, I fear, try to hush up the matter.) Hence Booth says that "one could demonstrate that [the poem] is just so much bombast." But he goes on to say that "having done so, one would have only to reread the poem to be again moved by it and convinced of its greatness." I think this dismisses the problem too readily. If one is moved or convinced by Sonnet 116, it must have something to do with its insistent rhetorical manner, and we must say how it speaks not bombastically, but with authority. In the lines we have been examining, modernist critics would like "whose worth's unknown" to register an ironic awareness on the part of a speaker who had just claimed to represent Love itself. But the oddness of this speaker is that he continues to assert his absolute knowledge of love: "Love's not time's fool," the poem continues, and the speaker's self-identification is clear in the last line of the third quatrain, "But bears it out even to the edge of doom." Looking back to lines 7 and 8, we can see that the speaker's self-identifications are suggested but not as definite as they might be in a poem by Donne. For as against what the image of line 8 seems to indicate—that the speaker is one of the wandering barks—the rhetorical manner of the line, its continuing the asseveration of line 7, suggests that the speaker still embodies the absolute love represented by the star. This is tantamount to saying "I know the worth of love," in the teeth of the possibility that its "worth's unknown." These lines are of a piece with the other asseverations in the poem. Like them, they combine a claim of absoluteness with a sense of human vulnerability. To look on tempests and never be shaken is to represent one's fixity as overcoming the possibility of being shaken. Indeed, the possibility of not standing firm underlies the most striking rhetorical fact about this sonnet—that its affirmations are cast as negatives. Its strange, defiant rhetoric reminds us that its author wrote not only *Julius Caesar* but also *Antony and Cleopatra*.

Shakespeare's Sonnets are so distinct individually that it is hard to generalize about them on the basis of one or two examples. But I think the problem presented by Sonnet 116 is representative. It gives a strong impression of what Joel Fineman, one of the most brilliant interpreters of the Sonnets, called "the subjectivity effect."[41] At the same time, the first person, the "I" of the poem, is mobile and elusive. One of the most interesting lines of inquiry into these poems is to locate the ways in which the speaker's pronoun, the "I," appears in them. It is often a case of "now you see him, now you don't," even when the subjectivity effect itself seems strong and constant. The way to address this difficulty, which baffled and frustrated Ransom and other modernist critics, is to keep in mind the fundamentally rhetorical character of these poems. Sonnet 116 is clearly a piece of rhetoric, and not only because of its moments of vocalizing and its mode of asseveration. The speaker's mobile identifications, the changing positions from which he speaks, recall one of the most persistent complaints, from ancient times to the present, about speechifying to an audience—that you cannot tell what the speaker really thinks, that he will say anything for an effect. In addition to this traditional complaint, the New Critics felt a social and cultural hostility to public speech: to them, language was sullied by being turned to practical uses or utilitarian purposes. Shakespeare's Sonnets are not public speech; the first notice of them, in Francis Meres' *Palladis Tamia* (1598), refers to "his sugared sonnets amongst his privy friends" (i.e., they circulated privately). But circulation among one's friends is still a social use of poetry, and we can see the rhetorical nature of the Sonnets in at least three respects. Many of them address another person in distinct social or interpersonal situations. "No more be grieved at that which thou hast done" (35); "No longer mourn for me when I am dead" (71); "Farewell, thou art too dear for my possessing" (87); "That you were once unkind befriends me now" (120). Second, even apart from such speaking in a situation, there are frequent apostrophes and other instances of strong vocalizing. "Devouring Time, blunt thou the lion's paws" (19); "O fearful meditation, where alack / Shall time's best jewel from time's chest lie hid" (65); "Alas 'tis true, I have gone here and there, / And made myself a motley to the view" (110). Both these traits connect the subjectivity effect to a speaker, but the third rhetorical aspect of the Sonnets does not. These poems are full of frank manipulation of words, of the sort that sixteenth-century rhetorical handbooks exhaustively described. These manipulations or, as they were called, ornaments of speech were thought to make discourse more impressive, attractive, persuasive. But they could also arouse suspicion, for you could not always be sure what motivated them. We still use "sweet talk" as a term for speech we distrust. One way to deal with the frank manipulations of language in the Sonnets is to attribute them to Elizabethan convention. But I think Ransom's way is truer—to acknowledge the attraction and even power of this sweet talk, but not know how to account for it or trust it. Ransom concluded *The New Criticism* with a chapter entitled, "Wanted: an Ontological Critic." Such a critic would give individual poems and poetry in general a concrete, objective existence in the order of things. This dream of securing a realm of poetry has been largely undone by the last forty years of literature and the other arts and by our understanding both of the uses of language in general and of the literary past. What is wanted, certainly for Shakespeare's Sonnets, is a rhetorical critic.

That critic is Kenneth Burke. To put it more precisely, an account of Shakespeare's Sonnets (and of Renaissance lyric in general) that seeks to be both formalist and rhetorical must work through Burke, who alone among modernist critics made it a principle that human uses of language, including literary uses, are inevitably rhetorical. Hence he proposes, in the opening section of *The Philosophy of Literary Form,* that "we think of poetry . . . as the adopting of various strategies for the encompassing of situations." "These strategies," he says, "size up the situations, name their structure and outstanding ingredients, and name them in a way that contains an attitude towards them."[42] Burke indicates two main categories of naming—the "magical decree," which deploys a vocabulary to represent a situation as such and such, as if to call it into being according to what one desires, and the realistic "chart," which seeks to gauge the situation as it actually is.[43] In speaking of poems this way, Burke represents them as responsive to position and circumstance. He does not think of them, in the words of a New Critical critique of him, as "entirely organized with reference to a dramatic structure or movement which is self-contained."[44]

To understand Burke's usefulness, let us return to Sonnet 35 and yet another expression of uneasiness with it, the commentary of Helen Vendler, perhaps our last important modernist critic.[45] Feeling the same difficulty as L. C. Knights had sixty years earlier, Vendler says, "The 'same person' cannot speak both the first quatrain and the second." She proceeds to redeem the lyric coherence of the two quatrains, but only by what seems to me a desperate maneuver. She first asks us to imagine that the commonplaces of the first quatrain are to be put in quotation marks as past utterances of the speaker. She then looks ahead to the line, "Such civil war is in my love and hate," and proposes that both quatrains "belong to *hate,* who scornfully summarizes his own former excusings of the friend, and savagely exposes his own fault in so doing." I find this prima facie implausible, but let me specify one cost of conceiving the speaker as dramatically coherent in this way. If the commonplaces of quatrain 1 are scornfully rejected and we do not feel the speaker's investment in them, then they lose all their force, in the present time of the poem, as instances of "authorizing thy trespass with compare."

How can Burke help us understand the way these two quatrains are motivated and connected? After proposing that imaginative works are *"strategic* answers, *stylized* answers" to the situations in which they arise, his first examples are not poems but proverbs, the least individuated kind of stylized speech. "Think of the endless variety of situations, distinct in their particularities, which [a single] proverb may 'size up,' or attitudinally name."[46] Just as he suggests several applications of the same proverb, so he encourages us to imagine the potential human presence and to hear the potential speaker in a commonplace phrase like "roses have thorns." Sonnet 35 would seem to bring alive this potential use: its first line, "No more be grieved at that which thou hast done," is a gesture within a present situation. For Vendler the first quatrain has no rhetorical presence whatsoever. "The flat, foolish, and debased" sentences, she says, "would not convince a flea." Her contempt for the very idea of such persuasion reflects her assumption that lyric poetry imitates "the performance of the mind in solitary speech."[47] But surely she has a point about what happens in this quatrain. I would say, prompted by Burke, that the opening address to the young man brings out one way in which these images might encompass the situation. "Clouds and eclipses stain both moon and sun," which recapitulates the imagery of the two preceding sonnets, could sustain a tone of generous forgiveness. But the images of the muddy fountain and the loathsome canker seem to lose touch with their conceived auditor; they seem to say not "I forgive *you*" but "I forgive *him*," and they name the situation in a way that conveys the speaker's resentment. The first quatrain thus enacts the ambivalence that is analyzed in the second.

Vendler's project, like that of her great modernist predecessors, is to ground the formalist analysis of lyric poems on accurate observation and sound principles. It would certainly be possible to discuss these principles, which are spelled out in the general account of lyric in her introduction and appealed to in her commentary. But the value of her commentary is in displaying the artistry of individual poems (sometimes with amazing precision), and I think we have most to learn from the way in which, in any specific case, she lays out and proceeds to make sense of "evidence that no interpretation can afford to ignore."[48] I therefore want to conclude by considering her account of Sonnet 116, where she bypasses much of what bothers Winters and arouses Booth's wonder and where she proposes terms that intriguingly approach Burke's—but that also seem to me to show that Burke's terms are more natural and productive.

Vendler takes her critical bearings from two evident features of 116— the persistently negative formulation of its assertions and the differences among its three quatrains. These observations are underpinned by and confirm her principle that Shakespeare's sonnets do not simply iterate a theme stated in the opening line but instead change dynamically, with the third quatrain often synthesizing or complicating what occurs poetically in the first two. But the key to Vendler's interpretation of 116 is something that is not at all an evident feature but rather her inference from what the poem presents. She claims that the poem has to be seen as "a coherent refutation of the extended implied argument of an opponent," and she further identifies this opponent as the young man, whom she imagines to have been justifying his inconstancy by a cynical characterization of love. She carries this imagined scenario very far. On the grounds that the first quatrain "replicate[s] the dishonest discourse of [the speaker's] interlocutor by mimicking it, even quoting it," she feels entitled to rewrite it as follows:

> Let *me* not to the marriage of true minds
> Admit "impediments": love is *not* love
> Which "alters when it alteration finds,"
> Or "bends with the remover to remove."

As the commentary proceeds, she treats the young man's inferred speech as if we actually had it before us, referring, for example, to the way "alter" and "bend" are "undefined in the young man's utilitarian rhetoric" and to the way "the impersonal phraseology of law," which returns in the third quatrain, is "at first the young man's euphemistic screen for his own infidelity."[49]

What is implausible about the hypothesis of a prior speech on the part of the young man is the specificity with which Vendler represents it and makes it motivate elements of the poem. It would not seem necessary to her point about the metaphoric star of the second quatrain; she says that as a transcendent model of love, it is superseded by the third quatrain, in which the constancy of love is affirmed, "triumphantly but tragically," within the limits of mortality. This in effect makes moot Winters' objection to the image, for Vendler could argue that its instability, as he describes it, is part of the intended effect; in any case, her interpretation shows the strength of attending, as she always does, to the dynamics of the quatrains.[50] But Vendler also feels it necessary to claim that the star symbol is motivated by the young man's prior speech: it has "been conjured up by the opponent's terms" (e.g., "ever-fixèd," which she views as proleptically applying to the star). We seem to have another instance of modernist insistence on a dramatic situation, but Vendler operates by no principles but her own, and she has no need here for New Critical modes of ironic awareness on the part of speaker or poet. What concerns her far more, I think, is that a sonnet so manifestly powerful be grasped as aesthetically complete. Her most important objection to Booth is his view that the critic, "helpless before the plurisignification of language and overlapping of multiple structures visible in a Shakespearean sonnet, must be satisfied with irresolution with respect to its fundamental gestalt."[51] In the case of 116, Vendler's insistence on coherence leads her to find a way of showing that the poem's asseverations are coherently motivated, to the point of downplaying their extravagance.

Despite its misplaced concreteness, Vendler's hypothesis of a prior speech makes us attend, as no other interpretation does, to the rhetorical energy of this sonnet. She rightly objects to treating it as a definition poem, a mistake due to "think[ing] of the *Sonnets* as discursive propositional statements rather than as situationally motivated speech-acts." Though we may not accept her account of the dramatic situation of the poem, we should still seek to define "what form of speech-act it performs."[52] It is here, I think, that it is useful to turn to Burke again—in this case to the alternative line of thought he opens up at the beginning of *The Philosophy of Literary Form:* "In addition to the leads or cues, for the analysis of poetic strategy, that we get from proverbs, with their strongly realistic element, we may get leads from magic and religion." What interests Burke is what he calls "the magical decree," which says, in effect, "*Let there be* such and such." In these terms, Sonnet 116 is negative magic—"Let it *not* be the case that such and such"—but we note that the speaker still, as Burke puts it, "share[s] in the magical resources of some power by speaking 'in the name of' that power."[53] The advantage of following Burke's lead here is that it allows us to feel the asseverative power of the poem. Where Vendler needs to attribute the phrases of lines 3 and 4 to the offstage young man, a Burkean reading retains the doublings and resonance of "alters where it alteration finds" and "bends with the remover to remove." After all, is it not plausible to think of these phrases as referring to the speaker himself, sensing his own possibilities of altering and bending with the remover and maintaining his devotion, as Empson says, "in spite of anything"?[54] I do not insist on this as the "correct" reading; but I want a way of recognizing what Vendler does that will allow this to be the possible force of these lines. (For one thing, this reading does not over-specify the poem's situation, which it leaves troublingly unclear, though not uselessly murky.) Similarly, Burke encourages us to see the shifting identifications in the lines about the star as capturing both the felt absoluteness of a human claim (in this case, a positive "decree") and a more realistic "sizing up" of the vulnerabilities of love—though at the same time, the situation represented in line 8, of wandering ships guided by the pole star, suggests why an ideal is felt to be imperative and therefore to motivate speaking on the scale of this poem. By comparison, Vendler's placing of the star leaves it rather too neatly behind (even though, as often, she mitigates her strong interpretive stipulations by subtle local shading: "the star lingers, semi-effaced, a rejected model"). Finally, a Burkean rhetoric recognizes on principle the force of "Love's not Time's fool"—that behind it is felt, "*I* am not Time's fool"—whereas Vendler's account, equally appealing to rhetoric, keeps this resonant phrase under control: it "keep[s] up the vehemence of refutation, remaining within the debater's genre."

Vendler begins her book with a disarming acknowledgment: "Perhaps total immersion in the *Sonnets*—that is to say, in Shakespeare's mind—is a mildly deranging experience to anyone, and I cannot hope, I suppose, to escape the obsessive features characterizing Shakespearean sonnet criticism." We cannot wish this obsessiveness otherwise, the issue of it being so proper, in critics like Booth, Fineman, and (if her self-impeachment is just) Vendler herself. But my own concern is less the Sonnets in and for themselves than Renaissance lyrics in general and the challenge of recovering a formalist criticism that is adequate both to them and to our present understanding of poetry and of literary history. If this is a worthwhile endeavor, Burke is our best guide in it. On the one hand, he does not box off literary works from other modes of discourse—everything from Spinoza to popular culture is grist for his mill—or from social and biographical circumstances and purposes: the "intentional fallacy" and the "affective fallacy" are not articles of his faith. At the same time, he shares the principles and protocols of modernist criticism in attending to the individuality of literary works and to the specifically literary usages that determine their individuality. (He resists "the heresy of paraphrase" as much as Brooks and Vendler, though he does not call it that.)[55] Burke wrote much less about lyrics than about novels and dramas, so a Burkean account of (Renaissance) lyric would have to be developed from his rhetorical principles and his dealings with these other instances of "literary form." This essay is, in effect, a prolegomenon to this larger project. But I hope readers will have been convinced by the way Burke, without rejecting the endeavors of modernist criticism or its ways of working, helps us out of its impasses and limitations in dealing with Shakespeare's Sonnets. For these poems are not only compelling and complex, sometimes to the point of insuperable difficulty; they must also be central to any account we offer of the lyric poetry of the English Renaissance.

Notes

1. Leah Marcus, "The Seventeenth Century," in *Redrawing the Boundaries: The Transformation of English and American Literary Studies,* ed. Stephen Greenblatt and Giles Gunn (New York: The Modern Language Association, 1992), 48.
2. Marcus, "The Seventeenth Century," 54.
3. Chaviva Hosek and Patricia Parker, eds., *Lyric Poetry: Beyond New Criticism* (Ithaca: Cornell University Press, 1985).
4. The essays, in the order in which they appear in the volume, are: Sheldon Zitner, "Surrey's 'Epitaph on Thomas Clere': Lyric and History"; Joel Fineman, "Shakespeare's Sonnets' Perjured Eye"; Stanley Fish, "Authors-

Readers: Jonson's Community of the Same"; Annabel Patterson, "Lyric and Society in Jonson's *Under-wood.*"
5. I use "New Criticism" to refer to critics with unambiguous allegiances to the school or movement defined by John Crowe Ransom, Cleanth Brooks, Allen Tate, and W. K. Wimsatt. I use "modernist criticism" as a term of broader scope, to include critics like Yvor Winters, Kenneth Burke, William Empson, and F. R. Leavis, who shared a sense of common endeavor with the New Critics but would not have so identified themselves.
6. John Crowe Ransom, "Shakespeare at Sonnets," in *The World's Body* (New York: Charles Scribner's Sons, 1938), 270. This essay was first published in *The Southern Review* 3 (1938): 531–53.
7. Though attention to the orthography and punctuation of the 1609 quarto of the Sonnets is often useful, a modernized text seems clearly appropriate for this essay. I have accordingly modernized all the passages quoted, which I base on Booth's edition cited in note 19.
8. Ransom, "Shakespeare at Sonnets," 280. (The phrase "failure of objectivity" is found on page 279.)
9. Ransom, "Shakespeare at Sonnets," 281, my italics.
10. Cleanth Brooks and Robert Penn Warren, *Understanding Poetry* (New York: Henry Holt, 1938), ix.
11. *Poetry* 53 (1939): 258–72, 320–35; 54 (1939): 35–51; reprinted in Paul Alpers, *Elizabethan Poetry: Modern Essays in Criticism* (New York: Oxford University Press, 1967), 93–125. The discussion of Shakespeare is in the last of these essays (pages 120–22 in Alpers).
12. John Crowe Ransom, *The New Criticism* (Norfolk: New Directions, 1941), 211.
13. Winters' long response to Ransom first appeared in *The Anatomy of Nonsense* (1943) and was collected in *In Defense of Reason* (1947; reprint Athens: Swallow Press/Ohio University Press, 1987), esp. 533ff. Winters quotes the phrase "a tissue of irrelevance" from Ransom, *The World's Body,* but the idea runs throughout Ransom's criticism.
14. This is the title of the last chapter of Cleanth Brooks, *The Well Wrought Urn* (New York: Reynal and Hitchcock, 1947).
15. John Crowe Ransom, *Selected Essays,* ed. Thomas Daniel Young and John Hindle (Baton Rouge: Louisiana State University Press, 1984), 197. Ransom's essay, "Poetry: I, The Formal Analysis," first appeared in *Kenyon Review* 9 (1947): 436–56.
16. The most important exception to this generalization is Empson. But although his discussion of the "bare ruined choirs" of 73 was one of the most notorious and controversial analyses in *Seven Types of Ambiguity* (perhaps because it is the first), there is less about the Sonnets in that book and in his other writings than one expects and hopes for. The great exception, the chapter "They That Have Power to Hurt" in *Some Versions of Pastoral,* is notable for its impurity, by New Critical standards—its willingness to go outside individual poems not only to Shakespeare's plays but also to fully imagined contexts, social and biographical.

17. Kenneth Burke, "Key Words for Critics," *Kenyon Review* 4 (1942): 126.
18. Burke, "Key Words," 130–1.
19. Stephen Booth, *An Essay on Shakespeare's Sonnets* (New Haven: Yale University Press, 1969), and Stephen Booth, ed., *Shakespeare's Sonnets* (New Haven: Yale University Press, 1977). Booth responds to the "red flag" of "Shakespeare at Sonnets" by saying, "I propose to implement Ransom's complaint, to expand it, and to redefine the failure as a strength" (*Essay,* 24–25).
20. Citations and quotations from Booth's edition are from his commentary on the sonnet under discussion, unless a page number is specified.
21. Booth, *Shakespeare's Sonnets,* x.
22. Yvor Winters, "Poetic Styles, Old and New," in *Four Poets on Poetry,* ed. Don Cameron Allen (Baltimore: The Johns Hopkins Press, 1959), 51.
23. Ransom, "Shakespeare at Sonnets," 286.
24. Ransom, "Shakespeare at Sonnets," 287.
25. Ransom, "Shakespeare at Sonnets," 289.
26. Allen Tate, "Tension in Poetry" (1938), in *The Man of Letters in the Modern World: Selected Essays, 1928–1955* (New York: Meridian Books, 1955), 68.
27. Ransom, "Shakespeare at Sonnets," 290.
28. Ransom, "Shakespeare at Sonnets," 291.
29. Jonathan Culler, "The Modern Lyric: Generic Continuity and Critical Practice," in *The Comparative Perspective on Literature,* ed. Clayton Koelb and Susan Noakes (Ithaca: Cornell University Press, 1988), 292.
30. Culler, "The Modern Lyric," 295.
31. Culler, "The Modern Lyric," 294.
32. Line 8, in the 1609 quarto, is: "Excusing their sins more then their sins are." "Thy . . . thy" is the most usual emendation, but the line appears in other forms in some of the recent editions (below, note 39).
33. L. C. Knights, "Shakespeare's Sonnets," in *Explorations* (1946, reprint New York: New York University Press, 1964), 62. This essay first appeared in *Scrutiny* 3 (1934): 133–60. Knights is speaking of lines in Richard II's soliloquy at Pomfret (*RII* 5.5.45–60), but he means this formulation to apply generally to early Shakespeare.
34. Knights, "Shakespeare's Sonnets," 65. Knights' analysis is quoted in extenso in Brooks and Warren's *Understanding Poetry* as an exemplary account of Sonnet 35.
35. Knights, "Shakespeare's Sonnets," 67.
36. Winters, "Poetic Styles, Old and New," 48, 50.
37. Winters, "Poetic Styles, Old and New," 50–1.
38. Arthur Mizener, "The Structure of Figurative Language in Shakespeare's Sonnets," *The Southern Review* 5 (1940): 730–47; revised in *A Casebook on Shakespeare's Sonnets,* ed. Gerald Willen and Victor B. Reed (New York: Thomas Y. Crowell, 1964), 222.
39. In reporting what editors say, I have in mind the following editions of the Sonnets: ed. Willen and Reed (above, note 38); ed. Booth (note 19); ed. W. G. Ingram and Theodore Redpath (London: University of London Press, 1964); ed. John Kerrigan (Harmondsworth: Penguin Books, 1986); ed. G.

Blakemore Evans (Cambridge: Cambridge University Press, 1996); ed. Katherine Duncan-Jones, "The Arden Shakespeare," 3rd series (Walton-on-Thames: Thomas Nelson, 1997); ed. Helen Vendler (below, note 45).
40. Michael Drayton, *Idea* 9, in Alastair Fowler, ed., *The New Oxford Book of Seventeenth Century Verse* (Oxford: Oxford University Press, 1991), 38.
41. See, for example, "Shakespeare's 'Perjured Eye'" in Joel Fineman, *The Subjectivity Effect in Western Literary Tradition* (Cambridge: MIT Press, 1991), 91–119, esp. 111.
42. Kenneth Burke, *The Philosophy of Literary Form*, 3rd ed. (Berkeley: University of California Press, 1973), 1. Original edition published 1941.
43. Burke, *Philosophy of Literary Form*, 4–7.
44. H. M. McLuhan, "Poetic vs. Rhetorical Exegesis," *The Sewanee Review* 52 (1944): 268.
45. Helen Vendler, *The Art of Shakespeare's Sonnets* (Cambridge: Harvard University Press, 1997). As with Booth's commentary, I do not give page references for Vendler's discussions of individual sonnets.
46. Burke, *Philosophy of Literary Form*, 1–2.
47. Vendler, *Art*, 2.
48. Vendler, *Art*, 24.
49. In her introduction, Vendler appeals to Sonnet 76, as well as 116, as a sonnet in which "the speaker indirectly quotes his antagonist" (21). But the effect of quoting an antagonist or critic seems to me distinctly clearer and more plausible, though not certain, at the beginning of 76: "Why is my verse so barren of new pride? / So far from variation or quick change?" By the same token, 117, which she cites as a "rebuttal-sonnet" (21), begins with two quatrains that clearly refer to, even quote, something the addressee has said: "Accuse me thus: that I have scanted all / Wherein I should your great deserts repay, / Forgot upon your dearest love to call," etc.
50. A good example is her account of Sonnet 33, in which she points out that the central metaphoric contrast, sun shining vs. sun clouded over, occurs in units of decreasing size—two quatrains, one quatrain, couplet. She argues that this structure explains why the apparent resolution of the couplet, especially the quasiproverbial last line, is felt to be unsatisfactory.
51. Vendler, *Art*, 13.
52. These are general principles—see Vendler, *Art*, 13–14, 22–3—but these quotations are from her commentary on Sonnet 116.
53. Burke, *Philosophy of Literary Form*, 3, 4.
54. William Empson, *Some Versions of Pastoral* (Norfolk: New Directions, 1960), 96.
55. Cf. his remarks, in the opening sections of *A Rhetoric of Motives*, about not reducing the complex of motivations in a poem (in this case, *Samson Agonistes*) to one "gist."

Undelivered Meanings

The Aesthetics of Shakespearean Wordplay

Mark Womack

Shakespeare's exuberant punning has always posed something of a problem for literary critics. Critical suspicion of wordplay derives, I believe, from concerns about the dignity of literature and about the dignity of studying it for a living. In this essay I would like to demonstrate that thoughtful study of trivial punning is not only possible but essential to a full appreciation of literary art. Far from distancing myself from the potential frivolity of wordplay, I intend to embrace and celebrate it even to the point of pursuing something as odd and insubstantial as the undelivered pun.

Samuel Johnson famously lists punning as one of Shakespeare's prime weaknesses:

> A quibble is to Shakespeare, what luminous vapours are to the traveller; he follows it at all adventures, it is sure to lead him out of his way, and sure to engulf him in the mire. It has some malignant power over his mind, and its fascinations are irresistible. Whatever be the dignity or profundity of his disquisition, whether he be enlarging knowledge or exalting affection, whether he be amusing attention with incidents, or enchaining it in suspense, let but a quibble spring up before him, and he leaves his work unfinished. A quibble is the golden apple for which he will always turn aside from his career, or stoop from his elevation. A quibble, poor and barren as it is, gave him such delight, that he was content to purchase it, by the sacrifice of reason, propriety and truth. A quibble was to him the fatal Cleopatra for which he lost the world, and was content to lose it.[1]

Note that Johnson sees puns as a temptation that leads Shakespeare off track, away from the important toward the trivial. Shakespeare pursues "delight" at the expense of "reason, propriety and truth," a serious error in

Johnson's eyes. Thus for Johnson, Shakespeare's punning exemplifies his primary defect as a writer: "He sacrifices virtue to convenience, and is so much more careful to please than to instruct, that he seems to write without any moral purpose."[2] Punning becomes a moral failing; Shakespeare wantonly neglects his moral duty to have his way with words.

While not everyone shares Johnson's moral distaste for quibbles, most people do regard puns as trivial; consider all the essays introducing students to Shakespeare's language that try so earnestly to convince readers that puns really can be serious. Puns seem to awake such a terror of the trivial in scholars that many choose either to ignore or casually disparage them, and even those contemporary critics who focus on wordplay usually go to extraordinary lengths to make it seem serious, dignified, and important. Patricia Parker, a vigorous defender of the importance of puns, assures us that "Shakespearean wordplay—the very feature relegated by the subsequent influence of neoclassicism to the rude and deformed as well as ornamental or trivial—provides a way into networks whose linkages expose the very orthodoxies and ideologies the plays themselves often appear simply to rehearse."[3] For Parker, puns provide a way of analyzing serious cultural and political issues and of showing how Shakespeare's plays interact with and comment on contemporary ideology. But this strategy often tends to marginalize the very puns it claims to champion.

Consider the following passage from *The Merchant of Venice:*

> LORENZO. I shall answer that better to the commonwealth than you can the getting up of the Negro's belly; the Moor is with child by you, Launcelot.
> LAUNCELOT. It is much that the Moor should be more than reason; but if she be less than an honest woman, she is indeed more than I took her for. (3.5.37–42)[4]

In her analysis of these lines Parker first chastises previous critics for their careless dismissal of the punning language here and then shows how the pun touches on serious issues:

> The association of "Moor" and "more," for instance, in the lines on the pregnant female Moor from *The Merchant of Venice* (III.v.37–42), is reduced to a mere linguistic "jingle" in the Variorum Shakespeare notes and by the Arden editor to speculation that the entire passage is introduced "simply for the sake of an elaborate pun on Moor/more." But as Kim F. Hall has observed, this reduction to mere quibble or jingle . . . makes an already invisible black female figure disappear even more effectively from these lines—a technique that parallels the effacing of any sense of coloring from Morocco's "complexion" elsewhere in the play. The common early modern linking of *Moor* and *more,* however, is an important part of the assumption of disruptive excess behind

Elizabeth's proclamation in 1601 banishing "Negars and Blackamoors" from England on the grounds of their "great numbers" (a perception that Hall cogently argues had very little to do with their actual numbers) or the sense of sexual excess in the description of Othello as a "lascivious Moor." It involves associations still being chronicled by contemporary writers on race such as Patricia Hill Collins or Angela Davis, words powerful in their effect (or the work they do in the world) despite their contradiction by documentable facts or statistics. The more/Moor link, then—even apart from the possibility of a topical reference in these lines on a pregnant female Moor—is part of a set of associations that, far from being reducible to a trivializing sense of the merely verbal, have influenced laws and social practices.[5]

This does indeed make the *Moor/more* pun seem very important, but only because Parker uses it as a launching pad to get to the important topic of racism. Although she decries the trivialization of wordplay in critical discourse, Parker's attitude toward punning here seems strangely similar to Johnson's. Both want to get Shakespeare away from the trivial and back to important matters. Johnson sees puns as trivial and criticizes Shakespeare for his love of them; Parker sees puns as good excuses to talk about more dignified topics, like race and gender, and criticizes those who don't do the same. In both cases, a sense of serious moral purpose triumphs over the dangerous temptations of aesthetic frivolity.

Much of our current disdain for wordplay may spring from the suspicion of formalism and close literary analysis that currently so dominates critical discourse. Before we can deal honestly with puns and wordplay, we need to rethink the purpose of close reading. I suggest that we can use the techniques of close reading in a new way, not to interpret texts but to analyze the pleasures they provide to audiences.

The most basic component of any close reading is the assumption that careful analysis can reveal multiple nuances of meaning not readily apparent to the casual reader. A critic will typically use the newly excavated meanings to provide supporting evidence for an interpretation, usually an interpretation guided by a pre-existing theoretical agenda. The plenitude of meanings that close reading reveals, however, often exceeds the needs of the particular critic. The gap between the multitude of verbal nuances and the monolithic nature of a final interpretation is a serious problem both for New Criticism and for all the subsequent critical schools that borrow its analytical techniques. As Charles Altieri points out, "The New Critics greatly expanded our sense of the semantic complexity of a text, but they did not develop adequate ways of showing how this information might be coherently processed."[6] Subsequent literary analysts have fared no better in this regard. I submit that the "semantic complexity" of cherished literary texts is *not* "coherently processed" by readers and audiences and that to try to provide some coherent schema for that heterogeneous complexity constitutes a denial of the very feature that makes literature appealing.

Close reading reveals an excess of possible meanings that interpretation-centered criticism has not found compelling ways to explain. Rather than trying to "interpret" verbal excess, we should try to see how it functions in our experience of the phrases, sentences, and speeches in which it occurs.

Attempts to systematize the multiple and conflicting connotations of literary language arise from the mistaken assumption that because literature is made of words, its only consequential action must be to transmit meanings. On the contrary, literary artifacts, especially those that constitute the Shakespearean canon, play with the formal properties of language in the same way musical compositions play with rhythm, melody, and harmony or the way works of visual art play with various combinations of forms, lines, and colors. Richness of connotation is one such formal property of literary language, and the patterns of potential meanings are as crucial to the experience of a work of literature as the modulations in key and rhythm in a musical composition or the patterns of shape, color, and light in a painting. In each case, the patterns are not conduits for messages but material properties of the work that engage the audience in a richly complex experience.

In short, Shakespeare does with meanings and connotations of words what a painter like Vermeer does with line, color, and shape: he organizes them into intricate and pleasing patterns. Vermeer's *Woman Pouring Milk* (also known as *The Kitchenmaid;* see figure 1) is richly patterned in visual relationships of simultaneously similar and different objects. Edward Snow elaborates on the web of contrasts that structure the painting:

> *Woman Pouring Milk* ... is a melody of contrasting textures. The pair of hanging baskets provides the key: rough and smooth, hard and soft, woven and molded, curved and angular, open and shut. They even initiate opposing vectors: one tilting downward toward the footwarmer on the floor, the other jutting outward toward the pitcher pouring milk. Similar oppositions create the weave, the weft and warp, of the painting. Consider especially the shifting interplay of organic and manufactured forms (the bread and milk against containers and the table; the wicker basket against the metal one; or both baskets against the footwarmer), or the counterpoint between various states of suspension (the hanging baskets and the cradled pitcher suggest contrasting modes) and groundedness (the things on the table evoke one mood, the footwarmer another), or the downward progression through things at hand (the baskets on the wall), in hand (the pitcher pouring milk), and abandoned, out of reach or ken (the footwarmer on the floor).[7]

The network of contrasts that Snow describes coexists with a network of further similarities among dissimilar items. Consider the two baskets

Figure 1 *Woman Pouring Milk* by Johannes Vermeer. Courtesy of The Rijksmuseum, Amsterdam.

hanging on the wall on the left side of the painting. They are linked not only by kind but by their position in the composition; they are distinguished because one is made of wicker, the other of copper. The two wicker baskets in the painting are linked by their common material but otherwise distinguished. One is rectangular, closed, and hanging on the wall. The other is round, open, and sitting on the table. The round wicker basket holds two loaves of bread: one round, the other rectangular. These simultaneously similar and different loaves both resemble and differ from the broken pieces of bread lying on the table between the bread basket and the milk bowl. The round basket echoes the round bowl into which the woman pours milk, but one is wicker and extravagantly porous, the other solid earthen ware. Note too that the semicircular handles on the bread basket point up, while the semicircular handles on the milk bowl point to the sides. The milk bowl is made of the same material as the milk pitcher and the cup inside the footwarmer sitting in the lower right hand corner of the painting. Although all three objects are linked by their kind, they are all markedly different in size, shape, and position in the composition. The milk pitcher is similar in shape to the pitcher that sits on the table, but one is earthen ware, simple, open, and aligned on a horizontal axis while the other is metallic, more ornate, closed, and aligned on a vertical axis. The table and the footwarmer are similar in shape but very different in scale and function.

Virtually every element of the painting has a complex compositional echo; consider, for instance, the dark round space of the open milk pitcher and the dark square space of the footwarmer, or the large white window and the small black mirror on the left wall, or how the tilt of the woman's head echoes the tilt of the hanging wicker basket, and so on. Suffice it to say that various networks of similarities and differences among compositional elements thread across the whole painting. Such networks—whether in a painting, a quartet, or a film—make the work that contains them exciting, eventful, brimming with patterns and relationships.

Close reading can reveal a similar wealth of linguistic activity in literary texts. Most critics impoverish that wealth by making it conform to the dictates of a theoretical agenda. But close readers do not have to make that assumption. Indeed, the very best close readers, I would argue, are those who can present the complexity of a text while resisting the impulse to interpretive closure. Consider William Empson's famous analysis of line 4 of Shakespeare's Sonnet 73 ("Bare ruin'd choirs, where late the sweet birds sang"):

> the comparison holds for many reasons; because ruined monastery choirs are places in which to sing, because they involve sitting in a row, because they are made of wood, are carved into knots and so forth, because they used to be surrounded by a sheltering building crystallized out of the likeness of a forest, and coloured with stained glass and painting like flowers and leaves, because they are now abandoned by all but the grey walls coloured like the skies of winter, because the cold and Narcissistic charm suggested by choir-boys suits well with Shakespeare's feeling for the object of the Sonnets, and for various sociological and historical reasons (the protestant destruction of monasteries; fear of puritanism), which it would be hard now to trace out in their proportions; these reasons, and many more relating the simile [sic] to its place in the Sonnet, must all combine to give the line its beauty, and there is a sort of ambiguity in not knowing which of them to hold most clearly in mind. Clearly

this is involved in all such richness and heightening of effect, and the machinations of ambiguity are among the very roots of poetry.[8]

Empson does not attempt to exclude any of the various meanings at play in these lines, nor does he try to reconcile them into a single, paradoxical statement. Empson finds lots of interconnected potential meanings and assumes that they all play some part in giving the line its impact.

The multitudinous relationships among the meanings in the line from Sonnet 73 resemble the multitudinous patterns of visual relationships in Vermeer's painting. A technique of close reading that pays full attention to richness of patterning can allow us to understand more fully the beauty of literary language rather than using such language as a pretext for talking about some other historically, politically, or philosophically solemn topic.

And now let us resume our pursuit of the luminous vapors of the pun, starting with the *Moor/more* pun that Parker analyzed from *The Merchant of Venice*. Moors appear in three of Shakespeare's plays, and in two of them Shakespeare overtly exercises the potential for a *Moor/more* pun. Here is an exchange from *Titus Andronicus*:

> NURSE. O, tell me, did you see Aaron the Moor?
> AARON. Well, more or less, or ne'er a whit at all,
>   Here Aaron is, and what with Aaron now?
>
>   (4.2.52–54)

In *Titus Andronicus*, as in *The Merchant of Venice*, Shakespeare exploits the *Moor/more* pun for comic effect. The puns in these plays are overtly clever.

In contrast to the simultaneously bland and ostentatious exploitation of the potential inherent in the words "Moor" and "more," consider how Shakespeare deals with the same potential in *Othello*. In *Othello*, Shakespeare creates an environment that brings together the elements necessary for a pun but keeps them from consummating their relationship. Instead of squandering the inherent energy of the pun, Shakespeare maintains all its unrealized potential. Consider the Duke's advice to Brabantio: "If virtue no delighted beauty lack, / Your son-in-law is far more fair than black" (1.3.289–90). Here the word "more" appears in a context that draws attention to Othello's race, yet Shakespeare does not permit that context to turn "more" into a pun on "Moor." The unactualized potential for a pun is inherent in these lines; Shakespeare has brought the ideas and sounds necessary for a *Moor/more* pun into near collision. Shakespeare plays with this linguistic potential throughout the play by putting the word "Moor" into close proximity with the word "much": "So much I challenge that I may profess / Due to the Moor my lord," "And by how much she strives to do him good, / She shall undo her credit with the Moor," "the Moor / May unfold me to him; there stand I in much peril" (1.3.188–89; 2.3.358–59; 5.1.20–21). The unrealized potential of linguistic events like the near-miss pun on *Moor/more* in *Othello* is, I believe, a primary component of Shakespeare's appeal to the minds and ears of audiences.[9]

Analyzing puns that never actually occur may indeed seem like chasing a will-o'-the-wisp. Even a radical post-structuralist like Joel Fineman sensibly insists that a "motivated homophone," or pun, "must be noticed as such for it to work its poetic effect."[10] The very existence of "undelivered" meanings might seem too bizarre to be believable. Yet such undelivered meanings have been studied by perceptual psychologists. Some experiments indicate that people do momentarily entertain meanings for words that cannot fit logically into the clear meaning of a sentence. David Swinney, for example, presented subjects with these sentences: "Rumor has it that, for years, the government building had been plagued with problems. The man was not surprised when he found several spiders, roaches, and other bugs in the corner of his room." Swinney discovered that for a few seconds, the length of two or three syllables, a person will register not only the delivered meaning of "bug" (insect) but also the logically impossible alternative: a concealed microphone.[11] Similarly, researchers have discovered that words like "tire," that can function as either verbs or nouns, momentarily evoke both noun and verb meanings even in contexts where one meaning would be nonsensical.[12] Such research suggests that the fleeting, unharnessed meanings that I point to are not just the products of a wantonly creative mind but have a basis in empirical fact.

Moreover, a number of critics have commented on the odd occurrence of unnoticed but poetically effective puns. Christopher Ricks coined the appropriately bizarre term "anti-pun" to describe the phenomenon: "The practice is a variety of pun, but it is an anti-pun; whereas in a pun there are two senses which either get along or quarrel, in an anti-pun there is only one sense admitted but there is another sense denied admission. So the response is not 'this means x' (with the possibility even of its meaning y being no part of your response), but 'this-means-x-and-doesn't-mean-y', all hyphenated."[13] Ricks' comments imply that readers are consciously aware of the excluded meaning.

William Empson discusses what he calls "subdued puns"[14] in Shakespeare, but finds the subject "puzzling and hard to approach directly."[15] He suggests that the presence of such puns may spring from Shakespeare's unique poetic gifts: "When I said that subdued puns were not the most important object of analysis, I meant that very few poets are so sensitive to the sounds of language, that very few poets can afford so to exploit their sensitivity to the sounds of language, and that perhaps no other poet had been able to concentrate, on the creative act of a moment, such a range of intellectual power."[16] Empson's commentary on various subdued puns makes it clear that some of them are not consciously noticed by readers.

Many critics mention this curious phenomenon in passing, particularly in discussions of Shakespeare's language. N. F. Blake notes the presence of "submerged linking": Shakespeare's "ability to unite a passage by using words which overlap in their semantic fields, even though the primary meaning intended in the passage is not that which creates an echo with other words."[17] Randolph Quirk analyzes the "lexical congruence working through, without, or in defiance of syntactic structure" in *1 Henry VI* 2.5.10–15.[18] In the Arden edition of *Macbeth*, Kenneth Muir notes in passing the presence, at 3.2.46–49, of a "concealed pun on *seeling/sealing.*"[19]

Most references to this poetic effect are incidental and brief. The one critic who has given sustained and elaborate attention to the bizarre topic of puns that aren't quite really there is Stephen Booth. His monumental analytic commentary on Shakespeare's Sonnets contains numerous references to the "unharnessed meanings" of words and to what he calls "ideational puns": "an interplay between an idea and a word that could—but does not— express or relate to that idea."[20] From his early work on the Sonnets to his most recent analysis of *Twelfth Night*, Booth has shown a consistent interest in the effect of the ideational pun.[21]

Booth is also unique among commentators on unharnessed puns in that he speculates on the aesthetic value and effect of the phenomenon. He argues that such patterns of wordplay provide a linguistic coherence that does not consist of delivered meaning. He sees ideational puns as an extension of such formal devices as rhyme, rhythm, and alliteration. All such devices give a work of literature rich, yet nonsubstantive, coherence, coherence that lies in patterns and forms that "can make an artificial construct feel almost as inevitable—as obviously a thing and not a conglomerate—as an object in nature."[22]

Undelivered puns may also enhance the experience of an audience in a way that normal puns never do. According to Booth, unharnessed puns are superior to delivered puns in much the same way that the experience of a pun maker is superior to the experience of a pun hearer:

> What the pun's audience hears is a mere gimcrack, a toy, something entirely irrelevant to the nature of things so suddenly linked. What the punster feels in the air before he/she brings it forth and exposes it for the mouse a pun inevitably turns out to be is thrilling, is a sense of a previously unsuspected new order to things. A comparable feel of limitless mental possibility, I suggest, derives to us from the presence of substantively irrelevant organizations in the literary constructs we value best and longest.[23]

Thus undelivered puns create a richer experience for audiences. Consider the common laudatory phrase "pregnant with meaning." That metaphor implies that the meanings it describes remain undelivered, potential, nascent. A delivered pun advertises its own cleverness, it requires us to acknowledge it. The raw materials for a pun that never reaches our conscious attention will have a radically different effect. The unharnessed pun creates an exciting and volatile mental environment, one that provides a vital component of the pleasure we take from Shakespearean language.

The philosopher J. F. Ross provides a vocabulary that may help clarify the nature of unharnessed meanings. As Ross points out, "Everyone who speaks one of the relevant natural languages . . . characteristically and automatically uses the same words in different meanings, sometimes related (*see*/light, *see*/point: *collect*/books, *collect*/friends, *collect*/debts, *collect*/barnacles), and sometimes unrelated (*charge*/enemy, *charge*/battery, *charge*/account)."[24] Ross calls this procedure "differentiation," the process by which words acquire different meanings in different contexts. He calls the linguistic and contextual forces that cause differentiation "dominance." Thus in the examples quoted above, the italicized words differentiate because their companion words dominate them.

Shakespeare skillfully manipulates linguistic dominance relationships to force words to differentiate, to assume contextually appropriate meanings. Note how Shakespeare exploits contextual signals to make "rivals" say the opposite of what it means: "If you do meet Horatio and Marcellus, / The rivals of my watch, bid them make haste" (*Hamlet* 1.1.12–13). The word "rivals" differentiates into the unconventional meaning "partners" because of the dominating context. Such manipulation of linguistic contexts reveals how Shakespeare employed the principles that Ross later explained.

Employing Ross's terminology for literary analysis, Ann and John O. Thompson suggest that while linguistic dominance can ultimately rule out a word's potential denotations, the process of differentiation may nevertheless leave traces of such discarded meanings. They assert that "readings which dominance renders 'impossible' can retain a ghostly life within a poem or speech. They are rejected hypotheses, but they are *conceptually pertinent* rejected hypotheses, and that pertinence is what makes entertaining them a proper part of the experience of reading or listening."[25] Meanings that do not fit into the clearly delivered surface meaning of a text (and that therefore do not become a part of our conscious understanding) but that do bear some conceptual pertinence to the linguistic context are unharnessed meanings.

When dominance forces a word to differentiate into two conceptually pertinent meanings, we call such an occurrence a pun. Like most other literary phenomena, puns enable readers to perceive simultaneous likeness and difference, but the similarity established by a pun is always and obviously an accidental one established by coincidental phonetic resemblance. Consider, for instance, the following pun from the opening of *Julius Caesar*. When asked what his trade is, the Cobbler tells Murellus that he is "a mender of bad soles" (*Julius Caesar* 1.1.13). The pun establishes a relationship between *sole* (the bottom of a shoe) and *soul* (the immaterial part of a human being), yet the pun also, simultaneously, advertises how tenuous and coincidental that relationship is.

Perhaps more than any other trope, puns call attention to themselves. But when they get the attention they crave, they also reveal their own insignificance. So, when the mortally wounded Mercutio tells Romeo, "Ask for me to-morrow, and you shall find me a grave man" (*Romeo and Juliet* 3.1.98–99), his wordplay calls attention to the wit that produced it rather than to some profound connection between tombs and dignity. Yet compare Hamlet's words as he drags Polonius's dead body from his mother's room:

> This counselor
> Is now most still, most secret, and most grave,
> Who was in life a foolish prating knave.
> (*Hamlet* 3.4.213–15)

Hamlet's lines create the occasion for a pun on *grave*, one that goes unnoticed even by professional noticers like the modern editors of the play. Although the context for a pun on grave is at least as rich here as in *Romeo and Juliet*, that context is not harnessed to bring the potential for punning to our conscious attention. Although unobserved, I believe that such unharnessed meanings are aesthetically potent. It is a commonplace that unobtrusive rhetorical effects are more pleasing than crude, heavy-handed ones. The concept of the unharnessed pun merely presents an extension of that principle.

Unharnessed meanings can have an effect even when the delivered meanings of a passage remain obscure or incomprehensible. Consider the following lines from *The Winter's Tale*:

> Most dear'st! my collop! Can thy dam?—may't be?—
> Affection! thy intention stabs the centre.
> (1.2.137–38)

Mark Van Doren called the speech these lines initiate "the obscurest passage in Shakespeare . . . Leontes means in general that the impossible has become all too possible, but the particulars of his meaning are his own."[26] An audience might say to Leontes what Desdemona says to Othello: "I understand a fury in your words, / But not the words" (4.2.32–33). These opaque lines do not deliver precise meanings to an audience, but they do contain a number of unharnessed meanings.

In the phrase "Can thy dam?—may't be?" for instance, unharnessed puns help relate the sounds of the words to the general topic of discussion. The potential *dam/damn* pun reflects and is echoed in the themes of punishment, torture, and damnation that weave through Leontes' lines in the scene. The subliminal play on *may't/mate* similarly connects to the immediate context, since Leontes is asking about his son's mother ("thy dam") who is also his own wife or mate. And consider the phrase "thy intention stabs the center." Here the potential for a play on "in" and "to tent," a surgical term meaning "to probe," sharpens the stabbing of the center that the line presents to us. Again, although such linguistic play probably never intrudes into the conscious awareness of an audience, it nevertheless adds an extra dimension of connection among the various linguistic elements.

In several plays, Shakespeare collects the raw materials for a pun on "peer" (person of noble birth/to look at intently) without ever bothering to process them. Consider the following examples: "O King Stephano! O peer! O worthy Stephano! look what a wardrobe here is for thee!" (*The Tempest* 4.1.222–23); "See you, my princes and my noble peers" (*Henry V* 2.2.84); "KING HENRY. We do salute you, Duke of Burgundy, / And, princes French, and peers, health to you all! / FRENCH KING. Right joyous are we to behold your face" (*Henry V* 5.2.7–9).

Shakespeare makes similar use of the term "peerless"; although the word means "without equal," Shakespeare seems to sense its potential as a pun meaning something like "without vision" or "unseen." Consider the following lines from *The Winter's Tale*:

> LEONTES.   but we saw not
>   That which my daughter came to look upon,
>   The statue of her mother.
> PAULINA.   As she liv'd peerless,
>   So her dead likeness, I do well believe,
>   Excels what ever yet you look'd upon.
>
>   (5.3.12–16)

Here the verbs *saw*, *look*, and *looked* and the general topic of something not yet seen all help to form a context for a pun on *peerless*, but that potential pun never reaches actuality; it remains unharnessed.

Often, potential or undelivered puns will create fleeting links between certain lines. For example, look at these lines in which Macbeth speaks to the ghost of Banquo and Lady Macbeth addresses the assembled guests:

> MACBETH. Avaunt, and quit my sight! let the earth hide thee!
> Thy bones are marrowless, thy blood is cold;
> Thou hast no speculation in those eyes
> Which thou dost glare with!
> LADY MACBETH.   Think of this, good peers,
> But as a thing of custom. 'Tis no other
>
> (3.4.92–96)

The noun "peers" by which Lady Macbeth addresses the lords provides an incidental link with Macbeth's terms "glare," "eyes," and "sight." A similar undelivered pun occurs earlier in the play. Just after Macbeth calls on the stars to hide their fires and the eye to wink at the hand, Duncan refers to him as a "peerless kinsman," providing a subliminal link to the blindness required for regicide in Macbeth's aside (1.4.58).

Another unharnessed pun that occasionally energizes passages in Shakespeare occurs with the word "weed." Here is the beginning of Gertrude's account of Ophelia's suicide:

> There is a willow grows askaunt the brook,
> That shows his hoary leaves in the glassy stream,
> Therewith fantastic garlands did she make
> Of crow-flowers, nettles, daisies, and long purples
> That liberal shepherds give a grosser name,
> But our cull-cold maids do dead men's fingers call them.
> There on the pendant boughs her crownet weeds
> Clamb'ring to hang, an envious sliver broke,
> When down her weedy trophies and herself
> Fell in the weeping brook. Her clothes spread wide,
> And mermaid-like awhile they bore her up
>
> (*Hamlet* 4.7.166–76)

The passage begins with a list of various plants Ophelia used to make garlands and ends with the image of her clothes floating in the water. The phrase "crownet weeds" forges a link between these otherwise unrelated topics. Here "weeds" refers to the catalogue of plants, but since "weeds" could mean "clothing" (and, in fact, here *does* name something to wear) it subliminally prepares the way for the reference to Ophelia's clothes, which like her "weedy trophies" float on the surface of the water. While this connection surely never intrudes into the thoughts of an audience to the speech, it does provide an extra level of formal connection among the speech's elements. Here the undelivered pun on *weeds* functions like a subtle repetition of color in a painting: it provides an extra degree of coherence to the work.

Note the similar wordplay in the following passage:

> Besides, they are our outward consciences
> And preachers to us all, admonishing
> That we should dress us fairly for our end.
> Thus may we gather honey from the weed,
> And make a moral of the devil himself.
>
> (*Henry V* 4.1.8–12)

Here the contextually unrelated words "dress" and "weed" relate to one another in the subterranean realm of undelivered meanings, once again supplying an extra-logical coherence to the passage in which they appear. Moreover, clothing becomes a focus of the scene when King Henry borrows Erpingham's cloak.

Shakespeare's language contains many, many similar examples of unharnessed puns, but rather than enlarge on a potentially endless list I would like to turn to two broad theoretical topics. First, I will consider how readers and playgoers might experience undelivered meanings differently. Second, I will address the concern that the potential punning I analyze was never an intentional part of the works in which it appears.

Throughout this discussion, I have made no distinction between two different kinds of audiences: readers and playgoers. A colleague has suggested that my analyses imply that every playgoer can instantly "close hear" a line in all the detail that I bring to close readings conducted at leisure. An examination of the debate between text-based and performance-based critics may help explain why I choose to ignore the distinctions between readers and playgoers.

A number of contemporary critics have taken sides in a debate about the relative authority of text-based and performance-based interpretations of Shakespearean drama. Some critics assume that anything revealed by close analysis of the text is a valid part of a play's meaning, but performance critics argue that meaning is properly limited to what a play can communicate in the theater. Harry Berger, in a formulation as witty as it is tendentious, presents the difference between these two groups as "a contrast between the Slit-eyed Analyst and the Wide-eyed Playgoer."[27]

J. H. P. Pafford, clearly a Wide-eyed Playgoer, provides a succinct statement of the performance critic's credo: "The play must be judged as by a spectator who is allowing himself to be caught up by it in performance and to be carried away into its illusion"; thus many things that might appear to a close reader of the text "do not worry an audience; they cannot indeed be noticed in the quick movement of the play."[28] Thus for Pafford, and for other performance-based interpreters, the performance sets the limits of interpretation.

According to Berger, a champion of the Slit-eyed Analyst, close reading can and should make manifest information unavailable to playgoers: "Decelerated microanalysis . . . enlarges and emblematically fixes features not discernible in the normal rhythm of communication," and when the text is "reaccelerated" the critic can "sense how much is withheld from an audience that can only hear and see, how much is occulted in the text they cannot read" (148–49). Thus for Berger, and for many other text-based interpreters, the text opens up realms of meaning inaccessible to playgoers.

Note that both sides of this debate are promoting methods of interpretation. They are trying to establish the procedure for understanding what Shakespeare's plays mean. I am more interested in what the language of Shakespeare's plays does to—or better for—an audience, whether that audience gets its Shakespeare from an Arden edition, the Shenandoah Shakespeare Express, or a hypertext web page.

According to Berger, "when Shakespeare is staged and you hear his language at performance tempo you are always haunted by the sense that you are receiving more information than you can process, and you wish you could slow the tempo down or have passages repeated or reach for a text."[29] I too believe that Shakespearean language presents us with more than we can consciously process. Unlike Berger, however, I celebrate that excess. The sense of excess does not "haunt" me, it delights me. Close reading of a text can help us analyze just exactly what has gone whizzing across our minds, but seeing all the excess more clearly after the fact does not imply that we should, or even can, make it a part of our conscious experience of the play. Knowing precisely how a particular process works does not change that process. Reading a detailed scientific analysis of how our bodies digest food will not alter our own digestive processes. Moreover, most readers are not close readers. Most readers outside the academy read plays in the same way playgoers hear them: one word at a time, at the speed of thought.

Playgoers are, perhaps, a bit more likely than readers to hear and brush from their understandings the sorts of shadow assertions that I talk about. An auditor inescapably hears each succeeding syllable as the defining one in an emerging constellation of ideas. But both the reader and the playgoer will miss, at least on the conscious level, most of the linguistic effects I point to. You need not be a close reader or a close hearer to experience a Shakespeare play fully.

A usual objection to the idea that undelivered meanings form a part of an audience's experience is that no one can prove that they were part of the author's design for the work in question. This is, of course, yet another version of the intentional fallacy. The idea that only intended effects are real will not stand up to serious scrutiny. If all unintentional phenomena were unreal, there would be no spelling errors. Probably some of the undelivered meanings I point to were never part of Shakespeare's conscious design, but the connections and patterns are no less real, no less a part of our experience, for being accidental. To demonstrate this point I would like to look at two examples of unharnessed puns that could not have been intended by Shakespeare.

Consider first Caliban's awed aside when he first sees Stephano and Trinculo: "These be fine things, and if they be not sprites. / That's a brave god, and bears celestial liquor" (2.2.116–17). Here the play on "liquor" and "sprites" or "spirits" gives precisely the kind of extra coherence and energy to the language that I have analyzed throughout this essay. One key difference is that that potential pun was unavailable to the minds and ears of early seventeenth-century audiences to *The Tempest*. The word "spirits" did not come to mean an alcoholic beverage until the mid-1680s.[30] But though I can say with great certainty that Shakespeare never intended any such wordplay, I need not conclude that the undelivered pun does not play a part in a contemporary audience's experience of the lines. The connection between *spirits* and *liquor* gives contemporary audiences a connection between two dominant topics in the scene. References to spirits on the island and to liquor run throughout this scene with Caliban, Stephano, and Trinculo, and their intersection here—though clearly a historical linguistic accident—reinforces a pattern already undeniably present in the play.

Near the end of *1 Henry IV* another historically impossible connection of potential meanings occurs. Standing over Hotspur's dead body, Prince Hal declares "This earth that bears thee dead / Bears not alive so stout a gentleman" (5.4.92–93). Hal then turns his attention to the apparently dead Falstaff and declares, "What, old acquaintance! could not all this flesh / Keep in a little life?" (5.4.102–03). The description of Hotspur as "stout" makes a pleasing parallel with the recognition of Falstaff's corpulence. However, the word "stout" did not acquire the meaning "fat" until the early 1800s. For a contemporary audience, nevertheless, the unharnessed verbal link between Hotspur and Falstaff is quite plausible because the early modern meanings of "stout" (strong, proud, bold) are virtually obsolete in modern English.

Here again, although the connection clearly results from a linguistic accident, it fits well into the patterning of the context in which it occurs. Even without the play on "stout," the lines on Hotspur and Falstaff deal with the contrasts of full and empty, living and dead, large and small. Hal's parallel elegies to Hotspur and Falstaff implicitly contrast Hotspur's metaphorical, martial greatness with Falstaff's literal, fleshy greatness.

Note the striking number of verbal parallels between Hal's two speeches:

HOTSPUR.   O, I could prophesy,
But that the earthy and cold hand of death

>   Lies on my tongue. No, Percy, thou art dust,
>   And food for—   *Dies.*
> PRINCE. For worms, brave Percy. Fare thee well, great heart!
>   Ill-weav'd ambition, how much art thou shrunk!
>   When that this body did contain a spirit,
>   A kingdom for it was too small a bound,
>   But now two paces of the vilest earth
>   Is room enough. This earth that bears thee dead
>   Bears not alive so stout a gentleman.
>   If thou wert sensible of courtesy,
>   I should not make so dear a show of zeal;
>   But let my favors hide thy mangled face,
>   And even in thy behalf I'll thank myself
>   For doing these fair rites of tenderness. (5.4.83–98)
>   . . . .
>   *He spieth Falstaff on the ground.*
>   What, old acquaintance! could not all this flesh
>   Keep in a little life? Poor Jack, farewell!
>   I could have better spar'd a better man.
>   O, I should have a heavy miss of thee
>   If I were much in love with vanity!
>   Death hath not strook so fat a deer to-day,
>   Though many dearer, in this bloody fray.
>   Embowell'd will I see thee by and by,
>   Till then in blood by noble Percy lie. (5.4.102–10)

Concepts relating to food and eating weave through both passages: Hotspur is food for worms and Falstaff is a hunted deer. And the number of incidental verbal parallels is striking: "Fare thee well" / "farewell"; "Lies on my tongue" / "by noble Percy lie"; "make so dear a show of zeal" / "strook so fat a deer to-day"; "the earthy and cold hand of death" / "Death hath not strook"; and so on. All these incidental contrasting parallels subtly reinforce the play-wide series of contrasts between Hotspur and Falstaff.

Even though Shakespeare could not have made a pun, harnessed or unharnessed, on "stout," that wordplay fits beautifully into the scene's intricate patterning. In this case, audiences today get an extra element in the lushly patterned design through a historical linguistic accident. The rich conceptual harmonies that relate these passages are the essence of the poetic richness that draws us so irresistibly to Shakespeare.

Any sustained analytical attention to wordplay is likely to make some critics fidgety. Talking about the aesthetic effect of potential wordplay probably seems even more frivolous, and asserting that undelivered meanings that could not have been a part of the original audience's experience do have an effect on modern audiences sounds, I know, ludicrous. But if we want to focus on texts as rich and extraordinary as Shakespeare's, we need to abandon the assumption that our investigations must lead to momentous insights. Shakespeare's language often works in bizarre and quirky ways, and more often than not the quirks aren't serious or important; they may be simply delightful, or curious, or lovely.

An inevitable sense of whimsy attends any analysis of something so obviously frivolous as an undelivered pun. It lacks the gravity and consequence we have grown to expect from the interpretation industry. But if we refuse to acknowledge the full reality of the texts we study, however wacky or trifling they may seem, we risk losing touch with the very power that draws us to literature in the first place. As Debra Fried reminds us, "It is dangerous to assume that the local tics of puns in lyric poems must serve a coherent reading of the poem, and that puns that do not mean anything in this sense are simply not there. Like the Augustan poetic of sound as echo to sense, this tendency toward making puns serve meaning robs them of some of their wildness and shimmering contingency."[31] Trying to tie every element of a literary text to a coherent, delivered message ignores the full extravagant beauty of poetic language.[32]

Notes

1. Samuel Johnson, "Preface to Shakespeare," in *The Yale Edition of the Works of Samuel Johnson, Volume VII: Johnson on Shakespeare,* ed. Arthur Sherbo (New Haven: Yale University Press, 1968), 74.
2. Johnson, "Preface to Shakespeare," 71.
3. Patricia Parker, *Shakespeare from the Margins: Language, Culture, Context* (Chicago: University of Chicago Press, 1996), 114.
4. All quotations from Shakespeare come from *The Riverside Shakespeare, Second Edition,* ed. G. Blakemore Evans, et al. (Boston: Houghton Mifflin, 1997); I silently omit the brackets with which Riverside signals deviations from its chosen copy text.
5. Parker, *Shakespeare from the Margins,* 4–5.
6. Charles Altieri, *Act and Quality: A Theory of Literary Meaning and Humanistic Understanding* (Amherst: University of Massachusetts Press, 1981), 216.
7. Edward Snow, *A Study of Vermeer: Revised and Enlarged Edition* (Berkeley: University of California Press, 1994), 10.
8. William Empson, *Seven Types of Ambiguity* (New York: New Directions, 1947), 2–3.
9. Compare "whit" in the passage from *Titus Andronicus* quoted above for its overt pun on "more" and "Moor"; "whit" opens the door to contextually pertinent play on "white" and "black," but Shakespeare's lines hold back from entering into such play.
10. Joel Fineman, *Shakespeare's Perjured Eye: The Invention of Poetic Subjectivity in the Sonnets* (Berkeley: University of California Press, 1986), 70.

11. David Swinney, "Lexical Access During Sentence Comprehension: (Re)consideration of Contextual Effects," *Journal of Verbal Learning and Verbal Behavior* 5 (1979): 219–27.
12. See Mark Seidenberg, Michael Tanenhaus, et al., "Automatic Access of the Meanings of Words in Context: Some Limitations of Knowledge-based Processing," *Cognitive Psychology* 14 (1982): 489–537.
13. Christopher Ricks, *The Force of Poetry* (Oxford: Clarendon Press, 1984), 265–66.
14. References to subdued puns occur throughout Empson, *Seven Types of Ambiguity*, but the most concentrated discussion occurs during Empson's analysis of the implications of scholarly annotation: 80–88.
15. Empson, *Seven Types of Ambiguity*, 87.
16. Empson, *Seven Types of Ambiguity*, 88.
17. N. F. Blake, *Shakespeare's Language: An Introduction* (New York: St. Martin's Press, 1983), 54–55. Blake cites W. Whiter's 1794 *A Specimen of a Commentary on Shakespeare* and analyzes *Coriolanus* 2.3.220–26, noted by Whiter for its network of clothing-related words.
18. Randolph Quirk, *The Linguist and the English Language* (New York: St. Martin's Press, 1974), 61–62.
19. *Macbeth,* ed. Kenneth Muir (London: Methuen, 1984), 85.
20. Stephen Booth, ed., *Shakespeare's Sonnets* (New Haven: Yale University Press, 1977), 465.
21. Booth's investigations of this phenomenon include: *Shakespeare's Sonnets* (esp. 203, 231, 364–72); "Exit Pursued by a Gentleman Born," in *Shakespeare's Art from a Comparative Perspective,* ed. W. M. Aycock (Lubbock: Texas Tech Press, 1981), 51–66; "Close Reading Without Readings," in *Shakespeare Reread: The Texts in New Contexts,* ed. Russ McDonald (Ithaca: Cornell University Press, 1994), 42–55; "Shakespeare's Language and the Language of Shakespeare's Time," *Shakespeare Survey* 50 (1997): 1–17; and *Precious Nonsense* (Berkeley: University of California Press, 1998), 194–202.
22. Booth, *Precious Nonsense,* 6.
23. Booth, "Shakespeare's Language and the Language of Shakespeare's Time," 12.
24. J. F. Ross, *Portraying Analogy* (London: Cambridge University Press, 1981), 4.
25. Ann and John O. Thompson, *Shakespeare: Meaning and Metaphor* (Brighton: Harvester Press, 1987), 159.
26. Mark Van Doren, *Shakespeare* (New York: Holt, 1939), 316.
27. Harry Berger, Jr., *Imaginary Audition: Shakespeare on Stage and Page* (Berkeley: University of California Press, 1989), xiv.
28. J. H. P. Pafford, introduction to the Arden edition of *The Winter's Tale* (London: Methuen, 1963), li-liii.
29. Harry Berger, Jr., "Bodies and Texts," *Representations* 7 (1984): 146.
30. The OED lists under definition 21b for "spirits" ("Liquid such as is obtained by distillation, *spec.* that which is of an alcoholic nature") a quote from Jonson's 1610 play *The Alchemist:* [Have I] "Wrought thee to spirit, to quintessence, with paines / Would twise haue won me the pilosophers work?"

(1.1.70–71). The quote is unconvincing as evidence because "spirit" is in apposition to "quintessence" and because the context implies alchemical rather than alcoholic distillation. The next quote for this meaning comes from 1688.
31. Debra Fried, "Rhyme Puns," in *On Puns: The Foundation of Letters,* ed. Jonathan Culler (Oxford: Blackwell, 1988), 99.
32. For their comments and suggestions on various drafts of this essay, I would like to thank Stephen Booth, Thomas Cable, Bridgit Drinka, Leah Marcus, Mark Rasmussen, and John Rumrich.

The Poetics of Speech Tags

William Flesch

Around songs, everything becomes a play.—Shakespeare

—*Kenneth Koch*[1]

Midway between punctuation and semantics, sometimes prominently stressed but often a kind of residual rhythm barely more temporal than the unarticulated speech prefix they approximate, frequently offered in the frame of the parenthetical lunulae, speech tags merge quoted speech or writing to the quoting context in a linguistic inlay. They can help provide valuable insight into the nature and effect of poetic form since in their use you can see the work a poem has to do in order to make a set of words conform to a prosodical template. A speech tag supplements the words it quotes, filling out rhythms and rhymes where necessary. As in marquetry, the shape of the speech tag fits the shape of the cited words, or at least of their rhythm, since it must provide the supplement and balance needed to assimilate them *to* a rhythm. (This metrical framing for notionally or actually pre-existent words makes for a kind of converse to troping, where words are chosen to match a pre-existent music; although in practice there may be little or no difference between them since the poet will invent words that will fit the poem.)

An obvious example of such conformation, not Renaissance, is Mariana's song in Tennyson:

> She only said, "My life is dreary,
>   He cometh not," she said;
> She said, "I am aweary, aweary,
>   I would that I were dead!" (9–12)[2]

Quoting just Mariana yields the far more prosaic: "My life is dreary, he cometh not; I am aweary, aweary, I would that I were dead."³ Pope's quotation of Sir Plume in *The Rape of the Lock* is similar: "'My Lord, why, what the Devil? Z——ds! damn the Lock! 'fore Gad, you must be civil! Plague on't! 'tis past a Jest—nay prithee, Pox! Give her the hair'" (4.127–30).⁴ It's the poetic context that fills it out and makes it conform. James Merrill is the most ingenious modern exemplar of this practice, which indeed might be described as the central formalized emblem of the themes of *The Changing Light at Sandover*, as it seeks to match and meld the language of people irrevocably separated from one another.

The simplest version of the way speech tags (or other articulated indices of quotation) merge quotation with quoter is the generally iambic "he said" or equally iambic "said she." Thus Spenser's *Amoretti* 75 has:

> Vayne man, sayd she, that doest in vaine assay
>   a mortall thing so to immortalize. . . .
> Not so, (quod I) let baser things devize
>   to dy in dust, but you shall liue by fame . . . (5–6, 9–10)⁵

But even this simple form of narrating talk is interesting. The two speeches are rendered parallel by the speech tags in their second feet. His reply balances her accusation. The placement of the tags conveys meaning, since they serve as placeholders for significant pauses that stress the first words of the speech, even as they stitch the eight syllable speech to the ongoing iambic line.⁶ That effect may seem purely instinctive on Spenser's part, purely a matter of ear, but it also has a larger role to play in the poem, since these opening lines from the second and third quatrains retrospectively organize the first:

> One day I wrote her name upon the strand
>   but came the waves and washed it a way:
> agayne I wrote it with a second hand,
>   but came the tyde, and made my paynes his pray. (1–4)

One day I wrote; agayne I wrote; Vayne man, sayd she; Not so (quod I): this is the trajectory of the poem in minature. The fragile temporality of the extrapoetic—her name, her words—is brought into conformity with the eternizing poem. The form mirrors the content: just as the poem says it will eternize her and does so by telling the story of the challenge that elicited it, it inlays the irregular and aleatory gestures and speeches it narrates into its strict iambic form.

Such speech tags provide very quick and compressed ways to perform this kind of inlay. They do more work when they assimilate speeches to rhyme⁷ as well as to meter,[8] as in the passage from "Mariana." There her word "dead" rhymes with the poem's report "she said." The unrhymed speech is made to rhyme with the speech tag.

Now, Renaissance poets can't much exploit this particular device because tagging a speech with a phrase like "she said" in terminal position is highly anomalous diction. "She said" may introduce a speech, but "said she" is invariable if the quoted speech has come to an end. (Note, though, Tennyson's resourcefulness in a similar grammatical pickle in "The Lady of Shalott," where he rhymes on *"said / . . . ,"* *"wrote / . . . ,"* and *"cried /* The Lady of Shalott.")[9] One reason for this requisite and invariant inversion of subject and predicate is the fact that typographic markers of quotation are very rare until the late seventeenth century, when the so-called quotation mark came into more general use: we move from the inverted syntax of "said she" to the inverted comma. In Renaissance poetry some other device must signal the end of reported speech, and the word *said* does this frequently. Obviously you won't get such inversion when the speech tag introduces the speech, since then again the word "said" will serve as the marker of quotation. The point is, *said* is always contiguous to the speech it reports. Thus I want to try to show that it's just this lack of a typographical convention for framing speech that gives the speech tag more semantic work to do and therefore makes it particularly interesting in Renaissance poetry.

Herbert's "Denial" does exploit the device of rhyming speech tag with speech convincingly, but note that it's in the present tense and that he's reporting his thoughts' continuous lament, not a specific utterance of a complaint:

> As good go anywhere, they say,
>   As to benumb
> Both knees and heart in crying night and day
>   *Come come, my God, oh come,*
>   But no hearing. (11–15)[10]

The thoughts say "As good go anywhere as to benumb both knees and heart in crying night and day, *Come come my God, oh come,* but no hearing." What they say doesn't rhyme (the rhyme between "come" and "benumb" requires the *thoughts* to quote the prayer), but they are assimilated to the slowly regularizing verse through the report of what "they say." Herbert similarly uses "reply" in "Love" (III):

> Love took my hand, and smiling did reply,
>   Who made the eyes but I? (11–12)

Note again that the speech tag precedes the speech. Juliet's witty response to the Nurse in *Romeo and Juliet* shows how the reporting verb must remain contiguous to the speech it reports:

> NURSE. Yea, quoth my husband, fall'st upon thy face?
>   Thou wilt fall backward when thou com'st to age,
>   Wilt thou not Jule? It stinted and said Ay.
> JULIET. And stint thou too, I pray thee, Nurse, say I. (1.3.55–58)

It said "Ay," the speech following the verb, and the other accounts put the verb before the subject: "quoth my husband," "say I." In general, Renaissance uses of the rhymed speech tag are rare because the "she said" form will tend to precede speech and so either close a previous rhyme (since *said* too obviously announces what will follow if it's an opening rhyme and is too redundant a parallel to grammatical form) or appear in midline ("Love said, You shall be he"); I can't think of any Renaissance examples of *said* rhyming with a word within the speech that it records. Since a rhyming "he said" always rhymes with a prior word in the poem's own voice, it tends to feel like a particularly weak introduction to the speech, a weak disposition of the expectation set up by the proposing rhyme word. This is just because "he said" is so unassuming, and therefore can stake no claim to surprise. It must always be anticlimactic as a rhyme word when introducing a speech. But for just this reason, its post-Renaissance use *after* the speech it records will be all the more supple. There it will mark a return to the quoting voice, and that return has the effect, just because the transition is so unassuming, of indicating that the poem's prosody has been steadily continuing all along. Thus Thom Gunn can write these great quatrains—

> Your pain still hangs in air,
> Sharp motes of it suspended;
> The voice of your despair—
> That also is not ended:
>
> When near your death a friend
> Asked you what he could do,
> "Remember me," you said.
> We will remember you. ("Memory Unsettled")[11]—

without our noticing that *a friend* and *you said* are only assonantial. Doubtless we've been primed for this by the doubling of these two assonances in the *ended* rhymes, but the effect really depends on our easy tacit acceptance of the anticipated speech tag. We anticipate the speech tag more than we anticipate even the rhyme, and so we accept the fulfillment of the one anticipation as the fulfillment of both.

I consider these examples so minutely because they may be regarded as exemplary instances of the more general phenomenology of the speech tag: its subliminal assimilative power.[12] The speech is the place in the poem where non- or extra-poetic matter is swept into the quoting poem's prosody, and it's as though in the speech tag we can see the ontogenic recapitulation of poetic phylogeny: we see the moment of application of poetic form on extra-poetic matter. Ordinarily, you might say, that form and matter are reciprocal entities: no form without matter and no poetic matter without form. But the speech tag lets you tease them apart and see the moment that form informs matter.

Moreover, this informing moment actually corresponds interestingly to the phenomenology of iambic pentameter in general, the rule of free onsets and strict endings.[13] Iambic lines also sweep into stricter form as they unfold, so that each line re-establishes the form. The simplest speech tags will be iambic: terminal *she said* and terminal *said she* will both be metrical. But the speech tag at the end of the line can also be thought of as a sort of semantic feminine ending—standing outside the reported words it helps render metrical because it provides a strict ending to an onset however free, it feels like an unassuming extra-prosodical moment innocuously polishing off the prosody it thereby retroactively regulates. Thus the speech tag may be taken as a representation of the way iambic pentameter lines work, while being sufficiently specific (unlike the free onset/strict ending rule) not to be simply categorized as part of the system of rules it brings its speech into conformity with.

As I say, the effect of the speech tag can be subtle, altering the free onset of prose to make it into verse; this can be true even when the tag precedes the quotation just by the way it frames it *as* a quotation, as may be illustrated by another exchange between the Nurse and Juliet:

> JULIET. Sweet, sweet, sweet Nurse, tell me, what says my love?
> NURSE. Your love says, like an honest gentleman, and a courteous, and a
>   kind, and a handsome, and I warrant, a virtuous—where is your mother?
> JULIET. Where is my mother? Why, she is within.
>   Where should she be? How oddly thou repliest!
>   Your love says like an honest gentleman
>   Where is your mother? (2.4.53–60)

Just by quoting it Juliet turns the Nurse's prose to verse. She doesn't need a speech tag to do so: all she needs is the retrospectively acting elision of most of what the Nurse says. The Nurse's *honest gentleman* is drawn into the ambit of the parenthetical list of virtues it introduces and so reads as part of the list's prosaic rhetorical scheme rather than as the culmination of a pentameter line. In the list, *honest* is stressed, since the list is a list of related adjectives. In the pentameter line, as Juliet quotes it, the stresses on *gentleman* are much more prominent. But the metrical transmutation is more particularly due to the way the rhythm of the first four syllables is altered in Juliet's quotation through the shift in connotation that enables her quibble. The Nurse stresses *says* in the prose, because *says* is the word modified by the complex list of Romeo's strengths in the Nurse's long adverbial phrase. Romeo *talks* like an honest gentleman, and a courteous, and a kind, etc. But in Juliet's quotation, the word isn't stressed. It is a speech tag, and so reads as an unstressed syllable: Your love says, "Where is your mother?" It's unstressed because speech tags almost always are unstressed when they are not the final foot of the line (and sometimes even then they'll fill the weakest of the strong positions; the speech tag would be the most likely candidate for the unstressed or superadded material in the four stress theory of English pentameter).[14] In Juliet's line it loses the stress the Nurse has given it and so fits neatly into her meter. This is a good example as well of the requirement of the strict-ending rule: the Nurse's prose is too metrically free for us to hear any of the iambic meter of her opening words.

I choose this passage because it both illustrates the way quotation can turn prose into verse and emblematizes the subliminal and unassuming role of the speech tag in doing so. The Nurse's speech tag is prose; Juliet's quotation of it makes it turn everything else she quotes into verse. That hushing of the speech tag has been our topic, and I would like to consider it in a few other cases, beginning with that species of quotation that Elizabeth Sagaser has called "quoting the beloved."[15]

In "They fle from me," Wyatt describes with elegiac awe the happiest moment of his erotic life:

> Thancked be fortune, it hath ben othrewise
> Twenty tymes better; but ons in speciall
> In thyn arraye after a pleasaunt gyse
> When her lose gowne from her shoulders did fall,
> And she me caught in her armes long and small;
> Therewithall swetely did me kysse,
> And softely said dere hert, how like you this? (8–14)[16]

The quotation of what she said becomes the center of the poem. She said it softly, and the softness of the speech tag governs the softness of the quotation. Metrically central, experientially privileged, but phenomenologically accurate in the hush the line reproduces, her question retains in the poem that soft centrality that it has had in his life. Again the effect can be traced in large part to the speech tag. Although in a strong position, it is less stressed than the spondee that follows it, her "dere hert," to which it nevertheless lends its introducing softness.

Like *Amoretti* 75 this poem is also organized around a subliminal parallelism of quotation. The bitter question it ends with ("But syns that I so kyndely ame serued, / I would fain knowe what she hath deserued" [20–21]) picks up and contrasts with her question at the end of stanza two (14); and that parallel in turn allows for seeing their busy seeking at the end of stanza one as also parallel to the continuous restless questioning that the poem describes. But her question to him—the question he quotes—resists assimilation into the indirectly reported questionings of stanzas one and three, and this gives it its sense of timelessness: "It was no dreme: I lay brode waking" (15).

That timelessness, as the philosophers of quotation from Goodman to Quine and Davidson have noted, is a feature of the display of words that defines quotation. Quotation takes utterance outside of time and makes it canonical (as I've argued elsewhere);[17] making utterance into poetry is a pretty good model of this canon-making. Quotation takes utterance out of time by displaying a token of that utterance—the quotation itself—and thereby making the quoted words into a type. This is an antithetical operation: the type depends on the token; it's the act of quotation that estranges the quoted words from any ordinary context. To quote is not to point accurately at an original event, or at least not *only* to point accurately at an original event: it is (to use Spenser's word) to eternize it. (Derrida's argument about the constitutive iterability of words makes a related but not identical point.) The quoted speech is said first in full voice, but all subsequent quotation displays the speech out of context, and that is just why Wyatt quotes it. And indeed the timelessness is captured also by the present perfect aspect of his report: "it hath ben othrewise."

A different version of such timeless quotation of the beloved in Wyatt is provided by "Who so list to hounte":

> And graven with Diamondes in letters plain
> There is written her faier neck rounde abowte:
> Noli me tangere for Cesars I ame,
> And wylde for to hold though I seme tame. (11–14)

The collar quotes the timeless typological admonition, as though Henry VIII is Caesar's correlative type or antitype, and Anne Boleyn the antitype of Caesar's hinds. At all events, the poem itself quotes a timeless and perdurable admonition. It quotes what all hunters will find, and not the unique event of an utterance directed at Wyatt. The quotation of the quotation around the hind's neck has the interesting effect of a unique refrain (whose meaning is: *refrain*). The poem ends with the inevitable refrain, and all who list her hunt will come upon the same inescapable ending.

The effect of timelessness is a general feature of the use of refrain, as is a sort of quotational aura, since refrains derive their effect from a repetition that preserves their identity through a varying context. Refrains therefore have an effect similar to quotation: the progressing poem unfolds into the refrain that has been *dictated,* so to speak, by its earlier utterance (at a minimum, earlier in the poem in its first appearance). Thus refrain and quotation have a natural affinity for each other. Wyatt's refrain "*Circa Regna tonat*" in "Who lyst his welth and eas Retayne" quotes Seneca's *Phaedra* but refers to Henry VIII and not to Jove and applies to the first-person story Wyatt retells in the poem; nevertheless the moral is timeless. Sidney makes Stella speak the refrain in the fourth song of *Astrophil and Stella:* "No no no no, my Deare let bee." Unlike Wyatt's quotation of the beloved in "They fle from me," this refrain isn't particularly magical. But its iteration makes possible the story implicit in the song, in which the refrain is turned from refusal to at least a partial vouchsafement of Astrophil's right to continue to love her:

> Sweete, alas why strive you thus?
> Concord better fitteth us;
> Leave to *Mars* the force of hands,
> Your power in your beautie stands.
> Take me to thee, and thee to mee.
> No no no no, my Deare let bee.
>
> Wo to me, and do you sweare
> Me to hate? but I forbeare,
> Curst be my destnies all,
> That brought me so high to fall:
> Soone with my death I will please thee.
> No no no no, my Deare, let be. (43–44)[18]

True, in Sidney you get a sort of dialogue, where Astrophil is speaking as well as Stella, but his speeches aren't quotations and repetitions. Like Juliet's Nurse he speaks in full voice, and his speeches provide the context for Stella's iterated refrain.

Quotational refrain can thus make for an interplay between the specifics of the context and the generality (Stella's) or universality (Seneca's) of the type whose token connects it to the context. Kant's name for such a manifestation of type within empirical specificity is *hypotyposis,* but in the ontology of quotation priority is reversed, since the individual instance of quotation creates the timeless type of which such a quotation then becomes just one instantiation. This dense formulation is simply illustrated by all those echo poems, so well analyzed by John Hollander,[19] in which the repetition of the local utterance declares itself a timelessly authoritative answer to the time-bound uncertain and anxious questioner. Echo poems often thematize this very fact: so at one point in Sidney's "Faire rocks . . ." Echo insists on the fact that when it speaks it echoes its own timeless authority:

> Yet say againe thy advise for th'ev'lls that I tolde thee.
> I tolde thee. (17)

And in the penultimate poem of *The Church*, where Herbert's Echo speaks for the Heaven that gives the poem its title and prefigures the voice of Love itself in the final poem, the poem alludes to its own repetitions as instantiations of timeless authoritative utterance:

> Are holy leaves the Echo then of blisse?
> *Echo.*   Yes. (11–12)

"Holy" "leaves" are indeed echoes since they are previous responses of Echo in the poem ("Were thou not born among the trees and leaves?" "What leaves are they? impart the matter wholly"). And do the eternal delights that Echo offers "persever? / *Echo.* Ever" (9–10).

Echo poems generally dramatize rather than narrate the events between the tokens, which is why the character of Echo tends to be introduced by a speech prefix rather than by a speech tag. Refrains can attach to their contexts in different ways. They may arise, as Stella's does in the fourth song of *Astrophil and Stella*, as an answer to a provocative utterance (note too that Sidney's Echo doesn't need a speech prefix either). They may be introduced by some nonce formulation such as those that Wyatt employs in "Who lyst his welth and eas Retayne": *for sure . . . , and sure . . . , of truth . . . , that yet . . . , for sure circa Regna tonat*. And they may be attached by speech tags ("Quoth the raven, Nevermore"), as in Mariana's song, or in Herbert's "The Sacrifice":

> Onely let others say, when I am dead,
>   Never was grief like mine. (251–52)

Here the refrain is very interesting indeed: it is a token from a typology wherein Christ is *quoting* Lamentations and also prophesying his persecutors' punishment, when they will be forced into the same inescapable lament to which they are already and eternally predestined. (Christ's mourners too will assent to the universal and eternal proposition that never was grief like his.)[20] What quotational refrains almost always do is show the interaction of the local incident and the quotation that transcends it. But really this is the work that all speech tags perform and that they best and most generally model: bringing utterances into relation with the local context that cites them.

Even the quotation of dialogue within a narrative does this, since it displays something that happened in the past as illustrative of the present narrative it gives of those past events. What the lady in "They fle from me" said has the untethered quality of a dream. But she did say it, and Wyatt can recall and cherish it. It transcends the local narrative just because it makes vivid the difference between its present context of quotation and the past that was otherwise, when she originally said it.[21] Thus too with "It stinted and said Ay," and with any narrative of the past that in the present flourishes the replica of an anterior token.

Speech tags connect the narrative voice to the words it cites in a different voice. In poems speech tags have two effects: a formal one, through which they bring the cited words into conformity with the citing poem's prosody; and a material or narrative one, through which they defer to the authority of what they adduce by showing and not telling.[22] An initial or terminal speech tag makes this double effect obvious. At one end such tags splice speeches into poems, or grade more or less insensibly into speeches (as I've been trying to argue); at their other end they glide into the rest of the poem's narrative. They narrate the transition from narrative to quotation. Thus in "Who so list" the unique refrain, or hapaxafrain (as a regretful respect for the necessity of an efficient technical vocabulary might condemn me to baptize it), follows two lines of a kind of participial narrative: "And graven with Diamondes in letters plain / There is written her faier neck rounde abowte / Noli me tangere . . ." The speech tag narrates the timely utterance of the local token of the timeless type.

There's a sense, then, in which you could see the speech tag and its relation to quotation as a brief and condensed model for the workings of the poem as a whole. Speech tags contextualize quotation, with respect both to prosody and to narrative. They set up the quotation, give it the effect the poem seeks. Where quotation or refrain occurs, the rest of the poem may be treated as a more or less extended setting for those repeated words. Of course figure and ground may change places; of course I don't mean to suggest, for example, that what's not quoted in a poem is simply a placeholder that makes the quotation work. Rather I mean to argue that speech tags can be seen as playing a far more central role than the subject seems to promise, since in speech tags you can see something like the whole work of the poem distilled. The last stanza of Herbert's "Home" provides a usefully clear illustration:

> Come dearest Lord, passe not this holy season,
> My flesh and bones and joynts do pray:
> And ev'n my verse, when by the ryme and reason
> The word is, *Stay,* sayes ever, *Come.* (72–76)

What the verse says is a surprise: it doesn't rhyme *Stay* with *pray.* Rather the last speech tag shows the quoted prayer trumping the prosodical context that quotes it, and the place where the context defers to the quotation is in the speech tag. The drama of this last stanza is rapid but real. Two varieties of token, and therefore two corresponding varieties of type, are considered. *Stay* would be the token of the available rhymes for *pray,* and as such would refer itself to the unchanging linguistic array that the versification must select from. *Come* is a token of an ever-renovated type, as Herbert prays without ceasing, and carries over the speech tags ("My flesh and bones . . . do pray"; "my verse . . . sayes") from the beginning of the prayer to the end: "Come dearest Lord . . . Come." An even more rapid compression occurs in Herbert's "Redemption," where the somewhat prolix and tardy speaker wastes the first thirteen lines of the sonnet before finally finding Christ, who has left only a single line to confer salvation and seal it with his blood:

> I straight return'd, and knowing his great birth,
> Sought him accordingly in great resorts;
> In cities, theatres, gardens, parks, and courts:
> At length I heard a ragged noise and mirth
> Of theeves and murderers: there I him espied,
> Who straight, *Your suit is granted,* said, *& died.*

The immediacy of his response, noted by the speech tag, stands for the fullheartedness of the sacrifice. When the speaker does something quickly ("I straight return'd"), it still takes him five lines to find Christ; when Christ does something straight, he goes straight into the saving speech.

Of course this argument risks seeming slightly tautologous, since the report of any climactic utterance is bound to be a culminating narrative incident.[23] What's been interesting me here, though, is the way the act of saying becomes particularly stressed: she said it to *me,* he said it *straight,* my verse says it *ever,* your love says like an honest gentleman, etc. The speech tag contextualizes the speech, shows the local significance of the type through the particular manifestation of the token, and this is how the type enters into the narrative. Indeed, the narrative element in a poem may become assimilated almost entirely to a single extended speech tag, as in Shakespeare's Sonnet 145:

> Those lips that love's own hand did make
> Breathed forth the sound that said I hate
> To me that languished for her sake;
> But when she saw my woeful state,
> Straight in her heart did mercy come,
> Chiding that tongue that ever sweet
> Was used in giving gentle doom,
> And taught it thus anew to greet:
> I hate she altered with an end
> That followed it as gentle day
> Doth follow night who, like a fiend,
> From heaven to hell is flown away.
> I hate from hate away she threw,
> And saved my life, saying not you.

The whole narrative occurs as medial speech tag. "I hate," she says, "not you"; and probably she didn't pause since *Straight* in her heart did mercy come. The anxiety is all the hearer's, and it all belongs to the narrative of her speech and not to what she actually says.

These two examples are further useful in that they show not only the formal ways that speech tags can telescope utterance with narrative context but also the temporal telescoping they can make possible. The speech occurs faster than its report possibly can: the speech tag (as we've already observed) alters the temporality of the report, so that the speech can happen to a narrative faster than a narrative can prepare to control or assimilate it. In Herbert the effect is one of Christ's inexhaustible rapidity: it's never too late to ask abundance of his grace. In Shakespeare the same effect supervenes upon the instantaneous anxiety of the narrator: she says "I hate . . ." and the sonnet gives you a long drama of woe and response, but still despite this she rescues the narrator like Christ without having to pause at all, simply by finishing her utterance. In a verbal analogue to Zeno's paradox, an extended focus on the instantaneous moment in which Achilles might catch the tortoise, the speech tag allows a syncopated effect, laying the immediate continuous speech over a narrative of anxiety that takes place between two contiguous moments of the speech.[24] A kind of counterpoint is set up, one in which one voice is actual and the other only potential.

The immediacy of the speech has the gratifying narrative effect of rescue. The narrative brings the protagonist to an unenviable position, and then the rescuer says something to save him. The supervention of the saving speech can occur in any relation to the speech tag. On "Redemption" it actually divides the speech tag itself ("Who straight, *Your suit is granted,* said"); in Sonnet 145 the speech tag divides the speech; in another scene in *Romeo and Juliet* it surrounds the significant speech on all sides. The Nurse seems to be reporting Romeo's death and does report his banishment; as in the other cases brief sounds determine weal or woe (here rescue and disaster coincide):

> NURSE.   Alack the day, he's gone, he's killed, he's dead!
> . . . .
> JULIET. . . . Hath Romeo slain himself? Say thou but Ay,
> And that bare vowel I shall poison more
> Than the death darting eye of cockatrice.
> I am not I if there be such an Ay,
> Or those eyes shut that makes thee answer Ay.
> If he be slain, say Ay; or if not, No.
> Brief sounds determine of my weal or woe.
> . . . .
> NURSE. Tybalt is gone and Romeo banishèd . . .

Juliet manages to interpose a long meditation into her consideration of this news, whose report she rehearses in her mind:

> My husband lives, that Tybalt would have slain;
> And Tybalt's dead, that would have slain my husband.
> All this is comfort. Wherefore weep I then?
> Some word there was, worser than Tybalt's death,
> That murdered me. I would forget it fain,
> But O, it presses to my memory
> Like damnèd guilty deeds to sinners' minds!
> Tybalt is dead, and Romeo banishèd.
> That banishèd, that one word banishèd
> Hath slain ten thousand Tybalts. Tybalt's death
> Was woe enough, if it had ended there;
> Or, if sour woe delights in fellowship
> And needly will be ranked with other griefs,
> Why followed not, when she said Tybalt's dead,
> Thy father, or thy mother, nay, or both,
> Which modern lamentation might have moved?
> But with a rearward following Tybalt's death,
> Romeo is banishèd—to speak that word
> Is father, mother, Tybalt, Romeo, Juliet
> All slain, all dead. Romeo is banishèd—
> There is no end, no limit, measure bound,
> In that word's death. No words can that woe sound.
>   (3.2.39–126)

News of Romeo ends the Nurse's one-line report, which Juliet has awaited so anxiously (as before she'd awaited the Nurse's report of what Romeo says like an honest gentleman). The news first is a relief: her comfort is that he's alive, and then as she reconsiders the import of that single line she gives the prolix narrative of the instantaneous disaster that the speech conveys.

I quote this to show Shakespeare's taste for the complexity of responding to reported speech, which you can see everywhere in his plays,[25] especially when he's indulging himself in the verbal dexterity of a character like Juliet. But the phenomenon of the clarifying supervention of continuous quotation onto a narrative that presents such quotation discontinuously is a pretty general one. And as I say, it's used to fine effect when the reported utterance can rescue the protagonist. Some of Milton's original effects in *Lycidas* work this way. That poem's notorious trick is that what had seemed to be spoken in full voice turns out to be quoted: "Thus sang the uncouth Swain to th'Okes and rills" (186),[26] and so here it's as though the speech tag rescues or assimilates or displays the resolution of the speaker's drama. The whole speech turns out to have been spoken in the past and thus eternized under the grammatical aspect of the past. The speech tag makes the body of the poem into a speech, and when it becomes perceived as a speech it has the effect of rescuing its speaker, or at least ratifying his rescue. Indeed this last effect of the poem is the corresponding converse of similar effects within its body:

>   Alas! What boots it with uncessant care
> To tend the homely slighted Shepherds trade
> And strictly meditate the thankles Muse,
> Were it not better don as others use,
> To sport with *Amaryllis* in the shade,
> Or with the tangles of *Neaera*'s hair?
> *Fame* is the spur that the clear spirit doth raise
> (That last infirmity of Noble mind)
> To scorn delights, and live laborious dayes;
> But the fair Guerdon when we hope to find,
> And think to burst out into sudden blaze,
> Comes the blind *Fury* with th'abhorred shears
> And slits the thin-spun life. But not the praise,
> *Phoebus* repli'd, and touch'd my trembling ears. (64–77)

Simultaneously with the report that "*Phoebus* repli'd" we learn: that the speaker has been complaining aloud, that Phoebus has been present to hear the complaint, and that the words of his reply are not spoken by the speaker but by Phoebus, by way of rescue. The interplay of utterance and narration of utterance is what keeps the poem going ("Return, *Alpheus,* the dread voice is past" 132).[27]

Lycidas turns out to be almost all quotation, and the speech tag ("Thus sang . . .") frames it after the fact. The quotation is made an element of a narrative we didn't even know was under way (*What the Swain Did*) and ceases to be the narrative itself.²⁸ The poem narrates the successful act of mourning made by the elegy that it quotes. The contrary effect may be found in another moment from *Astrophil and Stella,* the eighth song:

> Therewithall away she went,
> Leaving him with passion rent,
> With what she had done and spoken,
> That therewith my song is broken. (101–104)

The narrative turns out to be Sidney's song, or at least in the speech tag the song becomes aware of itself, much as Herbert's speech tag in "Home" will narrate the poem's own utterance. The unhappy ending breaks the frame of the quotation, and it's the very existence of the discursive acknowledgement that this *is* a song that ends and undoes it. In Milton the song can come successfully to an end, and the discovery vouchsafed by the speech tag that it has been a song frames the success of the process the song undertakes; here a similar discovery represents the song's failure.²⁹

In all these cases, the speech tag makes the utterance into a single object—even if the major object—in the discursive narrative to which it belongs. Narrative and speech tag interact and have the effect of telescoping different modes or realms of expression into one another. But what I am arguing is that this telescoping isn't just a technique that the poem employs: it is what poems will consistently take as their theme, since it's the possibility of such formal overdetermination that the works I've quoted keep making their very subject, whether occultly or openly. The poem displays the utterance it quotes as privileged, and while it urges that privilege in manifold ways, we can schematize its argument like this: the perfect fit of quotation to context shows the aptness either of the utterance quoted or of the context quoting, or of both.

As a matter of poetic practice, speech tags must assimilate quotation to prosodical context. But as a moment in the drama of versification, this assimilation can be variously felt to subsume the quotation to its context or to subsume the narrative context to the quotation. They merge, but which telescopes into which? The greater the effect of refrain, perhaps, the greater the sense that the speech tag dissolves narrative into the speech; the greater the effect of performative utterance, the greater the sense that speech is dissolving into an element of plot or context, introduced by the speech act as narrative element. Yet sometimes these two vectors may themselves coincide. As I'm about to argue, Spenser is particularly interested in the way the speakers referred to in speech tags can become assimilated to the things they say or sing, even within the unfolding of the narrative.

The perfect fit of apparently unrelated aspects of language—of rhyme and reason, as Wimsatt puts it—is one of the formal pleasures of poetry. Linguistic elements from independent sources merge in a single and seamless effect when sound seems to echo sense, that is, when matter complies with an independent form and becomes the form's perfect medium. The pleasure we take is the pleasure of seeing this falling-into-place of heterogeneous levels of language. This pleasure may be related to the pleasure of a jigsaw puzzle or of a crossword, but Merrill and Perec have taught us that these are pleasures not to be slighted.

My own not entirely modest aim here has been to show that to the list of the formal sites where independent elements may telescope into overdetermined phenomena—phenomena thus further overdetermined by the way they emblematize their own effects—to the list that includes rhyme, meter, enjambment, and phraseology, one should add quotation. I want to end with one final but extended example to show just how dazzling the combination and coordination of all these elements can be, an example from Spenser the structure of which has not, I think, ever been noticed.

As we have seen in looking at *Amoretti* 75, Spenser tends to place the speech tag in medial position. Thus a random example from *The Faerie Queene:* "In deed Sir knight (said he) one word may tell . . ."(3.7.57.1).[30] I think in *The Faerie Queene* this tends to be an effective use of report, because it combines speech and narrative into a single metrical unit, in a work whose every speech is also part of the action. It's significant that these parenthetical reports rarely occur in the alexandrine: Spenser doesn't want the possibility of a pentameter speech separating itself out from the extra foot that would report it in the alexandrine—he wants to keep them merged, and it is easier to bind them in the established unit of the pentameter line.[31] There's something typically Spenserian about these parenthetical speech tags, a distillation of the engaging leisure of all of Spenser's parenthetical comment: his poem is spacious and wide enough to allow for these remarks that we may not really need—but we're in no rush, and his prosody will take them in. Thus the famous parentheses like "(Who knows not Colin Clout?)" and "(Who knows not Arlo hill?)"; but also others in which he has room and time (his meter accommodates them) for an easy confirmation of what we already know: "It fortuned (high God did so ordaine)" (3.7.27.1).[32] This kind of parenthetical report is one of the many manifestations of the ways in which speaking, reading, or writing—articulating—the poem is also like being in the Faery Land, as Spenser puts it in the proem to Book VI:

> The waies through which my weary steps I guyde
> In this delightfull land of Faery
> Are so exceeding spacious and wyde,
> And sprinckled with such sweet variety
> Of all that pleasant is to ear or eye,
> That I, nigh ravisht with rare thoughts delight

> My tedious travell doe forget thereby;
> And, when I gin to feel decay of might,
> It strength to me supplies, and chears my dulled spright.
>   (6.Proem.1)

Writing the poem is a weary and tedious travail, but the experience of the poem—hearing himself speak it, reading himself write it—enables the poet to travel through the Faery Land and experience its delights. His weary steps—the meter of the poem—become, through the poem, the source of the delight that replenishes his strength, so that the stanza describing the weariness of those steps can nevertheless end in an alexandrine. In the same way, I think, the parenthetical speech tags merge the speaker with the meter of what he or she says and make the saying of it part of the world of the poem, one of the marvels of the Faery Land. Actions are attuned unto the lays of their speakers, as if in approuvance of their pleasing words.

This attunement is described and enacted in the Bower of Bliss section of Book II, which presents a more general version of this attempering of speech to narrative. Guyon and the Palmer have entered the Bower of Bliss, where they see sights of seductively heart-breaking loveliness and hear a gorgeous *carpe diem* song (translated from Tasso), introduced by a speech tag:

> The whiles some one did chaunt this lovely lay:
>   Ah! see, whoso fayre thing doest fain to see,
>   In springing flowre the image of thy day,
>   Ah! see the Virgin Rose, how sweetly shee
>   Doth first peepe foorth with bashful modestee,
>   That fairer seemes the less ye see her may.
>   Lo! see soone after how more bold and free
>   Her bared bosome she doth broad display;
> Lo! see soone after how she fades and falls away.
>
> So passeth in the passing of a day,
>   Of mortall life the leafe, the bud, the flowre;
>   Ne more doth florish after first decay,
>   That earst was sought to deck both bed and bowre
>   Of many a lady and many a Paramowre.
>   Gather therefore the Rose whilest yet is prime,
>   For soon comes age that will her pride deflowre;
>   Gather the Rose of love whilest yet is time,
> Whilest loving thou mayst loved be with equall crime.
>
> He ceast; and then gan all the quire of birdes
>   Their diverse notes t'attune unto his lay,
>   As in approuvance of his pleasing wordes. (2.12.74–76)

The song does not coincide with the Spenserian stanza, though, and at first seems to require the piecing-out of the introductory speech tag to achieve symmetrical form. Thus context would assimilate text, the narrative speech tag making the song part of the contextual form.

But it turns out, as I hope to show, that the song has its own free-standing form which can nevertheless be overlaid on the Spenserian stanza. Of course there is no doubt that part of what makes the lay so lovely is its participation in the structure that contextualizes it—there is no doubt that the song shows one of the glories of the Spenserian stanza, and that we read it within the context of that stanza. But it contributes to our fascination to see how Spenser works the dovetailing of two poetic forms within a single set of lines. Spenser does this through the play of the song's rhymes in / -ay /. The form of the Spenserian stanza is ababbcbcc, but stanza 74 repeats the a-rhyme / -ay / as the c-rhyme as well, so that the rhyme scheme here comes out as ababbabaa. It's as though the song is taking the framing rhyme from the speech tag ("some one did chaunt this lovely lay") into itself, lest it should lack its own rhyme, as it would if the c-rhyme were different. Imagine that stanza 74 read this perfectly permissable way:

> The whiles some one did chaunt this lovely lay:
> Ah! see, whoso fayre thing doest fain to see,
> In springing flowre the image of thy day,
> Ah! see the Virgin Rose, how sweetly shee
> Doth first peepe foorth with bashful modestee,
> That fairer seemes as ye see her the less.
> Lo! see soone after how more bold and free
> Her bared bosome she doth straight undress;
> Lo! see soone after how she fades from thy caress.

Why is this fairly minor alteration so jarring? It's not just my poetic clumsiness. This form of the stanza would leave line three rhymed in the stanza but unrhymed in the song (it would be the song's second line), and we'd notice this; it's not just familiarity that makes us yearn for the / -ay / rhyme. By using the apparently supererogatory rhyme sounds, Spenser can make every line in the song rhyme as well. The scheme of the *song's* first eight lines—lines 2–9 of the *stanza*—becomes abaababa (these *a*'s the framing stanza's *b*'s and vice-versa). In the spirit of John Hollander's stanzaic reframing of Adam and Eve's morning songs in *Paradise Lost* we can tinker with the display of the song to bring out its own internal form. Note first that 75.5 is possibly hypermetrical—"Of many a lady and many a Paramowre"—depending on how you scan it; it's one of those lines that phenomenologically allows for the telescoping of two scansions, since we can simultaneously register and elide the articles. If we scan it as an alexandrine we can use it along with the two terminal alexandrines as markers of stanza breaks within our modified layout of:

A Lovely Lay ("Ah! see . . .")

Ah! see, whoso fayre thing doest fain to see,	A	
In springing flowre the image of thy day,	B	
Ah! see the Virgin Rose, how sweetly shee	A	
Doth first peepe foorth with bashful modestee,	A	
That fairer seemes the less ye see her may.	B	5
Lo! see soone after how more bold and free	A	
Her bared bosome she doth broad display;	B	
Lo! see soone after how she fades and falls away.	B	
So passeth in the passing of a day,	B	
Of mortall life the leafe, the bud, the flowre;	C	10
Ne more doth florish after first decay,	B	
That earst was sought to deck both bed and bowre	C	
Of many a lady and many a Paramowre.	C	
Gather therefore the Rose whilest yet is prime,	D	
For soon comes age that will her pride deflowre;	C	15
Gather the Rose of love whilest yet is time,	D	
Whilest loving thou mayst loved be with equall crime.	D	

This is not perfectly regular, I admit, but it's as regular as the Spenserian stanzas which frame it, and almost perfectly symmetrical around the central line, which I've set off here. All the quatrains have an abaa rhyme scheme, each quatrain linked to the next by its second line. The first two stanzas have only two rhymes between them. This is necessary for the poem to rhyme every line and keep up the abstract abaa bcbb rhyme scheme: the c rhyme has to revert to a in the second stanza, otherwise the b would have nothing to rhyme with, since in this form the second rhyme always looks to the preceding stanza, but nothing precedes the first; after the second stanza new rhymes may be introduced, as they are here. If you think of the middle line of the song (line nine in my display) as a supernumerary line (which is why I set it off and indent it), the central line of the song links the two quatrains that precede it and the two that follow,[33] not unlike the fifth line of a Spenserian stanza, which links two interestingly overlaid quintaines, the closing couplet of the first forming the opening line of the second: the Spenserian stanza is already a scheme of superposition. Line nine of the song gives the b-rhyme a prominence after the first two quatrains something like the prominence the a-rhyme has in the first two, where otherwise the b-rhyme might feel isolated in stanza 3. The only real failure of symmetry is that the first stanza doesn't end with an alexandrine—but the stanza is about bashful modesty just peeping forth (4), not strutting its stuff.

What's important here is the extraordinary superimposition of a set of quatrains onto the very different prosodical form of the Spenserian stanza. (This is an elaborate version of the usual duck-rabbit game of prosody, where different groupings or chunkings will give rise to different rhythms: a line will feel different depending on whether we think of it as a headless iambic or a trochaic line.) Indeed Spenser continues the / -ay / rhymes into the next stanza, so that the song again does something different from the typical Spenserian progression, and merges with its narrative as that narrative gets picked up again in stanza 76 after the song is over. Naturally that continuation will at last rhyme with the word "say": "The constant payre heard all that he did say." (Note the pun in "p*ay*re," which also refers to the pairing of rhyming in the / -ay / rhymes, and may look back to "fayre" in 74.2: we fain to *see* what is *fayre*, the constant *payre hear* the song's distracting rhymes but do not swerve from their own original and still-continuing Spenserian scheme.) Spenser is also displaying his constancy in the rhyme scheme he keeps going after the interpolated material of the song:

>   The while some one did chaunt this lovely lay:
>   . . . .
>   He ceast; and then gan all the quire of birdes
>   Their diverse notes t'attune unto his lay,
>   As in approuvance of his pleasing words.
>   The constant payre heard all that he did say,
>   Yet swarved not, but kept their forward way. (2.12.74.1; 2.12.76.1–5)

Spenser returns to the originating word, "lay," and picks the narrative up, in a sort of combined *rime riche* and resumption *da capo*.[34]

Spenser's virtuoso performance might help to show something about the nature of poetic form. I've suggested that speech tags allow for an additional coordination of separate linguistic elements like those of sound and sense. Empson observes that we take pleasure in the graceful simultaneity "satisfying a number of independent conditions,"[35] like those of rhyme, meter, meaning, and phrasing. Overlaid quotation can impose another one of those independent conditions. It gives rise to the kind of additional effect that songs may also provide, when poems fit with music, and it's as though in quotation (an idea Spenser might be thought to be emblematizing) you get a perspectival representation of the effect of song: the third dimension coordinated in the music of a song is mapped into the two-dimensional space of the poem.

Why do we take pleasure in seeing the assimilation of these independent contexts and domains? Why is such an assimilation crucial, as Empson says, to the "distinctive feeling" of poetry? Quotation is the assimilation of the heard or the read utterance and the spoken or the written context, the assimilation of the material received with the receptive context. It's a sort of passing of the formal baton through the overlay of giver and receiver. As such it provides a representation of the experience of reading—certainly of reading formal poetry—itself. We receive the poem through a formal template of expectation—we time our steps to the prosody of the poem we run with—and the poem and our expectation temper themselves to each other, so that form and content become nearly inextricable, "as growne together quite" (1590 3.12.46.5). Speech tags allow us to perceive a place where this assimilation becomes unusually visible. But they stand for the experience of reading poetry itself, when we are most concentrating on internalizing and savoring words that come from elsewhere.

Notes

1. Kenneth Koch, *Straits* (New York: Knopf, 1998), 67.
2. Robert W. Hill, Jr., ed., *Tennyson's Poetry*, 2nd ed. (New York: Norton, 1999).
3. "Mariana in the South" works similarly to "Mariana."
4. See *The Rape of the Lock* (4:125–30) in Geoffrey Tillotson, ed., *The Poems of Alexander Pope*, vol. 2 (London: Methuen, 1940).
5. William A. Oram et al., eds., *The Yale Edition of the Shorter Poems of Edmund Spenser* (New Haven: Yale University Press, 1989).
6. This can be done in prose as well and can give the effect of a sort of phantom pause whereby the pause in quotation stresses an aspect of the unpaused speech: "'There's a man—' he did not gulp or hesitate over the word but he wanted to hesitate—'gutshot on the hill.'" (James Jones, *The Thin Red Line* [New York: Scribner, 1962], 255.) This is a vivid illustration of the kind of counterpoint between context and quotation that I am to consider in this essay; Jones makes the actual speech counterpoint a potential pause that is never voiced but only occurs silently: in the speaker's desire, in the narrator's and reader's reception. A more standard employment of this method may be found in George Eliot:

> At last Sir Hugo, who might have imagined that they had already spoken to each other, said, "Deronda, you will like to hear what Mrs Grandcourt tells me about your favourite Klesmer."
> Gwendolen's eyelids had been lowered, and Deronda, already looking at her, thought he discovered a quivering reluctance as

she was obliged to raise them and return his unembarrassed bow and smile, her own smile being one of the lip merely. It was but an instant, and Sir Hugo continued without pause—"The Arrowpoints have condoned the marriage...."

Daniel Deronda, ed. Barbara Hardy (Harmondsworth: Penguin, 1967), 459.

7. A very simple form of such assimilation can occur when one poem quotes another but rhymes the quoted line with a different word in the new context. "Where both deliberate, the love is slight, / Who ever lov'd that lov'd not at first sight." Marlowe, *Hero and Leander*, 1.176, in Roma Gill, ed., *The Complete Works of Christopher Marlowe* (Oxford: Clarendon, 1987); in *As You Like It,* Phoebe introduces the quotation with what is after all a speech tag: "Dead shepherd, now I find thy saw of might: / Who ever loved that loved not at first sight?" William Shakespeare, *As You Like It,* 3.5.82–83, in Stephen Greenblatt, ed., *The Norton Shakespeare* (New York: Norton, 1997).

8. Again from *As You Like It,* another saw, which a lord quotes Jacques saying: "'Tis right, quoth he, thus misery doth part / The flux of company" (2.1.51–52; see the whole context, lines 47–57). Jaques' balanced hexameter is distributed into two iambic lines in its quotation, and the speech tag does some of this work.

9. Thanks to Annabel Patterson for pointing this out to me. The typographical shift in "wrote / *The Lady of Shallot*" (125–26) is an elegant variation, since here her name is the direct object, not subject in inverted position; she's writing her own name.

10. F. E. Hutchinson, ed., *The Works of George Herbert* (Oxford: Clarendon, 1941).

11. Thom Gunn, *Collected Poems* (London: Faber, 1994).

12. Thus Coleridge also relies on the way we tacitly grant the speech tag the status of rhyme, a kind of blank square in the Scrabble of prosodic concatenation (like the recourse to "Word!" in rap as a placeholder for rhyme):

> He holds him with his skinny hand,
> "There was a ship," quoth he.
> "Hold off! unhand me, grey-beard loon!"
> Eftsoons his hand dropt he.

"Rime of the Ancient Mariner," 1.9–12, in H. J. Jackson, ed., *Samuel Taylor Coleridge* (Oxford: Oxford University Press, 1985).

"Quoth he" is made to rhyme with "dropt he," just on the repetition of the "he." We don't register it as a *rime riche*, though, and I think that this is because "quoth he," like "she said" or "said he," is so far ingrained in our sense of the appropriate poetic foot that we just assume the rhyme, which gives us, as it were, its moral equivalent.

13. The simplest instance of this rule is the ease and frequency of trochaic inversion in the first foot of the line and its rarity and anomalousness in the last two feet.

14. Consider the lines from *Amoretti* 75 quoted above, or: "I said: 'A line will take us hours maybe'" (Yeats, "Adam's Curse," in Richard J. Finneran, ed., *W. B. Yeats: The Poems* [New York: Macmillan, 1983]).
15. Elizabeth Sagaser, "Quoting the Beloved in Renaissance Poetry" (paper read at the Modern Language Association annual meeting, San Diego, December 1994).
16. Kenneth Muir and Patricia Thomson, eds., *Collected Poems of Sir Thomas Wyatt* (Liverpool: Liverpool University Press, 1969).
17. See "The Shadow of a Magnitude: Forgotten Quotations," in Kenneth Dauber and Walter Jost, eds., *Ordinary Language* (Evanston: Northwestern University Press, forthcoming); and "Analogy and the Inscrutability of Reference," *The Henry James Review* 18 (1997): 265–72.
18. William A. Ringler, Jr., ed., *The Poems of Sir Philip Sidney* (Oxford: Clarendon, 1962).
19. John Hollander, *The Figure of Echo: A Mode of Allusion in Milton and After* (Berkeley: University of California Press, 1981).
20. I'm agreeing with Empson's reading of the poem in *Seven Types of Ambiguity* (New York: New Directions, 1949), 228–29. The very idea of multiple reference within Empsonian ambiguity suggests the way the ambiguous token refers to pre-existent types. I analyze the typological play of quotation in this poem more extensively in *Generosity and the Limits of Authority* (Ithaca: Cornell University Press, 1992), 74–78.
21. Proust explores similar plangencies; consider the narrator remembering a privileged moment of kindness on his father's part:

    > It has been many years since then. The wall of the stairway where I saw the reflection of [my father's] lamp rising up hasn't existed for a long time. In me too many things have been destroyed that I thought would last forever and new things have been built giving birth to new pains and joys which I couldn't have then foreseen, just as the old have become difficult to understand. It has been a very long time too since my father ceased being able to say to mama, "Go with the little one." [*Va avec le petit.*] The possibility of such hours will never be reborn for me. But for the last little while, I have begun to perceive very clearly, if I lend an ear, the sobs that I had the strength to contain in my father's presence, and which only burst out when I was alone again with mama. In reality, they never ceased, and it is only because life is now more silent around me that I hear them again....

    Marcel Proust: *A La recherche du temps perdu*, ed. Jean-Yves Tadié (Paris: Gallimard, 1987), I, 37, my translation.
22. This double effect will occur in prose as well, of course, but it won't be so much connected to the question of prosody as to that of style. V. N. Voloshinov considers these effects in *Marxism and the Philosophy of Language* (Cambridge:

Harvard University Press, 1986), and so too does Mark Lambert in *Dickens and the Suspended Quotation* (New Haven: Yale University Press, 1981).

23. Henry James ends a passage thus:

> The supreme hour was to furnish her with a vivid reminiscence, that of a strange outbreak in the drawing-room on the part of Moddle, who, in reply to something her father had just said, cried aloud: "You ought to be perfectly ashamed of yourself—you ought to blush, sir, for the way you go on!" The carriage, with her mother in it, was at the door; a gentleman who was there, who was always there, laughed out very loud; her father, who had her in his arms, said to Moddle: "My dear woman, I'll settle *you* presently!"—after which he repeated, showing his teeth more than ever at Maisie while he hugged her, the words for which her nurse had taken him up. Maisie was not at the moment so fully conscious of them as of the wonder of Moddle's sudden disrespect and crimson face; but she was able to produce them in the course of five minutes when, in the carriage, her mother, all kisses, ribbons, eyes, arms, strange sounds and sweet smells, said to her: "And did your beastly papa, my precious angel, send any message to your own loving mamma?" Then it was that she found the words spoken by her beastly papa to be, after all, in her little bewildered ears, from which, at her mother's appeal, they passed, in her clear shrill voice, straight to her little innocent lips. "He said I was to tell you, from him," she faithfully reported, "that you're a nasty horrid pig!"

Henry James, *What Maisie Knew* (Harmondsworth: Penguin, 1966), 18.

24. The hero of Nicholson Baker's *The Fermata* can make time stop for everyone and everything around him, and sometimes will do so in the middle of a speech or even a piano note: this novel, along with *Tristram Shandy*, probably represents the longest narrative intervention within a speech presented as uninterrupted. The supplement to the argument in this essay, a supplement I've been tracking in the footnotes, concerns the relation of prose narrative to quoted speech, and here too a moment from *Daniel Deronda* is relevant. His mother is expostulating with Deronda:

> " . . . I had a right to seek my freedom from a bondage I hated." She seated herself again, while there was that subtle movement in her eyes and closed lips which is like the suppressed continuation of speech.

Eliot, *Daniel Deronda*, 689.

And so we're returned to narrative again.

25. Iago and Hamlet are obvious examples, but consider even Henry IV quoting Richard II about Northumberland, as he interposes speech tags into the (mis)quotation:

> But which of you was by—
> You, cousin Neville, as I may remember—
> When Richard with his eye brimful of tears,
> Then checked and rated by Northumberland,
> Did speak these words, now proved a prophecy?—
> Northumberland, thou ladder by the which
> My cousin Bolingbroke ascends my throne—
> Though then, God knows, I had no such intent,
> But that necessity so bowed the state
> That I and greatness were compelled to kiss—
> The time shall come—thus did he follow it—
> The time will come that foul sin, gathering head,
> Shall break into corruption; so went on
> Foretelling this same time's condition,
> And the division of our amity. (*2 Henry IV,* 3.1.60–74)

Henry alters to whitewash himself, and he interrupts the quotation at an apposite time, attempting to provide his own context for Richard's prophecy.

26. John Milton, *Poems, 1645. Lycidas, 1638* (Menston: Scholar Press, 1970).
27. "When I consider how my light is spent" works similarly, and also unfolds in the dialectic of utterance and speech tag. We mistake Milton's murmur for God's chastisement, but then we get Patience's truer reply, in vivid contrast to Milton's one-line question, and her reply rescues him.
28. Flaubert's "La Légende de St. Julien l'Hospitalier" provides a bravura example of this sort of ending. The whole story turns out to be in the first person, since the story is what the narrator, whose existence we discover in the last sentence, has learned about the medieval legend.
29. Compare with both *Lycidas* and the eighth song the "glad preamble" of *The Prelude,* where the rest of the poem extends from the speech tag, which narrates the disappointing fact that what seemed full-voiced in Wordsworth is a quotation and that what turned out to matter was that his own song was broken.
30. Edmund Spenser, *The Faerie Queene,* ed. Thomas P. Roche, Jr. (New Haven: Yale University Press, 1978).
31. An exception may prove the rule. Arthur is conversing with Una:

> O but (quoth she) great griefe will not be tould,
> And can more easily be thought, then said.
> Right so; (quoth he) but he, that neuer would,
> Could neuer: will to might giues greatest aid.
> But grief (quoth she) does greater grow displaid,
> If then it find not helpe, and breedes despaire.
> Despaire breedes not (quoth he) where faith is staid.
> No faith so fast (quoth she) but flesh doth paire.
> Flesh may empaire (quoth he) but reason can repaire. (I.7.41)

The alexandrine still stands out because there are so many earlier speech tags in this interchange; only the alexandrine sounds like it's quoting a complete and conclusive line. But without such a blizzard of speech tags, the alexandrine won't usually contain a speech tag in Spenser. Note too that the alexandrine here quotes a sort of rhymed proverb, with the speech tag as a caesura between the rhymed lines.

32. On Spenser's parentheses, see Hollander, *Figure of Echo*, and also Elizabeth Harris Sagaser, "Gathered in Time: Form, Meter (and Parentheses) in *The Shepheardes Calender*," *Spenser Studies* 10 (1992): 95–107.

33. It also adds another sort of link between the first 8 lines of the song and those that follow, as though Spenser is actually superimposing yet a third potential form on the first two. Taking the central line and supernumerary line as the first line in the third quatrain (instead of deferring it as I've done), you subliminally expect the rhyme scheme to go abaa babb bcbb cbcc, which has a binary palindromic symmetry (1211 2122 2122 1211). Spenser's superimposition of rhyme schemes is a far more complex version of what happens at the beginning of a terza rima poem, if not set off in tercets: you wouldn't suspect until the sixth line that you weren't reading abab quatrains, and you wouldn't know it for sure until the eighth line. You could have the experience of coming up short if you tried to parse it this way: abab c*b*cD. The italized *b* is a mild surprise since you're expecting a new rhyme: the capitalized D is a greater shock since it doesn't rhyme at all, and only after this will you have to reevaluate, retroactively, how you've been parsing.

34. The song reported here is also, of course, an almost literal translation from Tasso, but it's worth noting that in *Gerusalemme Liberata* Tasso isn't quite so virtuostic. The first line of the song in Tasso has to be shortened by its two-foot speech tag so that Tasso's first line can contain the song's report: "—Deh mira, egli cantò, spuntar la rosa," *Gerusalemme Liberata* 16.14.1, in *Opere*, ed. Bortolo Tomaso Sozzi (Turin: Unione tipografico-editrice torinese, 1974). Fairfax uses the more typical Spenserian formula to translate the song (in a translation that itself uses Spenser's liberally): "The gentle-budding rose (quoth she) behold." *Jerusalem Delivered*, trans. Edward Fairfax (London: Routledge, 1890). And Tasso doesn't produce Spenser's elaborate superimposition of rhyme schemes.

35. William Empson, *Argufying: Essays on Literature and Culture*, ed. John Haffenden (Iowa City: University of Iowa Press, 1987), 156.

Flirting with Eternity

Teaching Form and Meter in a Renaissance Poetry Course

Elizabeth Harris Sagaser

Teaching form and meter is essential to teaching Renaissance literature. Certainly, it is essential to bringing Renaissance poetry to life in all its drive for dignity, defiance of death, and seductive splendor. And it is essential to any inquiry into the nature and history of poetry. But even if one is not interested in teaching poetics per se in a Renaissance course, some attention to formal verse is essential. To skip over the question of meter is to encourage students to ignore a vital sixteenth- and seventeenth-century aesthetic and those aspects of early modern English culture within which that aesthetic thrived. It is to encourage them to believe that formal verse occurred arbitrarily—maybe simply because of poets' lack of sophistication, lack of enlightenment, or absence of rebellious spirit, while in many instances such assumptions could not be further from the truth. Indeed, the more one might want to ground a study of Renaissance literature in historical awareness or cultural criticism, the more one cannot ignore basic questions such as why—politically, philosophically, psychologically—a culture would develop form and meter so intensely.

However, teaching form and meter poorly can be worse than ignoring it. If students are taught that reading poetry in form is a technical science rife with Latin terms and correct or incorrect answers, they will feel even more estranged from these old poems than they already do and approach them not as representations of dramatic, seductive, or meditative voice but as relics of a foreign language or arcane, unclear—and unfair—math problems. Indeed, it is not hard to thwart a student's ability to listen to and begin to speak the poetry, especially as many undergraduates have assumptions about old poetry's dullness and irrelevance, and some feel at odds with poetry in general.

A metrical quiz, an unnecessarily technical lecture on form, or a discussion detaching formal issues from larger concerns in the class, will all backfire.

So, how can we help students think about form and meter more analytically, curiously, and imaginatively? How can we encourage them to bring large questions about life, death, and poetry to bear on specific poetic practices and to bring specific poetic practices to bear on those large questions?

I describe here the activities and assignments that have become a foundation for my teaching of poetry in form. Some of these activities develop students' linguistic and aesthetic understanding of form and meter, such as classroom games to demonstrate the accentual nature of English and verse-writing demonstrations and assignments. Others contribute more immediately to students' historical awareness, including a simple beastliness/godliness scale I draw on the board repeatedly and annotate according to discussions and close readings that suggest the period's obsession with death and concurrent anxiety about human nature. Memorization and recitation—my own and my students'—foster both aesthetic and historical insights into form and meter, as do our readings of Renaissance poetic theory, especially Sidney's *Defense of Poetry* and Daniel's *Defense of Ryme*.

My remarks are based on teaching undergraduate courses and senior seminars on sixteenth-century poetry, seventeenth-century poetry, Renaissance and Restoration poetry and politics, Shakespeare's Sonnets, Milton, early modern poetry by women, and a new course, "Love and Loss in the English Lyric."[1] I present strategies and themes here according to how soon in a course I might first introduce them or how important it is that they quickly become pervasive to student learning. However, most of the ideas I present are highly interdependent, and many I introduce more or less simultaneously in several overlapping lessons. For example, my own or student recitations at the start of class one day will set the stage for both iambic-writing demonstrations and some remarks on court culture. The recitations will make more vivid some fundamental points in Sidney's *Defense of Poetry* and will ready students for games we'll play that dramatize the accentual nature of our language. In the context of critical articles we are reading, the recitations may also make students think further about the political implications of Wyatt's bold individual voice and Sidney's *sprezzatura*. I encourage readers of this essay to be alert to a variety of ways the strategies I discuss here can and should be entwined.

I also hope readers will be inspired to remember that teaching form and meter is vitally allied to theorizing about it: form and meter only exist in practice—in reciting verse, listening to it, reading it, writing it, remembering it, teaching it. Indeed, it is hard to imagine how one would begin to examine "what a self-conscious return to formal analysis might look like within Renaissance studies today" without examining ways we might involve our students in this self-conscious return.[2] Therefore, by offering strategies for teaching form and meter, I aim to demonstrate ways that theory generates, and is generated by, active experiences of poetry. I also hope to demonstrate an approach to formal poetry fueled by respect for the fragility as well as the ingenuity of the human brain.

I begin class nearly every day with a poem I recite from memory. It is remarkably more captivating for students to hear verse recited from memory than to see it being read, and the experience provokes them to think about poetry as personally communicative and expressive, potentially spontaneous-sounding, a script for any number of live individuals to inhabit and perform.[3] Students of literature spend so much time in silence, immersed visually in the lines on the page, that they are in danger of not knowing something vital about poetry, *especially* poetry that predates free verse: its power is rooted in its aural as well as its visual effects.[4]

The opening poem is either a poem we'll discuss that day or a poem that speaks to the poems of the day though it is written in another era. For example, I've opened class with Keats' "This Living Hand" on a day we're discussing the corona of Daniel's *Delia* or Marvell's "To His Coy Mistress"; I've opened with "Divinity must live within herself" (lines 23–30 of Stevens' "Sunday Morning") on a day we're discussing book 12 of *Paradise Lost;* the next time I teach Katherine Philips' friendship poems, I'll begin one day with Millay's "Recuerdo." Poems that begin with apostrophes, questions, exclamations, declarations, and colloquial lines are great class openers; for example: "Who will believe my verse in time to come" or "What is your substance, whereof are you made" or "Busy old fool, unruly sun" or "How soon hath Time the suttle theef of youth / Stoln on his wing my three and twentieth year!" The trick in reciting many lyrics is to confide them to the class, as if off the record: "They flee from me that sometime did me seek"; "Whoso list to hunt, I know where is an hind"; "When I have seen by Time's fell hand defaced"; "When my love swears that she is made of truth"; "Love bade me welcome: yet my soul drew back"; "Methought I saw my late espoused saint."[5]

Recitations should also instantly reveal some of the power of poetry in form; for example, after listening to "The Passionate Shepherd to His Love" or the Bower of Bliss *carpe rosam* passages, no one should doubt that these poems are partly seductive because of their measure and rhyme. More specifically, I try to show how unexpected rhymes, especially those taking place in the authoritative momentum of formal meter, sometimes trick the brain into lending an automatic credence to the poem's words. Linguistically, the brain has experienced a surprisingly good fit, and it associates such experiences of fit with rightness and truth.[6] (I ask students if they ever read meaning into coincidences.) Meter and rhyme, therefore, can make a good joke better, as Marlowe's *Hero and Leander,* Shakespeare's *Venus and Adonis,* and Aphra Behn's "The Disappointment" demonstrate well.

Meter and rhyme can also make a sincere line sound all the more sincere. I regularly recite poems with this effect. They begin with a self-conscious, learned authority and often a sense of polished spontaneity. Several of the words are polysyllabic, often Latinate. But then, at the turn of the sonnet or at some other crucial point, the poem becomes simple in diction, mostly monosyllabic. My listeners feel that they are now receiving the unpremeditated, painfully sincere truth.[7] Here is but one of many such examples:

> Let others sing of Knights and Palladines,
> In aged accents, and untimely words:
> Paint shadowes in imaginary lines,
> Which well the reach of their high wits records;
> But I must sing of thee and those fair eyes . . .
> (Daniel, *Delia* XLVI)[8]

Starting in the first week of class, I also give students several chances to read poetry aloud. This is easy to do, as I precede every discussion of a poem with two readings of it, and mark our discussions with additional readings (to test out various claims and ideas—as sports analysts "go to the video"). If the poem is in couplets, I'll have each student read a couplet, working clockwise or counterclockwise around the room. (Arranging desks or tables in a circle is essential for speaking and hearing poems.) If the poem is in quatrains, I may split it up that way. Sometimes I have students read one line each; such reading can make more evident lineation strategies, rhyme scheme, and other aspects of a poem. I offer help in a low-key way to anyone hesitating or stumbling on a word, though I usually save pointers and reminders—about pronouncing "ed" versus "'d" for example, and about reading enjambed lines without pauses—until we've completed a round of reading. I convey these tips as matter-of-factly as possible, usually to the whole class in general. Of course you can read this beautifully eventually, I imply to everyone, and of course you need a few tips early on, as it hasn't been a big part of your education so far to read aloud Renaissance verse.

Such exercises show over and over again how necessary this reading together is; without it, clearly, most students would never read the verse skillfully and so would never really hear it. Most of all, students who are anxious about reading aloud gain confidence if they are neither ignored as potential readers nor asked to read too much at once. Further, once quiet students have heard their voices emerge in a particular class a few times as readers, they are more likely to volunteer comments during discussion. If I do have a few theater majors in class, particularly students who have performed

Shakespeare before, all the better; the whole class benefits from hearing lines performed well in different ways.[9]

Once the class is under way and students have had numerous opportunities to hear me recite and to read lines aloud themselves, I put the memorization challenge to them. I start small: for example, I assign a stanza per person of Marlowe's "The Passionate Shepherd to his Love" and Ralegh's "The Nymph's Reply to the Shepherd," or a quatrain or couplet per person of a Shakespearean sonnet, or a couplet per person of part of Marvell's "To His Coy Mistress" or Milton's "L'Allegro." Essential for these recitations to be enjoyable—and therein enlightening—is a low-key, supportive atmosphere. Therefore, students do not have to stand; they may have the text in hand, ready to glance at; and I prompt any student looking for a prompt. Anxiety or apathy (sometimes a close cousin to anxiety) would undermine the potential rewards of these efforts, particularly the pleasure of playing with words aloud; the fascination of expressively merging one's sense of self and mind with a representation of self and mind written by another; increased awareness of how meter and rhyme aid memory; and increased awareness of how memory fuels critical analysis. A particularly foolproof pair of poems early in the semester seems to be the Marlowe and Ralegh shepherd and nymph pair. Sometimes I give Marlowe stanzas to male voices and Ralegh stanzas to female voices and have them go through the poems twice, once listening only to the shepherd, once only to the nymph, and then once alternating the shepherd's stanzas with the nymph's to make more vivid the clever thoroughness of the nymph's reply.

The past couple of years, I've given several unconventional final exams: students have learned four to six poems of their choice (at least eighty-four lines, within certain distribution guidelines) and recited them to me in my office or at our downtown cappuccino place. Not one of the dozens of students who have completed this adventure has complained about it (including in confidential evaluations); on the contrary, most have praised highly this opportunity to make their favorite poems of the course truly their own.[10] Many also love the idea of speaking verse in a café! They are also often highly enthusiastic about how memorization forces them to observe—or forge—metaphors, connections, suggestions, and formal features in the poems that they would never have experienced otherwise. Memorizing a variety of poems, including end-stopped rhymed poetry and a section of *Paradise Lost*, demonstrates to students as no lecture or discussion could how specific poems enlist form and meter (including rhyme or the absence of rhyme) to win over a reader's memory and imagination.

Filling the classroom—and their lives—with the sounds of poems also helps students make connections between formal verse and music. Recent neurological research, especially great strides in understanding the rehabilitation of the brain after injury or disease, has affirmed what most people's life experiences have taught them—that music has a unique power on the brain. It can conjure memory and tap reservoirs of emotion that seem inaccessible otherwise. It is very basic logic to assume therefore that more musical verse—measured, stanzaic, sonorous—might also produce some of these powerful effects for many people (though surely some people are more susceptible to the powers of music than others). And because so much Renaissance poetry is explicitly about loss, longing, fleeting beauty, and memory, or because it aims to be emotionally persuasive, it makes sense that these poets would revel in and develop the musical effects of form.[11]

This logic may seem obvious, but again, students' routine of studying in silence (and of speed-reading) can keep the poems remote and mute on the page. I sometimes encourage everyone to postpone listening for sense and to listen first merely for the music of Petrarch's *rime,* Wyatt's lute songs, the songs in Sidney's *Astrophil and Stella,* Marlowe's "Passionate Shepherd," Spenser's *Epithalamion* and *Prothalamion,* Daniel's and Spenser's sonnets, the Bower of Bliss episode and other passages from *The Faerie Queene,* songs from Shakespeare's plays, Milton's nativity ode and "L'Allegro" and "Il Penseroso," to name just a few examples. One musical student noted last year that this emphasis on music completely changed his attitude toward poetry in form. With these appeals to common sense, I also try to make as vivid as I can for students a world in which the lyric poem and the song were still closely linked. It is helpful in reading Wyatt, Campion, and others to know they sometimes wrote lyric explicitly for music and other times imagined that their stanzaic poems might get set to music. I always hope to find time to bring in a few recordings or have a talented student play and sing the musical versions of some lyrics.

My insistence on the aural experience of poetry from the first day on prepares students for a more specific inquiry into the nature of meter. Usually in the third week of the semester, I'll begin one class asking, for example, "Is josh-SHOE-wa Lee here today?" Joshua will look confused but probably say he is here. "Is a-LISS-in an-DER-zin here? and Stephanie sa-VEE-oh?—I mean ste-FUNNY sa-VEE-oh ?" Alison will start to nod. "Stephanie . . . Savio," Stephanie will correct me, wondering what the game is. "How about chris-TOF-fer newTON?" Christopher will say, a little uncomfortably, "Newton." What is the matter with me? By now most of the students look bewildered. A few are amused, and all are quite awake. I place accents incorrectly on most students' first or last names, noting how a few names defy my game—"John Scott," for example—because they are made up of monosyllables.

My point is that one hesitates to claim as one's name a mispronunciation of one's name, especially a wrongly accented pronunciation. Why? *Accent is an innate quality of our language; we partly distinguish our words by which syllables we accent. One cannot speak English and hope to be understood without mastering accent.* I've underscored this point because it sounds obvious but usually has not been thought over by students, nor do they at first see what it has to do with poetry. I play more games with them: I see how fast they can guess a word I pronounce correctly in terms of phonemes but incorrectly in terms of accent—"in-AR-ti-KEW-lit," "AN-a-li-TICK-le." They are fair-LEE fast, but they see that if they neeDED that ex-TRA se-COND to re-COG-nize e-VREE word I speak in a par-AH-graph, they'd ra-PID-ly get CONfused.

If I have a student in class who can speak in a tonal language, I will ask that student to demonstrate how the vast majority of English speakers are unable to make distinctions in tone. If I do not, I explain the best I can how we cannot recognize tonal distinctions and could easily therefore say something highly embarrassing by getting the tone wrong if we were travelling, for example, in Taiwan. If we moved to Taiwan, we would probably struggle for years with tone, just as many persons whose first language is not English or another accentual language find accent the most difficult part of the language to master. For interested students, some discussion of recent studies of infants and language acquisition can underscore how languages have innate, natural qualities that involve making distinctions in speech and in hearing that may not be meaningful distinctions in other languages.

It might seem to some professors that there is not time for such games and discussions in a course aiming to cover at least two centuries' worth of poems or most of Shakespeare's or Milton's writings. However, these activities involve students in an insight about poetry that no student of Renaissance literature (indeed no English major, certainly no graduate student) can afford to miss: poetry exploits (for various purposes) to the furthest extent the defining features of the language in which it is written. A poem is therefore necessarily always about its native tongue—the very material of its being, even as it may be about other things. Formal verse has a particular use for the defining features of a language: it uses them to make patterns and structures. English metrical verse, for example, consists of patterns of accented and unaccented syllables. When I ask students to reflect on the difficulties—indeed, impossibilities—of translating (versus adapting) poems from one language to another, these points about language and poetry usually become particularly clear.

Once the students have at least a beginning sense of what meter is, they are ready for more specific involvement in that ubiquitous Renaissance meter, iambic pentameter. I want them to experience how well this metrical pattern represents an *individual* speaking and so invites individual versus collective speech, allowing for many variations in delivery while still conveying a distinctive sense of measure. I begin, therefore, by demonstrating how iambic pentameter takes its cues from occasional natural metrical patterns in our speech. I have students write down monosyllabic sentences beginning with "I want," "I wish," or "I'll have," sentences they could imagine saying in their everyday worlds. Some of these end up being accidentally iambic, such as "I want to sleep all day," "I wish that film would play again," or "I'll have a cup of tea with milk to go."

The point is that our default metrics as speakers of English are pretty much iambic. If we are not bound by putting accents in the right places within polysyllabic words for recognition's sake (which we always are, of course, in speaking prose), or because we are aiming to emphasize particular monosyllabic words for a desired meaning, then we tend to alternately stress and not stress syllables. This alteration seems maximally comfortable for our physiological-linguistic apparatus. I have students try to accent every syllable in a sentence, or three in a row with only one unaccented syllable in between the groups (or other such combinations) to demonstrate what an effort it is to accent or not accent successive syllables in any prolonged way, and how such a way of talking is at odds with our basic instinct to communicate.

It's important to emphasize, however, that no reader will produce all his or her stressed syllables as equally stressed nor all unstressed syllables as equally unstressed. Stress is relative; an unstressed syllable is unstressed because the syllables before and after it are stressed. If all readers produced all stresses equally, there would be no room for individual performance, and poetry in form would really be as dull as some students fear it will prove to be. For this reason, scanning is not at all synonymous with experiencing a poem metrically. It's merely a convenient system of notation, but highly misleading in its reducing of many variations to signs for two absolute values. However, a little scanning with a lot of disclaimers is useful during these introductory meter lessons.

So: because iambic meter sometimes occurs naturally in our speech, it is not highly artificial. Yes, it is artificial because it does not occur so perpetually in our speech as it does in blank verse or a sonnet, but one could also call it artificially natural—or naturally artificial. Next, I try to get students to feel for themselves how different meters and lines represent different kinds of voice. "Let's do an experiment," I'll say. "'Humpty Dumpty sat on a wall, / Humpty Dumpty . . . '—join in, you know this." The class recites in unison this verse (usually with hesitant pleasure) and other nursery rhymes nearly everyone remembers—"Little Miss Muffet," "Jack and Jill" (the pleasure increases)—discovering that the trochaic and dactylic meters and short lines make it relatively easy to do so, certainly easier than reading in unison dramatic lines from Marlowe, Sidney, Shakespeare, or Milton, as everyone reads those lines a little differently (we try that, too). I might also have the class compare the relative ease of reciting in unison Sternhold and

Hopkins' psalm 58 in poulter's measure versus Mary Sidney Herbert's psalm 58 in iambic pentameter.[12]

To emphasize not only the nature of iambic meter but also pentameter, I sometimes challenge students to abridge a sonnet or passage from Shakespeare into iambic tetrameter. Which words seem expendable? Usually students will discover that qualifiers and interjections are most expendable; the basic sense of the lines can be preserved without them. Pentameter's allowance for qualifiers and for conversational phrasing therefore is part of its ability to represent an individual voice. Also, the longer line encourages the connective phrasing integral to hierarchical syntax, as Antony Easthope demonstrates so well.[13] Tetrameter and shorter lines are more likely to represent paratactic grammatical structures.

These activities yield the most insight into iambic pentameter and other forms and meters when students finally write their own sonnets, Spenserian stanzas, heroic couplets, or blank verse.[14] No single exercise in my courses increases more effectively students' reading of poetry in various forms and meters, just as learning to play soccer or baseball increases dramatically one's involvement and pleasure when watching the sport, or making a film enhances one's ability to analyze one. Several students embrace these assignments, and practically all students find them valuable. They also enjoy hearing their classmates' work (I read select efforts anonymously). A few are hilarious and bring down the house; a few are seriously effective. The assignments are also helpful for making clear to me those students whose reading skills are flagging because of persistent unawareness of some technical basics.

The goal in these assignments is not necessarily for students to write good poems, but for them to meet the demands of the genre with any wit and creative awareness of form they can muster. If they do not meet most of the demands the first time, they simply have to do it again. The highest and only grade is a "bravo." I do not give these assignments until we draft together in class a sonnet or at least several lines of one. Collaborative versifying allows everyone to participate in and witness the process of composing in form (being behind the scenes of *sprezzatura*)—working on lines simultaneously or in constantly shifting order; tinkering with pronouns, verb tenses, and adjectives to alter a line to be iambic; figuring out sense; planning for rhymes; and changing those plans according to a new idea. Often I'll begin the class poem with one of the lines generated by the "I want," "I wish," or I'll have" exercise.[15]

How do we feel writing and speaking in iambic pentameter? What do we feel about characters that speak it—all Shakespeare's high and noble persons and some of his more regular ones? Much of our reading in class—certainly our study of sonnet sequences or seventeenth-century *carpe diem* lyrics— suggests that iambic pentameter and other meters can dignify desire, rather like the fox trot or other dances can—by yoking conventions of seduction and display that require patience, effort, and creativity with uncivilized, essential sexual desire, and yoking them so well that they cannot be distilled from each other. I also ask students how easily they can whine, sob, roar, scream, or otherwise lose control in iambic pentameter. If they can, or if they can think of examples of losing control in pentameter from Shakespeare or another poet (*Lear* and *Othello* offer many examples), I have them examine these lines to see how much the lines use metrical variation to gain their effects. In Donne's "Batter my heart" and other Holy Sonnets, for example, the counterpoint between the abstract pattern and individual intonation is powerful.[16] Also, I have students test out how an expression of excess would sound converted from lines to prose. I had one student rant and rave impressively in a sonnet, but still, he agreed, his bristling lines seemed more controlled than a prose tirade would. Imagine if children talking back to their parents or arguing with each other used only iambic pentameter; imagine if adults did. Imagine an exasperated coach speaking in sheer iambic pentameter, or an angry town meeting. These scenarios are goofy, but they help students understand how form—especially iambic pentameter—can convey dignity, self-possession, control, and therein, civilization. Form suggests faith in the innate capacities of human beings to be civilized—their ability to use those powers of reason that distinguish them from beasts and to strive toward heavenly order and proportion. As Edgar says, "The worst is not / So long as we can say 'this is the worst'" (*Lear* 4.1.28–9), and especially so long as we can say it in iambic pentameter.[17]

In general, iambic pentameter—well executed—sounds more authoritative, meditative, and dignified than natural speech; it is a hyper-civilized speech, as it were. Other lines from that great play about human nature, animal instinct, death, love and civilization—*King Lear*—are helpful printed across the board during this discussion. When Goneril grills Lear on his declared need for "five and twenty, ten or five" servants in a house that already has servants, and Regan demands, "What need one?" Lear responds:

> O, reason not the need! Our basest beggars
> Are in the poorest thing superfluous.
> Allow not nature more than nature needs,
> Man's life is cheap as beast's. Thou art a lady.
> If only to go warm were gorgeous,
> Why, nature needs not what thou, gorgeous, wear'st,
> Which scarcely keeps thee warm. (2.2.430–436)

I ask students if they can think of evidence in their own lives for the truth of this claim, and ask why I'd highlight these lines in a discussion of the hypercivilized speech of iambic pentameter. How might pentameter (on the Renaissance stage, in an epic poem celebrating the realm, in a lyric poem satirizing the court and despairing of human nature, in a lyric poem voicing desire for another) be something like a beggar's staff or a lord or lady's fur coat? Couldn't we say the intelligentsia of Renaissance England aimed to be superfluous and gorgeous, not merely alive and warm? We've established that poetry is always in part about the language in which it is written. Isn't it logical that Queen Elizabeth would pay for poetic glorification of her realm? Isn't it also logical that in a world of great death and danger yet a world that increasingly values the life of the mind, individuals would try to speak in a way that defies mortality and celebrates measured thought?

These questions will not push students far enough, of course, unless they have already let go of some of the assumptions and stereotypes about early modern times many bring to the first day of class. Therefore, as I immerse the class in aural experiences of poetry and demonstrate accent, meter, and iambic pentameter, I also try to increase students' insight into the past. This is no mean feat. Beneath the dread many students begin the course with—dread of what they think will be the metrical irrelevance, impenetrable language, and outdated religious concerns of older texts—lurks an assumption about the people of the time. Consciously or unconsciously, many students think, *we are better than they were*. It is ironic to my mind that our supposedly progressive students, some of them exhibiting proudly their multicultural interests and openness to otherness, are uncritical of their own biases against the past. Many have no real sense of intellectual or any other kind of history before the nineteenth century. They simply imagine earlier periods as progressively more extreme caricatures of the Victorian age; as a result, they often begin my courses imagining early modern persons as dutiful, prudish, pious, unenlightened, and resolutely dull.

Teaching form and meter well is impossible as long as these caricatures persist. Therefore, I begin every course with in-class writing that makes it plain to me once again just how little background the majority of my students have. I ask students to make a chart with a space for major poets—or more broadly, artistic and intellectual figures, even historical events—for each century, beginning in the 1500s. They are usually embarrassed about how poorly they fill in the spaces, but it's a productive embarrassment. They seem to wonder why they've never paused before to notice just how shoddy their overviews of literary history are, because surely if they had so paused, they would have done something about it. It is extremely tempting at the start of each semester to imagine or pretend my students know more than they do, but I shortchange them and myself if I don't face the reality from the get-go. When students reflect on what they don't know, they sharpen and direct their attention. I sometimes follow the in-class writing with a creative chronology assignment. Students must map out connections between poetic figures of earlier centuries and milestones in the history of one of their passions, such as music, a sport, food and drink, fashion, exploration, astronomy, political reform, painting, religion, domestic life, medicine, or dance.[18]

Above all, it is crucial that students learn that most sixteenth- and seventeenth-century English persons confronted disease, violence, and death frequently and graphically. Being lower class, especially as a woman, could make life particularly limited and grim. When late twentieth-century American students begin to imagine these realities, they understand better both the dark and the idealized imagery of the poetry; they hear more distinctly the despair or urgency of some voices; they are less likely to feel alienated by the religious or moral imperatives in much of the literature; and they become more attuned to the memento mori and carpe diem motifs. Therefore, they are more interested in the ways formal poetic practice in the Renaissance might be inseparable from poets' experiences of time and mortality. Film can most certainly help; *Shakespeare in Love,* although idealizing of upper-class Elizabethan life, contrasts well the squalor of ordinary life with the dignifying power of poetry.[19] The film is also valuable in representing Shakespeare as a young, virile man versus an aging, immobile bust.

A simple scale I sketch quickly on the board helps my students cultivate an awareness of the literature's obsession with mortality and anxiety about human worth. At the far left, I write BEASTLINESS, elaborating with phrases such as "animal instincts," "bodily functions," and "mortality/death/earth." I connect this display by a long horizontal line—a double arrow—to the word GODLINESS at the far right of the board, elaborating with "spirit/soul," "virtue," "civilization," "transcendence," "eternity/immortality/heaven." A vertical scale would make more sense, but leaves less room for additional notes. I remind students that the dichotomy is not up there on the board because I endorse it or because it is true in any essential way, but because it represents a vital tension in many Renaissance poems and much early modern thought. In addition to using the dichotomy practically as we read Renaissance poems, I urge them to think about it critically in light of their own world views. Should the straight line from one end of it to the other be wavy? Should it be a circle? Would you need a three-dimensional exhibit to demonstrate the relationship between these facets of humanity? Would you reject the terms of this dichotomy altogether?

I draw the scale repeatedly during various discussions through the course, connecting phrases and issues in the poems at hand to places on the scale. The scale helps students see that the very destiny of persons is at stake in Renaissance representations of humanity. Does the possibility of Christian transcendence and eternity define humanity, or is materiality and mortality—mutability, in Spenser's lexicon—the triumphant force? What would be the ramifications for politics and everyday life if human nature were not encompassed by the divine? Would any ramifications be good ones, or all disastrous? In what other ways do poets reinforce and challenge this beastliness/godliness dichotomy?

The scale is helpful in mapping out tensions, ambitions, ambiguities, and paradoxes in almost every sixteenth- and seventeenth-century text, particularly when the class and I annotate it to demonstrate how paradoxical this dichotomy can be. Annotating the scale makes more vivid the complexity of the physical and religious language in Pembroke's *Psalms,* the sexual and spiritual strivings in *Amoretti,* and the divine and the dangerous elements of music in *Comus.* It helps us organize and investigate the animal imagery in *Othello* and the argumentative discourse of Adam and Eve after the Fall. If I am teaching Petrarch in the course, I overlay a scattered/gathered dichotomy on the beastliness/godliness one. Students have noted that "scattered" suggested forgetting, loss, lack of meaning, and decay (and so death); "gathered" suggested wholeness, meaning, remembering, and enduring (perhaps immortality).

Sidney's *Defense of Poetry* clarifies particularly well the relevance of the dichotomy to poetry.[20] Sidney declares that the

> heavenly Maker of that maker [the poet], who having made man to His own likeness, set him beyond and over all the works of that second nature: which in nothing he showeth so much as in poetry, when with the force of a divine breath he bringeth things forth surpassing her doings . . . since our erected wit maketh us know what perfection is, and yet our infected will keepeth us from reaching unto it. (24–25)

Discussing the learning that poetry enables, he adds:

> This purifying of wit—this enriching of memory, enabling of judgment, and enlarging of conceit—which commonly we call learning, under what name soever it come forth, or to what immediate end soever it be directed, the final end is to lead and draw us to as high a perfection as our degenerate souls, made worse by their clayey lodgings, can be capable of. (28)

By "poetry," Sidney means poetry in form, of course, and reminds us that the prophets were poets: "may I not presume a little further, to show the reasonableness of this word *vates,* and say that the holy David's Psalms are a divine poem? . . . [They] are written fully in metre, as all learned hebricians agree" (22).

In Sidney's conclusions, his defense strategy shifts cleverly. He retreats from the godliness extreme of the scale to some human middle ground. Now poetry is important because it can procure essential human needs—to be loved and to be remembered. Addressing all those who still denounce poetry, he writes: "thus much curse I must send you, in the behalf of all poets, that while you live, you live in love, and never get favour for lacking the skill of a sonnet; and, when you die, your memory die from the earth for want of an epitaph" (75). When we read *Astrophil and Stella,* we return to the scale with even more ironic connections to make; Sonnet 71, for example, begins with conventional praise of Stella's godliness and ends with Desire crying for food.

Annotating the beastliness/godliness scale can also help students see what is at stake in two other important Renaissance texts of poetic theory, Thomas Campion's *Observations in the Art of English Poesy* and Samuel Daniel's *Defense of Ryme.* Campion expresses distrust of pleasure and ease and makes plain his suspicion that rhyming "is grosse, vulgare, barbarous"—a practice that drags people into the muck of easy sensuality—perhaps beastly instinct![21] Following the poetic example of the glorious ancients is the only way to guard against a destructive popularizing of verse, he claims.[22] Daniel accuses Campion of advocating *unnatural* and unmusical composition, of wanting to "torture sillables, and adjudge them their perpetuall doome. . . . As though there were that disobedience in our wordes, as they would not be ruled or stand in order without so many intricate Lawes, which would argue a great perverseness amongst them" (149).[23] He laments that English speakers, particularly poets, would be "unkinde, and unnaturall to our owne native language" (158). Having played the accent games and composed their own sonnets, my students usually grasp these accusations and concerns.

We annotate the beastliness/godliness scale according to Daniel's concept of nature and pleasure to discover the paradoxes inherent both in Daniel and in the simple dichotomy the scale suggests. For example, "Nature" in Daniel is clearly good. He claims it is "above all Arte" (131), and though he doesn't invoke it strictly as God's creation, he also doesn't make it synonymous with earthly mortality or animal instincts. "Delight" in Daniel means sensual pleasure in some contexts (albeit poetic sensual pleasure), suggesting it might lean to the left side of the scale, but Daniel also aligns delight with "grace" and "harmony," and he speaks approvingly of enjoyment. He therefore allies some sensual pleasure with goodness and civilization: "delight" reaches toward the right side of the scale after all.

What about Petrarchan sonnets versus Elizabethan ones, rhyme royale versus blank verse? Close reading in class helps students begin to learn how the "standard" or "traditional" forms set up particular kinds of reading expectations.[24] Readers recognize the form, and so they know the rules of the game. When a poem is particularly innovative within these rules, producing effects beyond what readers expect, that poem is expressive and memorable. Sports analogies are helpful for many students in these discussions, particularly baseball, as many fans of both baseball and poetry have eloquently explained. Baseball has nine innings; three outs are allowed per team per half inning; each batter is allowed two strikes before striking out and each pitcher three balls before walking a batter, etc. The rules are intricate, and they are consistent. Instead of making the game boring, these intricacies and consistencies make it thrilling and suspenseful. What could happen within this structure that has never happened before? What unlikely but possible feats of pitching, batting, fielding might be generated by the game's requirements and yield a memorable poem of a game?

As my courses draw to an end, some students not only find formal verse accessible but also fascinating, or at least addictive. If I teach well, I earn student-colleagues who have begun to think about form and construction of voice, form and the power of abstract pattern, form and its relation to time, form and its relation to memory, and all of these in personal and political contexts. I earn student-colleagues who inspire me to test out my own working hypotheses—particularly that reading poetry in form, memorizing it, teaching it, and writing it are finally rooted in our desire to master time and thwart mortality, our temporary and illusory successes, and our fundamental failures. In a sense, immersing oneself in poetry in form is an attempt to *name* time—to seize and control a part of the experience of time by rendering it linguistically palpable, identifiable, human-scaled, and ordered. Form seems to make time into something we can get a handle on, instead of something that always and finally gets a handle on us. I think here of both Samuel Daniel's vision of form as a response to chaos and Maurice Blanchot's reflections on naming. (I also think of the birth announcement custom of joining the baby's name with his or her birth weight and maybe length. Measurements go with names as proof and celebration of existence). Daniel writes in his *Defense of Ryme:*

> For the body of our imagination, being as an unformed *Chaos* without fashion, without day, if by the divine power of the spirit it be wrought into an Orbe of order and forme, is it not more pleasing to Nature, that desires a certaintie, and comports not with that which is infinite, to have these clozes, rather than, not to know where to end, or how farre to goe, especially seeing our passions are often without measure. (138)

Daniel opposes a negative kind of infinity—"unformed *Chaos*" and unmeasured passions—to the divine, transcendent power of the spirit. The "Orbe of order and form"—a metrical, rhyming poem—has a transformative function for the mortal being: it offers "a certainty," a kind of faith. Daniel's orbe is like a name or word in Blanchot's formulation in "Literature and the Right to Death":

> My hope lies in the materiality of language, in the fact that words are things, too, are a kind of nature—this is given to me and gives me more than I can understand. Just now the reality of words was an obstacle. Now, it is my only chance. A name ceases to be the ephemeral passing of nonexistence and becomes a concrete ball, a solid mass of existence; language, abandoning the sense, the meaning which was all it wanted to be, tries to become senseless. Everything physical takes precedence: rhythm, weight, mass, shape, and then the paper on which one writes, the trail of the ink, the book. Yes, happily language is a thing: it is a written thing, a bit of bark, a sliver of rock, a fragment of clay in which the reality of the earth continues to exist. The word acts not as an ideal force but as an obscure power, as an incantation that coerces things, makes them *really* present outside of themselves.[25]

Reading, writing in form—as well as teaching form—all are involved in making orbes in the midst of chaos and in trusting the creative, "obscure" power of naming and writing. Partaking of poetry in form is longing put into practice: a kind of flirtation with eternity, perfection, and transcendence.[26] Indeed, flirting does often involve self-conscious uses of names and nicknames; I imagine the sonnet form as a kind of nickname for eternity. We could argue that this flirtation was optimistic and earnest for most readers and poets of the sixteenth and seventeenth centuries—really a courtship more than a flirtation, though a complex one. Today, most often, immersing oneself in form is a flirtation that readers or poets must value for its own sake; we know it will end bitterly and darkly if allowed to develop into an affair.

But what do I mean by these easy terms, "eternity, perfection, transcendence"? Is reading and writing poetry in form more specifically a flirtation with the possibility of one's own voice going on forever (for readers, perhaps going backward in time as well as forward)? Is it an attempt to name that mortal voice as it *lives* in time, to separate its power from its mortality, to make it renew old voices or reincarnate itself in new voices and so prove the endurance of eloquence and music? Yeats' image for form—the preservatives, ice and salt—argues as much. This formulation also echoes Renaissance poets' own eternizing claims for the poems, especially ones in which Spenser and Shakespeare really imagine their future audiences: "Where whenas death shall all the world subdew, / Our love shall live, and later life renew" (Spenser, *Amoretti* 75, couplet);[27] "So long as men can breathe or eyes can see, / So long lives this, and this gives life to thee" (Shakespeare, Sonnet 18, couplet); "So, till the Judgement that your self arise, / You live in this, and dwell in lovers' eyes" (Shakespeare, Sonnet 55, couplet).

But how can formal verse be conciliatory and soothing at the same time it can be desperate and bold, the last flight out of quotidian finitudes? Repetition is about beginning again instead of ending once and for all.[28] In its repetitions, formal poetry not only provides the means for flirting with eternity, but for doing so without naiveté. Adam Phillips critiques Freud's negative opinion of flirtation: "For Freud . . . flirtation was the relationship for those who were too fearful of death, those who must agree to make nothing happen. But like the continental lovers, of course, they cannot agree not to die. Defiance can be a form of acknowledgment."[29] Defiance is finally poetic form's acknowledgment of death. Form's insistence to begin again and again betrays its awareness and fear of the final impossibility of beginning again. However, this insistence—this defiance—also testifies to and generates for its participants two empowering states of mind.

First, the insistence sustains faith that at least if these speakers do not begin again, other ones will, and with this faith, the small consolation that maybe voices and selves are not so discrete—not so unique—as one had wished, once upon a time, and therefore, not so mortal. In other words, form can lower the stakes. Immersing oneself in poetic form can be a way to appropriate for one's self one's own final irrelevance. Spenser and Shakespeare demonstrate this appropriation in the couplets I quote above (and of course, in many of their poems). Keats demonstrates this appropriation when he concludes in this heroic couplet his representation of a mind compulsively rehearsing its fear of death: "then on the Shore / Of the wide world I stand alone and think / Till Love and Fame to Nothingness do sink.—"[30]

The second empowering state of mind that form's defiance of death enables is a tiny but lively childlike hope that one time the same act repeated over and over will yield a different result: this time the key will work; this time I'll leap the fence; this time the letter will be in the box; this time the sonnet will win the beloved; this time the song will lift us into eternity. We should remember that for children, life does sometimes happen this way because they grow so rapidly, refining fine motor and mental skills continually. A feat they attempted many times without success, such as turning off a faucet or reaching a doorknob, suddenly one day is possible, though the effort they make to achieve the feat does not seem very different to them from the effort they always make. Maybe those early seemingly miraculous victories of childhood leave us in later years still believing that enough repetition will yield a breakthrough.

Both empowering states of mind are enabled by Geoffrey Hill's short poem "Veni Coronaberis." The lyric is about meter and rhyme's enactment of the desire to transcend mortality; I began a Milton class reciting this poem last spring before discussing Adam's longing and reflections on the impossibility of ever again having face-to-face encounters with God. More specifically, Hill's poem is about how sexual and poetic expressions of the desire for transcendence are entwined. The poem enacts a philosophical decision, a conclusion that illicit sex is more a fool's gold than poetry is:

> The crocus armies from the dead
> rise up; the realm of love renews
> the battle it was born to lose,
> though for a time the snows have fled
> and old stones blossom in the south
> with sculpted vine and psaltery
> and half-effaced adultery
> the bird-dung dribbling from its mouth;
>
> and abstinence crowns all our care
> with martyr-laurels for this day.
> Towers and steeples rise away
> into the towering gulfs of air.[31]

Shelley's "One Word is Too Often Profaned" is also engaged in a comparison of sexual and metrical responses to desire for transcendence and seems especially suited to end (or resist ending) this essay, as I have recited it as an epigraph to discussions of sonnet sequences from the *Rime Sparse* to Shakespeare's Sonnets, as well as classes on Herbert's *The Temple* and the parts of *Paradise Lost* most about human loss and longing:

> One word is too often profaned
>   For me to profane it.
> One feeling too falsely disdained
>   For thee to disdain it.
> One hope is too like despair
>   For prudence to smother,
> And pity from thee more dear
>   Than that from another.
> I can give not what men call love,
>   But wilt thou accept not
> The worship the heart lifts above
>   And the heavens reject not,—
> The desire of the moth for the star,
>   Of the night for the morrow,
> The devotion to something afar
>   From the sphere of our sorrow?[32]

Notes

1. The seminars have had fifteen students; the other courses have had up to thirty-four but usually enrollments are between eighteen and twenty-seven.
2. Mark Rasmussen, description of special session "Toward a New Formalism in Renaissance Studies," Modern Language Association convention, 1997.

3. I dare to say "captivating" as it is a word a student used on an evaluation to describe my habit of beginning class with a poem recited from memory. Most students seem very attuned to the recitations, and in their evaluations, many mention their pleasure in them.
4. The master of formal analysis of the aural versus the visual effects of poems is John Hollander; his *Vision and Resonance* (New Haven: Yale University Press, 1985) and *Melodious Guile: Fictive Pattern in Poetic Language* (New Haven: Yale University Press, 1988), are two of the best books on form and meter.
5. These first lines are from, respectively, Shakespeare's Sonnets 17 and 53, Donne's "The Sun Rising," Milton's Sonnet 7, Wyatt "They flee from me" and "Whoso List to Hunt," Shakespeare's Sonnets 64 and 138, Herbert's "Love III," and Milton's Sonnet 23. All quotations from Shakespeare's Sonnets are from Helen Vendler, *The Art of Shakespeare's Sonnets* (Cambridge: Harvard University Press, 1997); all quotations from Milton are from *The Riverside Milton*, ed. Roy Flannagan (Boston: Houghton Mifflin, 1998); all other poems in this paragraph are quoted from *The Norton Anthology of Poetry*, ed. Margaret Ferguson, Mary Jo Salter, Jon Stallworthy (New York: Norton, 1996).
6. I could explain this basic phenomenon of poetic effect in terms of Hollander's idea that poems present their own fictions; see *Melodious Guile*, particularly the preface and introduction.
7. Shakespeare of course is the master of this effect. There are examples in every play, especially the late tragedies. My favorite example in the Sonnets is in Sonnet 64 (here printed through the line with that effect):

> When I have seen by Time's fell hand defaced
> The rich proud cost of outworn buried age,
> When sometime lofty towers I see down razed,
> And brass eternal slave to mortal rage;
> When I have seen the hungry ocean gain
> Advantage on the kingdom of the shore,
> And the firm soil win of the wat'ry main,
> Increasing store with loss, and loss with store;
> When I have seen such interchange of state,
> Or state itself confounded to decay,
> Ruin hath taught me thus to ruminate:
> That Time will come and take my love away. . . .

8. All quotations from Daniel are from *Poems and a Defense of Ryme*, ed. Arthur Colby Sprague (Chicago: University of Chicago Press, 1972, orig. pub. 1930). Consonantal *i* and *u*, as well as initial *v*, have been modernized.
9. Another way to aurally immerse students in poetic language is to have a reading marathon, such as a *Paradise Lost* marathon like those described in the past few years on Milton-L, the electronic list for Milton scholars (based

at the University of Richmond). I have had four marathons now with students in my Milton and seventeenth-century poetry courses, always with superb results. Three marathons ran on weekend days from about noon until midnight; one ran through the night, from 4 p.m. until 4 a.m., on a Friday. The marathons have provided students and me with immersion experiences in Miltonic blank verse. They have also yielded delightfully unpredictable group intellectual adventures.

10. This year, I am sponsoring a "senior scholar project" (twelve credit hours at Colby College) inspired by the memorization challenges in my courses. John Monty Hobson, an English and theater major, will memorize all 154 of Shakespeare's Sonnets and perform them in different venues on campus throughout the year. He will also set some to music; he has already written and recorded a song with acoustic guitar accompaniment called "Astrophil" that incorporates about a dozen lines from *Astrophil and Stella.*

11. As I write about filling the classroom with the sounds of poems, I think gratefully of Alan Levitan's lovely recitations of the *rime sparse* in a Brandeis University seminar on the Renaissance lyric.

12. Excellent analyses of meter's representation of collective versus individual voice are in Antony Easthope, *Poetry as Discourse* (London: Methuen, 1983), especially chapters 3–5, and John Thompson's *The Founding of English Meter* (New York: Columbia University Press, 1961). Students with a theoretical bent should read Easthope, and art majors and minors especially might like to consider Easthope's comparison of iambic pentameter in poetry to the discovery of perspective in art. These students might also benefit from S. K. Heninger, Jr., *The Subtext of Form in the English Renaissance: Proportion Poetical* (University Park: Pennsylvania State University Press, 1994); Heninger emphasizes the kinship between poetic form and contemporary art.

13. See in particular Easthope, *Poetry as Discourse,* chapters 3–5.

14. I have always remembered how effective for me the sonnet-writing assignment was in the late Sears Jayne's continental Renaissance course when I was a sophomore at Brown University and how much insight I gained in Michael S. Harper's numerous assignments to write form in his excellent advanced poetry workshop my senior year at Brown.

15. Next year, I am sponsoring an English thesis inspired by the sonnet writing exercises in my courses. Jaime Muehl will study the evolution and resilience of the sonnet form and write her own contemporary sonnet sequence.

16. On counterpoint, see Thompson, *The Founding of English Meter.*

17. References to *Lear* are to *The Tragedy of King Lear* in *The Norton Shakespeare,* ed. Stephen Greenblatt (New York: Norton, 1997). These lines of Edgar's prefigure for me Milton's invocation in Book 7 of *Paradise Lost,* especially the poet-narrator's assertion:

> More safe I Sing with mortal voice, unchang'd
> To hoarse or mute, though fall'n on evil days,

> On evil days though fall'n, and evil tongues;
> In darkness, and with dangers compast round,
> And solitude; yet not alone.... (24–28)

18. Most students enjoy this assignment, but one or two seem to object in some classes, thinking it is some kind of old-fashioned busy work. It *is* most definitely a useless assignment, I tell them, if they do not make it useful. Aren't there connections they want to establish between things they sort of know about? Don't they want to clarify blurry knowledge? One student who didn't like this assignment as a sophomore ended up doing an independent study his senior year mapping out an extensive chronology and making a postgraduate reading canon for himself.
19. The film also dramatizes well the prominence of poetry in the entertainment, business, political, and personal worlds of Elizabethan England. I also assign short readings in history and critical articles that make more vivid the culture at large, and I use the terrific resources in our library's special collections. Historical awakenings should also include disabusing students of the notion that sex is a relatively recent invention. When I discuss ancient and continental influences on the poetry, for example, I mention the explicit erotic verse of Catullus and Aretino's *Positions*.
20. All quotations to Sidney's *Defense* are to *A Defense of Poetry*, ed. J. A. Van Dorsten (Oxford University Press, 1966).
21. Campion, Thomas, *Observations in the Arte of English Poetry*, in *Elizabethan Critical Essays*, ed. G. Gregory Smith (Oxford: Clarendon Press, 1904), 129.
22. Of course, to be fair to Campion, his youthful rebellious-conservative assertions must be read in the context of later poems like "Celia" and "Those Winter Nights."
23. All quotations from Daniel's *Defense of Ryme* are from Sprague's edition cited above, note 8.
24. "Standard" and "traditional" are troublesome terms as they mask the fact that there were founding moments for all forms, and they mask the fact that forms continued to evolve because of the genius and daring of the best practitioners. Shakespeare left blank verse a different form than it had been before, and Milton left it more different still (left it practically as free verse, according to T. S. Eliot). Almost no one wrote in the Spenserian stanza after *The Faerie Queene*; it was hardly a standard or traditional thing for Keats to do.
25. Maurice Blanchot, "Literature and the Right to Death," in *The Gaze of Orpheus and Other Literary Essays*, trans. Lydia Davis, ed. P. Adams Sitney (New York, Station Hill, 1981), 46.
26. See Adam Phillips' book, *On Flirtation* (Cambridge: Harvard University Press, 1994). In the book's introduction, Phillips observes: "Flirting creates the uncertainty it is also trying to control" (xviii); "In flirtation, you never know whether the beginning of the story—the story of the relationship—will be the end.... Flirtation, if it can be sustained, is a way of cultivating wishes, of playing for time. Deferral can make room" (xix). See also chapter

one, "Contingency for Beginners": "What kind of love affair is a person having with time, and what kind of object is it for them?" (8).
27. Quoted from *The Yale Edition of the Shorter Poems of Edmund Spenser,* ed. William A. Oram et al. (New Haven: Yale University Press, 1989).
28. The eclectic reading list for William Flesch's superb graduate course, "The History and Theory of Versification" (Brandeis University, spring 1991) included Freud's *Beyond the Pleasure Principle* and Kierkegaard's *Repetition,* among many other suggestive texts.

"... nine, ten, begin again!" Children's rhymes sometimes make explicit the effect most measured and rhyming verses have on the brain—the urge to repeat them. The fun of declaring, "a big fat hen!" instead of "begin again!" is in resisting the momentum that would have you repeat the nursery rhyme yet again. This phenomenon can easily be demonstrated in the classroom.
29. Phillips, *On Flirtation,* xxii-xxiii.
30. Quoted from *John Keats,* ed. Elizabeth Cook (Oxford: Oxford University Press, 1990).
31. Quoted from Geoffrey Hill, *New and Collected Poems, 1952–92* (Boston: Houghton Mifflin, 1994).
32. Quoted from *Shelley's Poetry and Prose,* ed. Donald H. Reiman and Sharon B. Powers (New York: Norton, 1977). Dickinson's "I cannot live with You" also compares richly to Hill's poem and is a great epigraph for the Renaissance texts I list. I quote from *The Poems of Emily Dickinson, Variorum Edition,* ed. R.W. Franklin (Cambridge: Harvard University Press, 1998). The poem ends:

> So we must meet apart—
> You there—I—here—
> With just the Door ajar
> That Oceans are—and Prayer—
> And that White Sustenance—
> Despair—

Afterword

How Formalism Became a Dirty Word, and Why We Can't Do Without It

Richard Strier

I'm afraid that in my rather eighteenth-century title, "Wherein the author, etc.," I certainly promise more than I am going to deliver. In particular, I am not going to give a proper historical account but only the merest sketch of a history. I am also not truly going to show why—in absolute terms—we can't do without formalism. Much of my effort will go into distinguishing between two different kinds of "formalism" and considering the implications and underlying premises of each of them. I will argue that we give up a lot if we do, in fact, want to do without "formalism" in either of these senses. And I will argue this in relation to both literary and historical studies.

My modest and inadequate historical sketch is as follows. Formalism got to be a dirty word partly through essays like de Man's "The Dead-End of Formalist Criticism," written (in French) in the fifties but widely disseminated (in English) in the seventies (and echoed in Hartman's *Beyond Formalism* in 1970); partly through the resurgence of a certain kind of Marxist criticism; and partly through a very widespread misunderstanding of the phrase, "new historicism." To begin where I have begun, de Man's essay, when one actually looks at it and reads more than the title, turns out (like so many things) to be rather peculiar and complex. The "Dead-End" (or, properly, "Impasse") essay is deeply involved with Hegelian and Heideggerian notions like "the deep division of Being itself."[1] The central premise of the essay is the necessity of "the unhappy consciousness" which literature, especially poetry, is said to dramatize or reveal. Formalist criticism in its *echt* or naive state is held to be criticism expressing the false or "happy consciousness," which believes in a perfect adequacy of language and the world, and of intention and meaning. I. A. Richards in the Anglo-Saxon world and Roland Barthes in France are associated with this position. De Man's major point about the "impasse" of formalism is that it must necessarily, by following out the logic of its own premises and techniques, produce deconstruction. In "Form and Intent in American New Criticism," he states the point clearly. New Criticism, he there argues, starts with the assumption of wholeness, unity, and reconciliation, but ends by revealing ironies, ambiguities and discontinuities.[2] Empson is the hero of the "Impasse" essay because Empson recognized this.

Yet despite de Man's stated desire to open criticism to "the sorrowful time of patience, i.e., history" ("Impasse," 245), deconstruction was too easily seen not as a negation but as a version of formalism—as one that privileged the aesthetic by giving up the category, and remained focused on textual matters. New historicism has been widely taken as announcing the arrival of "historicism" on the literary-critical scene—and this despite the deterministic premises of nineteenth-century "historicism," and despite the historical fact that the point of the phrase "new historicism" was the contrast with an older kind of historicism, not with formalism.[3] The point was *new* historicism, not new *historicism*—though "the profession" has steadfastly refused to see this. There is a great desire to see historicism—in some loose sense—as in itself the new thing, and therefore to demonize "formalism" as its (falsely) presumed opposite. We are "new" in that we are historicists, not formalists. This claim is particularly odd in fields like Renaissance and Romantic studies, where historical work continued to thrive through the heyday of the New Criticism. But the myth—like all successful myths—retains its power in the face of facts. The bad consequences of this include not only the demonization of literary formalism—even while a formalism is established elsewhere—but also the production in current graduate students of a remarkable and complacent ignorance of earlier (pre-1980) works of historical scholarship as well as of "formalist" criticism.[4] It seems to me that as few of my graduate students have read Rosemond Tuve or D. C. Allen as have read Cleanth Brooks or, for that matter, William Empson. But that's an initiative for another occasion—the defense of "old" historicism.[5]

With regard to formalism, I want to distinguish formalism as an ideology from formalism as a practice, and then to make some distinctions within the realm—not, of course, entirely nonideological—of practice. By formalism as an ideology, I mean the view that literature, like all other arts, is best studied by the detailed observation of what is taken to constitute the formal structure of individual works. As the mention of other arts suggests, literary formalism in this sense is part of general aesthetics. The critic's aim is to reveal the significant patterns within the work, and the assumption is that the revelation and "explication" of these patterns will serve to demonstrate (or, more rarely, establish) the aesthetic value of the work in question. This kind of criticism is necessarily committed to the question of value (and, somewhat against its will, to that of disvalue).[6] Explication, as W. K. Wimsatt explained, becomes criticism insofar as it reveals value.[7] This kind of criticism is also committed to an interest in what makes works of art special—in the case of literature to some conception of "literariness." This quality can be conceived in different ways, just as quite different formal features can be held to be crucial (imagery versus plot, for instance), but the question of literary value is built into the approach.[8] In giving up formalist ideology, we tend, therefore, to give up both the question of value and the conception of "the literary." Perhaps we (collectively) do want to give up these things, but surely we need (collectively) to think much more about this than we have.

One of the ways that the ideology of formalism expresses itself is in the importance it attaches to phrases like "in itself" and "as such"—the work "itself" or "in itself" or "as such." We should all remember (and some of us do) books with titles like "the poem itself." The idea was, first, that the work of (literary) art was different from other things (other kinds of writing); and second, that such a work was, if valuable, a worthy object of study on its own, without "external" materials. This is a position that is easily parodied. As René Wellek (who popularized the "internal-external" distinction) says, "A straw man is set up: the New Critic who supposedly denies that a work of art can be illuminated by historical knowledge at all."[9] But in practice the critic can indeed focus on formal patterns—imagery, plot, or whatever—that are intelligibly regarded as internal to the work. If one is interested in individual works (or texts) at all, one cannot avoid attempting analysis something like this. But perhaps we are not interested in individual works. I will return to this.

The "internalist" critic runs into trouble when the work "itself" is filled with allusions or, especially, references.[10] Allusions can keep us within a formal system of works, but references are trickier. In a once-famous essay attempting to sort out the relations between "criticism" and "history," Cleanth Brooks rather bravely took Marvell's "Horatian Ode" to Cromwell as his test case. Although Brooks disingenuously claimed that he did not choose the "Ode" as a hard case but as a normal one, Brooks acknowledged the debt of the figure he called "the critic" to the lexicographer for access to the meanings of words in the text, and he noted that since, in this particular (but supposedly non-special) case, "many of the words of this poem are [historical] proper nouns," the critic owes a debt to the historian as well.[11] Brooks nonetheless argued that despite these unavoidable debts, the critic, meaning the formalist, "has a significant function even in relation to this text." Despite some false steps, I think that Brooks does, in fact, prove this. Most of the false steps in Brooks' analysis derive from implicit historical and political assumptions that have nothing to do with his general procedures. For reasons that have to do more with his own politics than with his critical method, Brooks has trouble believing that any intelligent person could *praise* Cromwell. So Brooks devotes himself to finding implied criticisms and undercuttings in Marvell's poem, and these are often forced, over-ingenious, and conventionally moralizing. Yet some of Brooks' formal observations are simply true. In the early part of the poem, Cromwell *is* treated as a force rather than as a person; "the thunderbolt simile of the first part of the poem" *does* give way "to the falcon simile" in the second; and this latter figure surely "revises and qualifies the former" (116–17). I take it that such observations are data about the poem "as such." I also take it that such observations are data about Andrew Marvell's attitude toward Oliver Cromwell in 1650. Brooks backs away from the latter—"I have tried to read the poem," he says, "not Andrew Marvell's mind." But this retreat is not a very happy, stable, or successful one. Brooks goes on to concede that the poem "may tell us a great deal about Marvell's attitude toward Cromwell." He even goes so far as to say that "it probably does" so before he begins (partially) backing away again (125). But he needn't have backed away at all. Despite some confusion on the matter, formalist ideology is only committed to rejecting a crude form of intentionalism.[12]

When Brooks asserts that what the poem "says" is a question "for the critic rather than for the historian to answer" (127), he means that what the poem "says" can be ascertained only by detailed analysis that takes imagery and development into account and does not rely on quotations out of context or on gross generalizations. Brooks makes the (I think) extremely important point—though not one that he was in fact very interested in—that the critic, who is reading with "literary" sensitivity, "may on occasion be able to make a return on his debt to the historian" (127). The results of a formalist analysis, in other words, may themselves be *data* for historical understanding. The "literary" nuances of the poem "itself" may help us understand its historical moment, just as, in turn, detailed knowledge of the historical moment may—in a richer way than Brooks suggests—help us understand the nuances of a poem.

Moreover, and here I move from the ideology to the practice of formalism, the literary scholar trained in, let's call it, internalist reading can "make a return on his debt to the historian" in another way as well. Once we discard, at least for most purposes, Wellek's distinction between "monuments" and "documents"—between works and texts—and recognize that, insofar as the historian's sources are written, the analyst has as direct access to them as to literary works, then "internalist" reading of (so-called) documents becomes a possible practice.[13] And, I would argue, a highly desirable and informative one. Very few historical documents—meaning nonliterary and practically significant texts—have been subjected to "close reading" in the formalist sense. They have been very closely read for factual references and implications (names, places, dates, and datable references) and, occasionally, for keywords and key concepts (as in Hexter, Pocock, and Skinner), but they have not been *read* in the formalist sense at all.[14] Their patterns of imagery and rhetorical development have overwhelmingly not been noticed. I can testify from my own experience that surprising insights emerge when such patterns in "documents" are perceived. I tried the experiment of attempting an "old-fashioned close-reading" of two famous "documents" from early in the English Revolution. The results were startling. I discovered that the first of these documents, now always known as the "Root and Branch" Petition, should not properly be referred to in this way, since the title phrase never, in fact, appears in the text in the grammatically singular form. Moreover, it turns out that the plural form—"roots and branches"—is crucial to the vision of widespread corruption that the text is presenting. A close reading of the "Grand Remonstrance" was equally productive, showing this text to be much more optimistic and consciously revolutionary than it is normally taken to be.[15]

But let me return to formalist practices in relation to literary texts. When one takes as model formalists figures like Leo Spitzer or Eric Auerbach, rather than Cleanth Brooks, one moves into a different world of formalist ideology and practice. The essential premise of critics like Spitzer or Auerbach is not the importance of detecting formal patterns within texts but the premise, as de Man puts it, of a "continuity between depth and surface"— the belief, that is, that formal features of a text, matters of style, can be indices to large intellectual and cultural matters.[16] I would call this practice and ideology "indexical" rather than aesthetic formalism. In his most famous book, Auerbach took on the task of studying "the representation of reality in Western literature" by considering minute details of style in selected passages from selected texts. In the famous opening chapter, on Homer and the Hebrew bible, Auerbach moves from kinds of syntax to kinds of narrative to matters of social, psychological, and religious world-view.[17] It does not matter, for my general point, whether Auerbach's conception of Homer is adequate (I think that it is suggestive but oversimplified); what matters is the premise that questions of style, minutely conceived, can be indices to large issues. This premise can be used by thoroughly historical critics. It is meant, in fact, to be a historical tool. In English Renaissance studies, for instance, we can think of the extraordinarily rich work of Morris Croll on the implications of baroque or Attic or Senecan style.[18] Even closer to Auerbach, we can point to how richly an Auerbachian insistence on "mixed" style and diction in Shakespeare has borne fruit in the work of Robert Weimann.[19] This kind of formalist believes, with Empson—who was himself a formalist *of this kind*—that "a profound enough criticism could extract an entire cultural history from a simple lyric."[20]

Let me give a brief and spectacular but by no means unusual example of this sort of "extraction," an example not tied to a particular conception of style. The procedure at issue is that of noting and giving full cultural weight to tiny anomalies and discontinuities. The point of such an analysis is not to deconstruct the text but to understand it. In Herbert's "Longing," this stanza (addressed to God) occurs:

> Indeed the world's thy book,
> Where all things have their leafe assign'd:
>   Yet a meek look
>   Hath interlin'd.
> Thy board is full, yet humble guests
>   Finde nests. (49–54)[21]

What struck me, on reading this stanza "closely"—that is, with attention and with the assumption that details matter—was the concessive and insistently adversative structure of it. "*Indeed* the world's thy book . . . *Yet* a meek look . . . Thy board is full, *yet* . . ." I wanted to know why the speaker was not, like Dante at the ecstatic end of the *Paradiso*, happy that the cosmos was God's "book, / Where all things have their leafe assign'd." Why did he have to introduce the messy intrusion of "interlining"? Similarly, I wanted to know why the vision of "fullness"—Pleroma—was not ecstatic.[22] To get an answer required recognizing in the image of the book and the mention of "fullness" the cosmology of the Great Chain of Being, which, as Lovejoy has taught us, places great weight on inclusiveness, position, and plenitude.[23] And one then had to recognize that the stanza dramatized the difference between what Tertullian called "the God of the Philosophers," whose glory is cosmological, and the God of devotion, whose glory is dynamism and immediate responsiveness.[24] All this out of an "indeed" and two "yet"'s.

But why would one *want* to do "cultural history" in this way, from a (not so) simple lyric? Why begin at the micro-level? If there is a "continuity between depth and surface," why not skip the surface? Why not go to the grand issues directly? The answer to these questions has to do with a belief that one has to know the texture as well as the content of ideas to do intellectual or cultural history with true sensitivity, and with a corollary belief that this texture is most fully experienced at the level of verbal and stylistic detail, where tensions are manifested in texts in very subtle and unpredictable ways. The level of style and syntax is the true level of "lived" experience.[25]

Finally, let us consider what it would mean truly to give up all formalist premises. It would mean that we would give up on taking matters of style and textual disruptions as loci of significance. It would mean giving up on the individual literary work as a significant object of study. New historicism comes close, at times, to doing these things. It tends, first of all, to proceed from passages rather than from works as a whole. It will rightly be noted that a formalist like Auerbach does this as well, but the relevant difference is that new historicists tend to treat their passages almost entirely in terms of content. The relation between formalism of any sort and new historicism in literary studies might be captured by the "use-mention" distinction familiar in the work of Quine and other analytic philosophers.[26] Formalists are concerned with the uses to which details in literary (and other) texts are put. Their premise is that *the work provides the initial context* for understanding the significance of any particular item in a text. The question is "How is feature X used in this text?" New historicism, like very old historicism, is concerned with mentions. The fact that some item that is taken to be culturally or politically significant is mentioned in a text—in passing, in a metaphor, it doesn't matter how—is sufficient to get the machinery of "archeology" and archive-churning going.[27] Much that is rich and strange is turned up in this way, but the object of this kind of study is not literature, or any text, but some aspect of a culture in general. Ultimately, I think, the question of formalism is tied up with the question of whether a *literary* approach is valuable and worthwhile—both "in itself" and in relation to the whole world of texts, including "documents."

Notes

1. Paul de Man, "The Dead-End of Formalist Criticism," in *Blindness and Insight: Essays in the Rhetoric of Contemporary Criticism,* 2nd ed. (Minneapolis: University of Minnesota Press, 1983), 229–245.
2. Paul de Man, "Form and Intent in American New Criticism," in *Blindness and Insight,* 20–35, esp. 28.
3. For Stephen Greenblatt's struggle with the term "historicism," see his "Resonance and Wonder" in *Learning to Curse: Essays in Early Modern Culture* (New York: Routledge, 1990), 161–183, esp. 164–5.
4. On the formalism of Clifford Geertz's anthropological work—the model for much new historicism—see, *inter alia,* my remarks in "Historicism Old and New: Excerpts from a Panel Discussion," in *"The Muses Commonweale": Poetry and Politics in the Seventeenth Century,* ed. Claude J. Summers and Ted-Larry Pebworth (Columbia: University of Missouri Press, 1988), 214; and Vincent P. Pecora, "The Limits of Local Knowledge," in *The New Historicism,* ed. H. Aram Veeser (New York: Routledge, 1989), 243–276.

5. For an attempt at a balanced assessment of the need for and accomplishments of both "new" and "old," see Richard Strier, *Resistant Structures: Particularity, Radicalism, and Renaissance Texts* (Berkeley: University of California Press, 1995), ch. 4.
6. See the wonderful chapter "Badness in Poetry" in I. A. Richards, *Principles of Literary Criticism* (New York: Harcourt, 1925), 199–206.
7. See Wimsatt's title essay in *Explication as Criticism: Selected Papers from the English Institute, 1941–1952* (New York: Columbia University Press, 1963), 1–26; also W. K. Wimsatt, *The Verbal Icon: Studies in the Meaning of Poetry* (Lexington: University of Kentucky Press, 1954), 234–265.
8. The sometimes bitter conflict between the "Chicago school" and the Yale and other New Critics was entirely a matter of which formal features were held to have priority. See the essays by R. S. Crane and W. R. Keast on New Criticism in *Critics and Criticism, Ancient and Modern*, ed. R. S. Crane (Chicago: University of Chicago Press, 1952). I took my stand with the "Chicago school" in "The Poetics of Surrender: An Exposition and Critique of New Critical Poetics," *Critical Inquiry* 2 (1975): 171–189.
9. René Wellek, "Literary Theory, Criticism, and History," in René Wellek, *Concepts of Criticism*, ed. Stephen G. Nichols (New Haven: Yale University Press, 1963), 6.
10. Quentin Skinner's distinction between "relatively autonomous" and "relatively heteronomous" works is of use here. See Skinner, "Hermeneutics and the Role of History," *New Literary History* 7 (1975): 209–232, esp. 222–3.
11. Cleanth Brooks, "Literary Criticism: Marvell's Horatian Ode" (1946), in Wimsatt, ed., *Explication as Criticism*, 106. Further page references will appear in the text.
12. For Empson's puzzlement at the anti-intentionalism of Brooks and Wimsatt, see his review of Brooks' *The Well Wrought Urn*, "Thy Darling in an Urn" (1947), reprinted in William Empson, *Argufying: Essays on Literature and Culture*, ed. John Haffenden (Iowa City: University of Iowa Press, 1988), 282–88; and Empson's comments upon Wimsatt's *The Verbal Icon*, "Still the Strange Necessity" (1955), reprinted in *Argufying*, 120–128.
13. For the distinction between "monuments" and "documents," see Wellek, "Literary Theory, Criticism, and History," 15.
14. See the textual analyses in J. H. Hexter, *The Vision of Politics on the Eve of the Reformation: More, Machiavelli, and Seysell* (New York: Basic, 1973); in J. G. A. Pocock, *The Machiavellian Moment: Florentine Political Thought and the Atlantic Republican Tradition* (Princeton: Princeton University Press, 1975); and in Quentin Skinner, *The Foundations of Modern Political Thought*, 2 vols. (Cambridge: Cambridge University Press, 1978). For calls for what Hexter calls "macroanalysis" of historical "documents," see J. H. Hexter, "The Rhetoric of History," in *Doing History* (Bloomington: University of Indiana Press, 1971), 48–50, and Dominick LaCapra, "Rethinking Intellectual History and Reading Texts," in *Rethinking Intellectual History: Texts, Contexts, Language* (Ithaca: Cornell University Press, 1983), 32–35.

15. See Richard Strier, "From Diagnosis to Operation: The 'Root and Branch' Petition and the Grand Remonstrance," in *The Theatrical City: Culture, Theatre, and Politics in London, 1576–1649,* ed. David L. Smith, Richard Strier, and David Bevington (Cambridge: Cambridge University Press, 1995), 224–244
16. De Man, "Form and Intent in American New Criticism," 23.
17. Eric Auerbach, *Mimesis: The Representation of Reality in Western Literature,* trans. Willard R. Trask (Princeton: Princeton University Press, 1953), ch. 1. For Spitzer, see Leo Spitzer, *Essays on English and American Literature,* ed. Anna Hatcher (Princeton: Princeton University Press, 1962).
18. See Morris Croll, *Style, Rhetoric, and Rhythm: Essays by Morris W. Croll,* ed. J. Max Patrick and Robert O. Evans, with John M. Wallace and R. J. Schoeck (Princeton: Princeton University Press, 1966).
19. See, for instance, Robert Weimann, "'Appropriation' and Modern History in Renaissance Prose Narrative," *New Literary History* 14 (1983): 459–95; and Weimann, "History and the Issue of Authority in Representation: The Elizabethan Theater and the Reformation," *New Literary History* 17 (1986): 449–76.
20. William Empson, "The Verbal Analysis" (1950), in Empson, *Argufying,* 107. On the historicism of Empson, see Strier, *Resistant Structures,* ch. 1.
21. From *The Works of George Herbert,* ed. F. E. Hutchinson (Oxford: Clarendon, 1941).
22. For the "Pleroma," see Hans Jonas, *The Gnostic Religion: The Message of the Alien God and the Beginnings of Christianity,* 2nd ed. (Boston: Beacon, 1963), esp. ch. 8.
23. See Arthur O. Lovejoy, *The Great Chain of Being: A Study of the History of an Idea* (Cambridge: Harvard University Press, 1936), ch. 1.
24. For a fuller version of this reading, see Strier, *Love Known: Theology and Experience in George Herbert's Poetry* (Chicago: University of Chicago Press, 1983), 166–173.
25. For defense and exemplification of this claim, see the "close reading" of Donne's third satire in Strier, *Resistant Structures,* ch. 6.
26. W. V. Quine, *Methods of Logic,* 4th ed. (Cambridge: Harvard University Press,1982) 50, 146n., 268.
27. This model of "archeology" derives, of course, from Foucault. See Michel Foucault, *The Archeology of Knowledge* [1969], trans. A. M. Sheridan Smith (New York: Pantheon, 1972), and *The Order of Things: An Archeology of the Human Sciences* [1966], trans. A. M. Sheridan Smith [?] (New York: Pantheon, 1970).

Contributors

PAUL ALPERS is Class of 1942 Professor of English Emeritus at the University of California, Berkeley. He is the author of books on Spenser's *Faerie Queene* and Virgil's *Eclogues* and, most recently, of *What Is Pastoral?* (Chicago, 1996), winner of the Christian Gauss prize of Phi Beta Kappa.

DOUGLAS BRUSTER is Assistant Professor of English at The University of Texas at Austin. He is author of *Drama and the Market in the Age of Shakespeare* (Cambridge, 1992) and *Quoting Shakespeare* (Nebraska, 2000), as well as textual editor of *The Changeling* for *The Collected Works of Thomas Middleton*.

STEPHEN COHEN is Assistant Professor of English at the University of South Alabama. His publications include essays on legal ideology in *The Merchant of Venice* and the uneasy relationship between form and politics in *Measure for Measure*. His current work is on tragicomic form and the politics of justice in early Jacobean drama.

HEATHER DUBROW, Tighe-Evans Professor and John Bascom Professor at the University of Wisconsin-Madison, is the author of five scholarly books, of which the most recent is *Shakespeare and Domestic Loss: Forms of Deprivation, Mourning, and Recuperation* (Cambridge, 1999). Her publications also include a co-edited volume of essays, numerous articles on Renaissance literature and on pedagogy, and two chapbooks of poetry.

WILLIAM FLESCH teaches English at Brandeis University. He is the author of *Generosity and the Limits of Authority: Shakespeare, Herbert, Milton* (Cornell, 1992). He is writing a book on vicarious experience and another on quotation in literature and philosophy, of which the essay included in this collection is a part.

JOSEPH LOEWENSTEIN teaches at Washington University and writes on Renaissance poetics and on institutional history. He is the author of *Responsive Readings: Versions of Echo in Epic, Pastoral, and the Jonsonian Masque* (Yale,

1984) and of two forthcoming books: *Authorial Impression: The Production of Intellectual Property in Early Modern England* (Chicago, 2002) and *Jonson and Possessive Authorship: "Meum Theatrum"* (Cambridge, 2002). He is currently preparing an edition of *The Staple of News* for *The Cambridge Ben Jonson*.

MARK DAVID RASMUSSEN is Associate Professor of English at Centre College, where he teaches medieval and Renaissance literature. He has published essays on Chaucer, Spenser, and the poetics of complaint.

ELIZABETH HARRIS SAGASER is Assistant Professor in sixteenth- and seventeenth-century literature at Colby College. She has published essays on Spenser, Shakespeare, and Samuel Daniel and is currently writing on Mary Sidney Herbert. Her book-in-progress is "Solitude in the Early Modern Love Lyric: Anticipatory Elegies, Elegiac Intimacies." Her poetry has been published in several journals, most recently in *The Southern Review*, and a personal essay appeared recently in *The Chronicle of Higher Education*.

RICHARD STRIER is Frank L. Sulzberger Professor in the Department of English and the College at the University of Chicago. His books include *Love Known: Theology and Experience in George Herbert's Poetry* (Chicago, 1983) and *Resistant Structures: Particularity, Radicalism, and Renaissance Texts* (Berkeley, 1995); he has co-edited a number of important collections, including *Writing and Political Engagement in Seventeenth-Century England* (Cambridge, 1999), and is currently working on an edition of the Quarto King Lear with contextualizing documents.

MARK WOMACK is Assistant Professor of English at the University of Texas at San Antonio. His essay "On the Value of Lycidas" won the Monroe Kirk Spears Award. The essay in the present volume is part of a work in progress entitled "Shakespearean Delights: A Poetics of Pleasure."

Index

Adorno, Theodor, 70, 86n11
aesthetics, 5–7, 14n19, 68–70, 139–56, 208–9
Allen, D. C., 208
Alpers, Paul, 5–6, 8–9, 14n22
Althusser, Louis, 3, 19–22, 24, 35nn11–13, 15, 36n19
Altieri, Charles, 141, 156n6
Anderson, Judith, 45
Attridge, Derek, 91, 107nn6, 7
Auerbach, Erich, 211, 213, 215n17

Bacon, Francis, 31, 106
Baker, Nicholson, *The Fermata*, 182n24
Baldwin, T. W., 50
Barthes, Roland, 208
Bathe, William, 105
Beebee, Thomas O., 40n52, 73, 87n26
Bell, Clive, 70, 86n10
Bell, Ilona, 14n24
Bennett, Tony, 19, 35n10
Berger, Harry, Jr., 152–3, 157nn27, 29
Berry, Edward I., 66n25
Bevington, David, 48
Blake, N.F., 147, 157n17
Blanchot, Maurice, 199–200, 205n25
Block, Alexandra, 88n42
Bloom, Harold, 66n31
Bolchazy, Ladislaus, 87n34
Booth, Stephen, 1, 7, 11n4, 14n22, 119–22, 125–9, 135, 137nn19–21, 147–8, 157nn20–23

Bradshaw, Graham, 14n23
Brannigan, John, 18, 34nn6, 8, 38n32, 39n37
Brecht, Bertolt, 19
Brenkman, John, 10n1
Brennan, Anthony, 57, 59, 65nn20, 23
Brinsley, John, 105
Brooks, Cleanth, 1, 10nn2, 3, 117–18, 135, 136nn5, 10, 14, 208–11, 214nn11, 12
Brown, Marshall, 13n11
Bruster, Douglas, 3–4, 9, 13n15, 63n1, 64n10, 65n21, 66nn28, 31
Burke, Kenneth, 6, 118–19, 131–5, 136n5, 137nn17, 18, 138nn42, 43, 46, 53, 55
Bush, Douglas, 1, 10n3
Butler, Charles, 105, 111n43

Campion, Thomas, 198, 205nn21, 22
Carew, Thomas, "To Saxham," 74, 76–8
Carroll, Noël, 69, 76, 85n9
Chapman, George, 60, 107n10
Chicago school, 214n8
children's companies, 101–2
Clark, Michael P., 13n11, 14n19
Cohen, Ralph, 67, 85n2, 86n23
Cohen, Stephen, 2–4, 9, 11n6, 40nn44, 51
Cohen, Walter, 34n8
Coiro, Ann Baynes, 45

Coleridge, Samuel Taylor, 10n2, 180n12
corporeality, 97–101, 103–6
country house poems, 4–5, 68, 74–85
Crane, Mary Thomas, 45
Crane, R. S., 214n8
Crawford, Donald W., 69, 85nn6, 9
Croll, Morris, 211, 215n18
Culler, Jonathan, 123, 137nn29–31
cultural materialism, 18, 46
cultural studies, 1, 3–4, 8, 23–4, 26, 37nn28, 29, 38n30, 46–8, 73
culture, 23–4, 46–7

Dalechamp, Caleb, *Christian Hospitalitie*, 74–5, 87
Daniel, Samuel, *Defense of Ryme*, 186, 198–9; *Delia*, 187, 190
Danto, Arthur, 70, 86n12
deconstruction, 7
de Grazia, Margreta, 13n16
De Luna, B. N, 50
de Man, Paul, 126, 207–8, 213nn1, 2, 215n16
Derrida, Jacques, 36n19, 72, 165
Dickinson, Emily, 206n32
Dollimore, Jonathan, 34n5
Donne, John, 1, 118, 122, 129, 187
Dowland, John, 111n43
Dowland, Robert, 105
Drayton, Michael, 128–9
Dubrow, Heather, 2, 4–5, 9, 11n8, 13nn13, 17, 14n18, 40n52, 45, 64n3, 78, 86n16, 87n32, 88nn38, 39
Duncan-Jones, Katherine, 138n39
Dunn, Kevin, 45
Dürer, Albrecht, 27–8
During, Simon, 37n28

Eagleton, Terry, 3, 19, 21–2, 35nn9, 14, 16, 36nn17, 18, 37n26, 38n31, 39n44
Easthope, Antony, 36n19, 37nn26, 29, 38n30, 193, 204nn12, 13

Eliot, George, *Daniel Deronda*, 179n6, 182n24
Eliot, T. S., 1, 10n2, 102, 205n24
Elsky, Martin, 87n30
Empson, William, 1, 10nn2, 3, 136 nn5, 16, 138n54, 144–7, 156n8, 157nn15, 16, 178–9, 181n20, 184n35, 208, 214n12, 215n20
Evans, G. Blakemore, 48, 137n39

Fairfax, Edward, 181n34
Felperin, Howard, 34n8
feminist criticism, 9, 72
Fineman, Joel, 130, 135, 135n4, 138n41, 146, 156n10
Fischlin, Daniel, 45
Fish, Stanley, 14n19, 135n4
Flaubert, Gustave, 183n28
Flesch, William, 7–9, 165, 181nn17, 20, 206n28
flirtation, 200–1
formalism, 1–9, 17–18, 21–3, 31–3, 44–6, 67–74, 84–5, 90–1, 106, 115–16, 141, 207–13
Foucault, Michel, 3, 13n14, 215n27
Fowler, Alastair, 65n15
Freer, Coburn, 106n5, 110n40
Fried, Debra, 156, 158n31

Gadamer, Hans-Georg, 62–3, 66n32
Gaines, Barry, 50, 64n11
Gaut, Berys, 70, 86n13
Geertz, Clifford, 3, 13n14, 37n29, 213n4
gender, 72, 80–1
genre, 22, 72–3, 76–7, 79–81, 84, 92
Goldberg, Jonathan, 29, 34n5, 38n33, 40n25
Goldmann, Lucien, 19, 35n9
Graff, Gerald, 71, 86nn15, 18
Greenblatt, Stephen, 2, 11nn5, 7, 9, 12n10, 14n23, 17–18, 25–32, 33nn2, 3, 34n8, 35n16, 38nn32–34, 39nn38–44,

40nn46–50, 49, 64nn8–9, 68, 85n3, 213n3
Greene, Thomas, 66n30
Greenfield, Matthew, 14n23
Grossberg, Lawrence, 37n28, 38n30
Grossman, Marshall, 14n24
Guillory, John, 67, 69, 85nn2, 7
Guilpin, Edward, *Skialetheia,* 96
Gullette, Margaret Morganroth, 83, 88n46
Gunn, Thom, 162–3
Gurr, Andrew, 46, 59, 64nn5, 6, 65n24

Hall, Joseph, 95–6, 105n13, 108n20
Hall, Stuart, 37n28
Hardison, O. B., 106n5
Hart, John, 105, 111n43
Hartman, Geoffrey, 207
Harvey, Gabriel, 91
Helgerson, Richard, 11n5, 75, 87n32
Heninger, S. K., Jr., 204n12
Herbert, George, 7, 202
  works: "Denial," 161; "Heaven," 166; "Home," 168–9, 183; "Longing," 212; "Love III," 161, 187; "Redemption," 169–70; "The Sacrifice," 1, 167–8
Herbert, Mary Sidney, 193, 197
Hernadi, Paul, 86n21
Herrick, Robert, 74, 77, 80–1
Hexter, J. H., 214n14
Hibbard, G. R., 87n30
Hieatt, A. Kent, 1, 11n4, 65n15
Hill, Geoffrey, "Veni Coronaberis," 201–2
Hillman, David, 11n42, 112n45
Hoggart, Richard, 37n28
Hollander, John, 104, 111n41, 167, 176, 181 n19, 184 n32, 203nn4, 6
Hosek, Chaviva, 116, 135n3
hospitality, 74–7, 84, 87n34
Howard, Jean, 11n5
Hunt, Lynn, 37n29

Hunter, G. K., 11n5, 106n4, 110n33

Ishiguro, Kazuo, *The Remains of the Day,* 5, 81–4

James, Heather, 46, 64n5
James, Henry, *What Maisie Knew,* 182n23
Jameson, Fredric, 3, 19, 21–3, 24–5, 35n10, 36nn20–22, 86nn17, 25
Javitch, Daniel, 5n11
Jenkins, Hugh, 88n42
Johnson, Samuel, 57, 65n19, 73, 139–41, 156nn1, 2
Jonas, Hans, 215n22
Jones, James, *The Thin Red Line,* 179n6
Jonson, Ben, 62, 102–6, 110nn38, 39
  works: *Every Man Out of His Humor,* 109n29; *Poetaster,* 103–4, 106, 110n36, "To Penshurst," 74–80, 84–5.

Kant, Immanuel, 4, 68–70, 85n4, 166
Keast, W. R., 214n8
Keats, John, 89, 104, 187, 201, 205n24
Kerrigan, John, 137n39
Knights, L. C., 124–6, 131, 137nn33–35
Knowles, Richard, 46, 64n5
Koch, Kenneth, 159

LaCapra, Dominick, 214n14
Lambert, Mark, 181n22
Lanyer, Aemilia, "Description of Cooke-ham," 74, 79
Leavis, F. R., 136n5
Lerner, Laurence, 54, 65n14
Lever, J. W., 73, 86n24
Levine, George, 11n9, 14n19, 68, 85n5
Liu, Alan, 12n9, 33, 34n8, 40nn53, 54, 71, 86n19
Loewenstein, Joseph, 5, 8–9
Lovejoy, Arthur O., 212, 215n23
Lukács, Georg, 19, 35n9

Lynch, Stephen J., 46, 64n5
lyric poetry, 5–6, 115–6, 135

Macherey, Pierre, 20–1, 35nn14, 15
Magnusson, Lynne, 45
Mallin, Eric, 46, 64n5
Marcus, Leah, 115, 135nn1, 2
Marlowe, Christopher, *Hero and Leander,* 180n7; "The Passionate Shepherd to His Love," 187, 189–90
Marotti, Arthur, 14n20
Marston, John, 5, 89–106
works: *Antonio and Mellida,* 99, 107n8, 109n22, 110 nn33, 34, 38; *Antonio's Revenge,* 90–1, 93–5, 97, 99–101, 103, 108nn11, 13, 19, 109 n22, 110n33; *Certaine Satyres,* 95–6; *Historiomastix,* 102–3, 110n38; *The Malcontent,* 100–1, 104, 108nn14, 17, 109n22, 110n38; *Satyres,* 92–3; *The Scourge of Villainie,* 96–8, 110nn37, 38
Marvell, Andrew, "An Horatian Ode," 1, 209–10; "To His Coy Mistress," 187, 189; "Upon Appleton House," 78–81, 84
Marxist criticism, 3, 19–25, 32–3, 67
Masten, Jeffrey, 13n16, 111n42
Mattick, Paul, Jr., 86n20
Mazzio, Carla, 111n42, 112n45
McClung, William, 87n30
McEachern, Claire, 46, 64n5
McGuire, Mary Ann C., 87n29
McLeod, Randall [Random Cloud], 14n24
McLuhan, H. M., 138n44
mediation, 32–3
Meredith, George, 73
Meres, Francis, *Palladis Tamia,* 130
Merrill, James, 160
meter and prosody, 5, 7–8, 77, 91–106, 159–79, 185–202

Millay, Edna St. Vincent, "Recuerdo," 187
Miller, Carolyn R., 87n28
Milton, John, "L'Allegro," 189; *Comus,* 197; *Lycidas,* 172–3, 183n29; *Paradise Lost,* 187, 197, 201–2, 203n9, 204n17; sonnets: "How soon hath Time," 187; "Methought I saw," 187; "When I consider," 183 n27
Miola, Robert, 46, 64nn4, 5
Mirror for Magistrates, 91
Mizener, Arthur, 127, 137n38
Monette, Susan, 88n44
Montrose, Louis, 11n9, 24–7, 30–1, 34n4, 37n29, 38nn33, 34, 39nn35–7, 40n49
More, Sir Thomas, *Utopia,* 1
Moretti, Franco, 40n52
Morley, Thomas, 111n43
Morton, Donald, 38n31
Moss, Ann, 45
Muir, Kenneth, 147
Mullaney, Steven, 34n8, 38n34
Munns, Jessica, 37n28
music and poetry, 105, 189–90

Nashe, Thomas, *The Unfortunate Traveller,* 55–62, 66n30
Nelson, Cary, 37n28, 37n30
New Criticism, 1–2, 6, 17–19, 24, 71, 115–31, 136n5, 141, 208–10, 214n8
new formalism (critical method), 1–9, 31–3, 44–6, 90
New Formalism (poetic school), 9, 25n14
new historicism, 2–5, 17–33, 46–8, 62–3, 90, 208, 213
Norbrook, David, 87n25

old historicism, 1, 19, 49–50, 52, 64n10, 208
Orgel, Stephen, 11n5, 13n16, 25, 34n5, 39n35, 105, 111n42

Pafford, J. H. P., 152, 157n28
Parker, Patricia, 45, 116, 135n3, 140–1, 156nn3, 5
Paster, Gail Kern, 12n10, 105, 111n42
Patterson, Annabel, 45, 65n13, 136n4
Paul, Henry, 49
Pecora, Vincent, 11n6, 213n4
pedagogy, *see* teaching and pedagogy
Petrarch, Francesco, 190, 197, 202
Pettet, E. C., 49
Philips, Katherine, 187
Phillips, Adam, 201, 205n26, 206n29
Pieters, Jürgen, 38n32
Pigman, G. W., III, 52–3, 64n12
Pitt-Rivers, Julian, 87n34, 88n47
Pocock, J. G. A., 214n14
Pope, Alexander, 160
prosody, *see* meter and prosody
Proust, Marcel, 181n21
puns, 6–7, 139–56
Puttenham, George, 75, 91

Quine, Willard, 213, 215n26
Quint, David, 45
Quirk, Randolph, 147, 157n18
quotation, poetic, 159–79

Rabinowitz, Peter, 87n27
Rajan, Gita, 37n28
Ralegh, Sir Walter, "The Nymph's Reply," 189
Ransom, John Crowe, 6, 116–31, 136nn5, 6, 8, 9, 12, 15, 137 nn23–25, 27, 28
Rasmussen, Mark David, 90, 186–7, 202n2
recitation, poetic, 187
Reed, Victor B., 137nn38, 39
refrain, poetic, 166–8
rhyme, 77, 81, 160–3, 169, 176–8, 187–8, 198–9
Richards, I. A., 208, 214n6

Rickert, Edith, 49
Ricks, Christopher, 146, 157n13
Ritvo, Harriet, 72, 86n22
Rollins, Hyder, 124
Rooney, Ellen, 3, 10n1, 13nn12, 13
Rorty, Richard, 8, 14n23
Ross, J. F., 148, 157n24
Ryan, Kiernan, 33n1, 34nn7, 8, 38 n32

Sagaser, Elizabeth Harris, 7–9, 164, 181n15, 184n32
Saito, Yuriko, 70, 86n14
satire, 95–99, 108n17
Schoenfeldt, Michael, 112nn44, 45
Scodel, Joshua, 45
Second Return from Parnassus, 96
Seidenberg, Mark, 157n12
Shakespeare, William, 7, 55–61, 116–35, 139–56, 190, 201
editions: New Arden, 50; *Norton Shakespeare,* 48–50
puns in: 139–58
works—plays: *As You Like It,* 180 nn7, 8; *Coriolanus,* 100; *Hamlet,* 148–9, 151; *1 Henry IV,* 154–5; *2 Henry IV,* 182n25; *Henry V,* 55–62, 150, 152; *Julius Caesar,* 149; *King Lear,* 109n23, 194–5; *Macbeth,* 150–1; *The Merchant of Venice,* 140–1, 144; *Othello,* 1, 145–6, 194, 197; *Romeo and Juliet,* 57, 149, 162–4, 170–2; *The Tempest,* 108n17, 154; *Titus Andronicus,* 145, 156n9; *Twelfth Night,* 105; *The Winter's Tale,* 149–50
works—poems: Sonnets, 1, 116–35, 202; Sonnet 17, 187; Sonnet 18, 200; Sonnet 33, 116–17, 119–20, 138n50; Sonnet 35, 124–6, 131–2; Sonnet 53, 187; Sonnet 55, 200; Sonnet 64, 187, 203n7; Sonnet 76, 138 n49; Sonnet 116, 120–1, 126–30,

132–5; Sonnet 138, 187; Sonnet 145, 169–70
Shakespeare In Love, 196, 205n19
Shelley, Percy Bysshe, 202
Shirley, James, *The Cardinal*, 89–90
Sidney, Sir Philip, 7, 186
  works: *Astrophil and Stella*, 190, 198, "Fourth Song," 166–7, "Eighth Song," 173; *Defense of Poetry [Apology for Poetry]*, 31, 60, 186, 197–8; "Faire rocks . . . ," 167
Skinner, Quentin, 214nn10, 14
Smith, Bruce, 105–6, 112nn46, 47
Smith, Nigel, 87n25
Snow, Edward, 142, 156n7
Soderholm, James, 12n11, 14n19
source study, 3, 43–66
speech tags, 7, 159–84
Spenser, Edmund, 1, 7, 91, 104, 146, 165, 174–9, 187, 190, 197, 201
  works: *Amoretti*, Sonnet 75, 160, 165, 200; *Epithalamion*, 1, 54, 190; *The Faerie Queene*, 171–9, 183n31, 184nn32–34; *Prothalamion*, 190
Spitzer, Leo, 211, 215n17
Stallybrass, Peter, 13n16, 105, 111n42
Stevens, Wallace, 104, 87
Strier, Richard, 1, 8, 10n3, 33n1, 34n8, 213n4, 214nn5, 8, 215nn15, 24, 25
Swinburne, Algernon, 93, 107n10
Swinney, David, 146, 157n11

Tannenhaus, Michael, 157n12
Tasso, Torquanto, 174, 184n34
Tate, Allen, 122, 136n5, 137n26
Taylor, Gary, 65n22, 66n27
teaching and pedagogy, 7–8, 91–2, 105, 107n7, 185–206
Tennyson, Alfred, 159–61, 179n2, 180n9
Thaler, Alwin, 66n26

theatricality, 28–30
Thomas, Brook, 39n39
Thompson, Ann, 148, 157n25
Thompson, John, 204nn12, 16
Thompson, John O., 148, 157n25
Tiffany, Grace, 46, 64n5
Tobin, J. I. M., 55, 65n16, 66n29
Tolman, Albert H., 66n25
Tompkins, Jane, 73, 87n28
Treichler, Paula A., 37n28, 38n30
Tricomi, Albert H., 64n2
Turner, James, 77, 88n36
Tuve, Rosemond, 1, 10n3, 208

Van Doren, Mark, 149, 157n26
Veeser, H. Aram, 11n6, 34n4, 38n32
Vendler, Helen, 6, 14n21, 131–5, 138nn39, 45, 47–52
Vermeer, Johannes, *Woman Pouring Milk [The Kitchenmaid]*, 142–5
Voloshinov, V. N, 181n22

Walter, J. H., 66n26
Warren, Robert Penn, 117, 136n10
Wayne, Don E., 34n8
Weever, John [?], *The Whipping of the Satyre*, 98
Weimann, Robert, 211, 215n19
Wellek, René, 209–10, 214n9, 13
Wharton, T. F., 108n15
Whigham, Frank, 46, 64n5
Wicks, Robert, 85n8
Wilde, Oscar, 124
Willen, Gerald, 137nn38, 39
Williams, Raymond, 3, 19, 23–5, 36nn23, 24, 37nn25–28, 38nn31, 34, 39n36, 47, 64n7, 77, 88n36
Wilson, John Dover, 49, 66n25
Wimsatt, W. K., 34n3, 136n5, 173, 209, 214nn7, 12
Winstanley, Lilian, 49
Winters, Yvor, 6, 117–9, 121, 126–7, 136nn5, 11, 13, 137nn22, 36, 37

Wolfson, Susan J., 13n11, 40n52, 86n20, 87n25, 88n43
Womack, Mark, 6–9
Woodbridge, Linda, 63n1, 75, 87n32
Wordsworth, William, 124, 183n29
Wyatt, Sir Thomas, 1, 7, 186
  works: "They flee from me," 164–5, 168, 187; "Who list his wealth and ease retain," 166; "Whoso list to hunt," 165, 168, 187

Yates, Frances, 49
Yeats, W. B., 181n14, 200

Zavarzadeh, Masud, 38n31
Zitner, Sheldon, 135n4